# SOE IN THE FAR EAST

The author of this as of other official histories of the
Second World War has been given free access to
official documents. He alone is responsible for the
statements made and the views expressed.

# SOE in the Far East

CHARLES CRUICKSHANK

Oxford   New York
OXFORD UNIVERSITY PRESS
1983

Oxford University Press, Walton Street, Oxford OX2 6DP

London Glasgow New York Toronto
Delhi Bombay Calcutta Madras Karachi
Kuala Lumpur Singapore Hong Kong Tokyo
Nairobi Dar es Salaam Cape Town
Melbourne Auckland

and associates in
Beirut Berlin Ibadan Mexico City Nicosia

Oxford is a trade mark of Oxford University Press

British Library Cataloguing in Publication data
Cruickshank, Charles
SOE in the Far East
1. Great Britain. Army Special Operations Executive
2. World War, 1939–1945 – Campaigns – Asia, Southeastern
I. Title
940.54'25   D767
ISBN 0-19-215873-2

Printed in Great Britain
at The University Press, Oxford
by Eric Buckley
Printer to the University

# Preface

EVER since the publication in 1966 of Professor M. R. D. Foot's admirable official history of *SOE in France* there has been a case for a companion volume on the Special Operations Executive in the Far East, where conditions, and the contribution called for from the organization, were very different. The Government agreed in 1980 that this work should be put in hand and I was appointed to write it, being given the same facilities as my predecessor. Like him, I have had access to all the relevant papers of SOE, and with minor exceptions to other closed papers bearing on the subject.

There is, however, one major difference between the sources we have drawn on. The research for *SOE in the Far East* was carried out twenty years later than that for *SOE in France*, with the inevitable consequence that the number of survivors who could provide evidence was much reduced. On many occasions I have hoped to discuss an operation or a policy decision with one or other of the principal actors, only to find that they had disappeared from the stage.

The introduction in 1968 of the 'thirty-year rule', which allows the use of most official records formerly withheld for fifty years, has had a significant effect on the nature of scholarly research. Few survive the events they shape by half a century, so that before the thirty-year rule the historian of recent events had little oral evidence to corroborate or disprove the story told by the documents. He had to rely almost exclusively on the papers as they became available fifty years on. Now he may draw on the evidence of many more survivors, which poses a new problem – the reconciliation of the documentary evidence and the evidence of the surviving protagonists. However, he is still denied the evidence of those who have not survived, so that his stock of oral evidence is incomplete. Again, some remember clearly, while others do not. Some witnesses, apparently equally well qualified to give evidence, contradict each other. Some may distort their evidence to cover up personal shortcomings, or perhaps to help a friend's reputation – wittingly or unwittingly. One may play down his contribution to affairs, another exaggerate his. Not all witnesses saw the events in which they participated with the same degree of perception. By definition, most of the survivors occupied junior posts and were perhaps unaware of the background to decisions made by those in greater authority. The Official Secrets Acts, supposed to seal for all time the lips of those privy to national secrets, inhibit some witnesses more than others. In short, the quality of oral evidence thirty years after the event is as varied as human nature and as difficult to evaluate.

The documents are more reliable. The ink may have faded like the memory of the actors, but the message is unchanged. Nevertheless, their evidence may also be less than the whole truth. The papers of a secret wartime organization may have been destroyed for security reasons after they served their immediate purpose. Further, it is unusual in the middle of a war, especially if things are going badly, to pay much attention to the needs of the future historian. Some papers may have been destroyed by enemy action, some simply lost, some disposed of through lack of storage space. Others, seemingly valueless to the 'weeders' – the band of officials charged with the impossible task of deciding what should be retained for posterity and what should be sent for pulping – might have thrown light on a particular transaction. Of course, documentary evidence reflects some of the weaknesses of oral evidence listed in the preceding paragraph. There is no absolute certainty that a paper, whether written by a single hand or by a committee, can be taken at its face value. The essential difference is that, unlike the human memory, documentary evidence is unaffected by the effluxion of time. True or false, it speaks with the same voice through the decades.

These considerations apply to the evaluation of papers released for study in the ordinary course under the thirty-year rule, and of the related 'survivor evidence'. The scholarly historian must judiciously weigh and honestly reconcile the two sorts of evidence: and he will count himself lucky if he never has to make a subjective judgement, or to toss a coin to decide which sort is to be believed when there is a conflict. The official historian with the privilege of access not only to papers withheld from the ordinary scholar under the thirty-year rule, but also to many which will not be released for much longer periods, and in some cases perhaps never, is faced with a much more daunting responsibility. He is denied the comfort of knowing that his readers can refer to his paper sources to judge whether he has fairly interpreted the evidence. If a survivor, or anyone else, disputes his conclusions he cannot summon up the closed papers to support his contention.

There is therefore a particularly heavy onus on him to make dispassionate and careful use of the papers; and this I have striven to do. It is necessary to emphasize this point in the case of the present work since information provided by survivors who have been kind enough to help sometimes does not tally with the records. Indeed, there have been striking discrepancies between contemporary reports of events and the recollection of those who prepared them.

I am indebted to the many members of the Special Forces Club who sent working material in response to the Club's appeal, to others who helped to fill out the story of the Oriental Mission and the India Mission, and to the staff of the Public Record Office at Kew for the unvarying excellence of their service. I must express my thanks to Lieutenant-Colonel E. G. Boxshall, the Foreign and Commonwealth Office custodian of the SOE papers, and his successor Mr Christopher Woods, both of whom were most generous with help and advice. Finally, I thank the four secretarial hands and their aiders and abettors for conjuring up papers from the depths of an archive which in the nature of things is not the easiest to fathom.

*November 1982*                                                    C. G. C.

# Contents

## APPENDICES

# Illustrations

Maps

# Abbreviations

| | |
|---|---|
| ABDA | American-British-Dutch-Australian |
| AEBUS | Anti-Enemy Backing-up Society |
| AFO | Anti-Fascist Organization |
| AJA | Anti-Japanese Army |
| AJU | Anti-Japanese Union |
| AJUF | Anti-Japanese Union and Forces |
| ALFSEA | Allied Land Forces, South East Asia |
| BAAG | British Army Aid Group |
| BDA | Burma Defence Army |
| BIA | Burma Independence Army |
| BIC | Burma Intelligence Corps |
| BNA | Burma National Army |
| C | Symbol, Head of Secret Intelligence Service |
| C-in-C | Commander-in-Chief |
| CAS(B) | Civil Affairs Service (Burma) |
| CBI | China-Burma-India |
| CCAO(B) | Chief Civil Affairs Officer (Burma) |
| CD | Symbol, Head of SOE |
| CLI | Corps Léger d'Intervention |
| CND | Chinese National Dollars |
| COPP | Combined Operations Pilotage Parties |
| COS | Chiefs of Staff |
| D. Div. | Deception Division, SEAC |
| DGER | Directeur Général Études Recherches |
| DGSR | Director General Shipbuilding and Repairs |
| DICA | Deputy Chief of Staff, Information and Civil Affairs |
| EWS(I) | Eastern Warfare School (India) |
| FANY | First Aid Nursing Yeomanry |
| FEB | Far Eastern Bureau |

GS(R)        General Staff (Research)
GSI(k)       India Mission's first cover symbol

IFBU         Indian Field Broadcasting Unit
IIR          Institute of International Relations
IIS          International Intelligence Service
ISLD         Inter-Services Liaison Department

JPS          Joint Planning Staff

KMT          Kuomintang

LCR          Landing Craft, Rubber

MCP          Malayan Communist Party
MCR          Miniature Communications Receiver
MEW          Ministry of Economic Warfare
MFU          Mobile Floating Unit
MI R         Military Intelligence, Research
MOI          Ministry of Information
MPAJA        Malayan People's Anti-Japanese Army

NCAC         Northern Combat Area Command

OM           Oriental Mission
OM/P         Oriental Mission, Propaganda Section
OSS          Office of Strategic Services
OWI          Office of War Information

PIAT         Projectile, Infantry, Anti-Tank
PWD          Psychological Warfare Division, SEAC
PWE          Political Warfare Executive
PWJC         Political Warfare (Japan) Committee

QOps         Quartermaster, Operations

RAPWI        Repatriation of Allied Prisoners of War and Internees
RII          Research and Investment Institute
RU           Research Unit

SA           Service d'Action
SACSEA       Supreme Allied Commander, South East Asia

| | |
|---|---|
| SB | Sleeping Beauty |
| SD | Special Duties |
| SEAC | South East Asia Command |
| SEI | School for Eastern Interpreters |
| SFDC | Special Forces Development Centre |
| SIS | Secret Intelligence Service |
| SO | Symbol, Minister in charge of SOE |
| SOA | Special Operations, Australia |
| SOE | Special Operations Executive |
| SRD | Services Reconnaissance Department |
| STS | Special Training School |
| | |
| USAAF | United States Army Air Force |
| | |
| W/T | Wireless Telegraph |

# Origin

THE Special Operations Executive (SOE) was conceived on 1 July 1940 when Ministers and officials, with the Foreign Secretary in the chair, examined a proposal that sabotage, subversive activities, and black propaganda in enemy, enemy-controlled, and neutral countries should come under the control of the Director of Military Intelligence (DMI). At this time propaganda, run by a secret body known as 'Electra House' from its office building, and ostensibly part of the Foreign Office, had not got into its stride. A second group known as 'Section D', also with Foreign Office cover, was investigating 'every possibility of attacking potential enemies by means other than the operations of military forces'. Thirdly, War Office Branch Military Intelligence, Research (MI R) (formerly General Staff (Research) (GS(R)) was developing methods of guerrilla warfare.* It was now mooted that these activities should be brought together under DMI, ministerial responsibility being shared between the Foreign Secretary, Secretary of State for War, and the Minister of Information, except that on sabotage in enemy countries he would be responsible to the Minister of Economic Warfare and the Secretary of State for War.

The Minister of Economic Warfare (Dr Hugh Dalton, later Lord Dalton) argued against the proposal. The new organization must be kept away from the War Office and headed by a single Minister. Next day he wrote to the Deputy Prime Minister (Mr Clement Attlee, later Lord Attlee): 'I did not mention your name, though I clearly had you in mind for the performance of this function.' DMI (Major-General F. G. Beaumont-Nesbitt) had claimed that these activities, being operations of war, should be directed by the General Staff; but he (Dalton) considered that 'the war from without' (i.e. military operations) was distinct from 'the war from within' which was of quite a different character, and must not come under military

---

* For detailed accounts of these bodies see M. R. D. Foot, *SOE in France* (HMSO, 1966); and Charles Cruickshank, *The Fourth Arm: Psychological Warfare 1938–1945* (OUP, 1981).

control. 'Regular soldiers are not fit to stir up revolution, to create social chaos, or to use all those ungentlemanly means of winning the war which come so easily to the Nazis.' What was needed was absolute secrecy, political reliability, fanatical enthusiasm, and willingness to work with people of other nationalities. 'One of the reasons why regular soldiers cannot be trusted to make a good job of this business is because of their distaste for foreigners and dislike of working with them.'

Dalton in effect applied for the command of the new body, availing himself of a ploy much loved in Westminster and Whitehall: 'So far as I myself am concerned, I am conscious as you know, of not being at present fully extended, and I should be very glad to assist you in this work, if you took it over.' He knew of course that Attlee did not want the job; and he even went so far as to choose his lieutenant – Sir Campbell Stuart, the Canadian then in charge of propaganda, whom he described as a 'civilian thruster with a large capacity of making use of foreigners'. An interesting choice, for a few weeks later Stuart was sacked from Electra House on Churchill's direct instructions, Dalton being required to hand him his letter of dismissal.[1]

The weakness in the argument that the new organization should not be under military control was masked by the purple passages and passion in his letter to Attlee, who had no hesitation in backing him for the Ministerial post. On 19 July 1940 the Lord President (Mr Neville Chamberlain) recorded that the Prime Minister had decided that 'the sabotage service' (i.e. Section D), MI R, and Electra House would be amalgamated to form the Special Operations Executive under the Minister of Economic Warfare. On 22 July the War Cabinet formally approved the arrangements.

Through his contention that regular soldiers are not fit to stir up revolution and the creation of a civilian body to do the job, SOE's first Minister imposed a handicap on the British clandestine forces in the Far East, where there were already more than enough natural difficulties. Some regular soldiers may have been incapable of grasping the potential of special operations, but not all. Equally, all civilians do not take to subversion as ducks to water. What Dalton failed to see, or more likely to admit, was that most soldiers in 1940 were 'amateurs' from all walks of life. Some would reveal in the army the qualities needed for special operations, and so would some of their professional colleagues. Happily his misconception did not preclude the recruitment of the best men (how, incidentally, did he rationalize the presence of large numbers of regulars in SOE?), but hindsight suggests that by keeping the Executive separate from the Chiefs of Staff organization he did a considerable disservice.

SOE headquarters were themselves divided on the point. In March 1942 it was argued that the failure of the Oriental Mission (OM)* proved that SOE in the Far East should become the responsibility of the Commander-in-Chief (C-in-C), India, whose approval was in any case necessary for all special operations in his Command; and that the Joint Planning Staff (JPS) should be consulted about 'the best method of imposing military direction over SOE activities'. The proposal filled one member of the headquarters staff (Lieutenant-Colonel Leslie Sheridan) with 'alarm and despondency'. It would create an organization run by regular service officers on regular service lines, which he admitted some believed to be ideal. He added: 'This may be true, but it cannot be regarded as true by SOE . . . What is left for the new SO [the symbol for the Ministerial head, Lord Selborne, who had just replaced Dalton] or CD [the symbol for the head of the organization, at this time Sir Frank Nelson] to administer if such an organization is set up?' The answer was that they would be out of a job. This was a clear case of empire-protection; but those who favoured integration with the military, and almost certainly greater effectiveness, lost the day.

About this time Mr Anthony Eden (later Lord Avon), Halifax's successor as Foreign Secretary, told the Prime Minister that SOE needed

a thorough overhaul and probably a severe pruning . . . My view has long been that SOE should be under the control of the Chiefs of Staff. Much of their work is military in character, all of it is connected either with military operations or with political activities which of course concern the Foreign Office. It is incongruous that the Minister of Economic Warfare should control SOE. The Minister is neither a member of the War Cabinet, nor of the Defence Committee. He cannot therefore be aware of our secret policies and purposes.

His attitude may have been influenced by the effect of some SOE activities on Foreign Office policies, although he did claim that he had never refused permission for 'any escapade which might profit our

---

* See Part II, Chapter 1.

war effort'. Surprisingly Churchill ignored this common-sense proposal.*[2]

In 1943 the Minister of State resident in the Middle East (Mr Richard Casey) who was Chairman of the Middle East Defence Committee urged that SOE Cairo should become a Directorate of GHQ, Middle East Forces, directly responsible to C-in-C. When this was discussed in a stormy meeting of the War Cabinet Defence Committee on 14 September 1943 Eden naturally supported the change. Only thus would 'the Aegean [sic] stable of SOE in the Middle East be cleaned up'.† Attlee, deputizing for the Prime Minister, said he understood this type of activity was better done 'by a not entirely military organization' – the seed planted by Dalton had not perished. Selborne fought desperately to save his empire. When it became clear that agreement was impossible the Minister of Production (Mr Oliver Lyttelton, later Viscount Chandos), who had preceded Casey as Minister Resident in the Middle East, was asked to act as referee. He consulted everybody concerned and decided that SOE activities *must* be taken over by a Directorate under C-in-C. The Chiefs of Staff advised independently that there would be great military advantage. Yet, most surprisingly, Selborne again won. The final decision was 'SOE will preserve its integrity under the Minister of Economic Warfare' – in short, the mixture as before.[3] Although the debate had been conducted with regard to the Middle East the arguments in favour of a similar change in the Far East were perhaps stronger.

SOE was set up with an eye to Europe – the Japanese war was still eighteen months distant. However, the Far East was not forgotten. Both War Office and Colonial Office advised the authorities in British territories to prepare to wage guerrilla warfare; and in June 1940 the War Office offered to collaborate in organizing paramilitary activities ranging from raids in uniform to sabotage in civilian clothes. On 19 November 1940 Major-General R. H. Dewing, Chief Staff Officer to C-in-C, Far East (Air Chief Marshal Sir Robert Brooke-Popham), told London there had been no attempt to initiate 'what used to be called MI R activities'. He urged the War Office to take the matter up.[4]

This was duly done. Terms of reference for an SOE group in

---

* At the beginning of 1944 Eden minuted the Prime Minister: 'If a change is to be made then in my view it [SOE] should be put under you as Minister of Defence with day-to-day control by the Chiefs of Staff, in consultation with me only in respect of policy.' (FO 954 24, ff. 173–4.)

† We shall never know if this was a joke or a typist's error.

Singapore were settled by SOE headquarters on 26 November 1940; and on 24 January 1941 the Governors of the Straits Settlements (Sir Shenton Thomas) and Hong Kong (Sir Geoffry Northcote) were formally told that 'the Oriental Mission' would be operating in their territories under C-in-C, Far East.[5] The magnitude of the task assigned to the infant Mission is reflected by the catalogue of countries in which it was instructed to operate: Free and occupied China; Manchuria; the Japanese Empire; Siberia; French Indo-China; Siam; the Philippines; the Dutch East Indies; Burma; Malaya; Hong Kong; Borneo; Sarawak; and to make sure that not even the smallest island slipped through the net, 'other British, French, Dutch and Portuguese possessions in the area'.

The OM's directive followed the model provided for SOE operations in Europe; and it seems that here a fundamental mistake was made. The Far Eastern theatre had nothing in common with the European. A whole range of factors made it difficult to carry out SOE's tasks as defined by Churchill – 'to create and foster the spirit of resistance' in occupied countries; and 'to establish a nucleus of trained men who would be able to assist as "a fifth column" in the liberation of the country concerned'.*

In every occupied country in Europe there was a resistance movement desperately anxious for help against the common enemy. In Burma, Malaya, Sumatra, and French Indo-China there was often doubt as to who *was* the real enemy – the invading Japanese, or the colonial power they had thrown out? In the last country SOE's hands were tied for a long time by American anti-colonial policy. The embryo guerrilla movement among the hill tribes in Burma which SOE developed successfully was based as much on hostility to the Burmese of the plains as on loyalty to the British regime.

Agents could be dropped into the countries of the compact European theatre with comparative ease. The vast distances between the SOE bases in India and Ceylon and the Japanese-occupied countries meant that they had to be carried many hundred miles in submarines or aircraft – and it was not until late in the war that aircraft capable of covering the whole theatre became available. A European agent had a good chance of passing unnoticed in any European country, but a white man could not pass unremarked through the streets of Tokyo or occupied Rangoon. Even in the

* M. R. D. Foot, pp. 10–11.

remotest jungle he could not remain forever invisible. The jungle itself and monsoon climate made for difficulties not encountered in the West. Men and equipment alike suffered from their effects. Highly vulnerable camps in the mountains took the place of safe houses in populous cities. The predominantly agricultural economies of the countries of the Far East meant that there was less scope for the devices of the saboteur than in the industrial economies of the West, where a handful of men could cripple a power-station or an aircraft factory in a single night. Sumatra, with its important oil production, was an exception; but despite repeated pleas from the Chiefs of Staff for attacks on oil installations, SOE found it impossible to move against the oilfields there.

Finally, the great distance from headquarters placed administrative strains on SOE in the Far East not experienced in Europe. It is never easy to manage an organization, especially when it is highly secret and personal contacts are limited to rare visits by headquarters staff to the field. Cabled correspondence lacks the human touch essential to good management, and it sometimes leads to misunderstandings that impair efficiency. This remoteness from headquarters certainly contributed to the failure of OM,* and it helped to allow the India Mission to deviate from its original terms of reference, which, it is argued below, was a mistake.†

It was no doubt natural that SOE should provide its outposts in the Far East with terms of reference modelled on those current in Europe, although it may be felt that the differences enumerated above should have been recognized and legislated for. What is more surprising is that as the war went on and the impossibility of carrying out 'European-type' special operations became evident, there was no deliberate attempt to redeploy SOE's resources in the Far East so that they might make a more effective contribution to the war effort. It is true that before the Japanese occupation was complete in the various countries there *was* scope for special operations in the accepted sense. 'Left-behind parties' established behind Japanese lines could have caused a great deal of trouble through activities in their own right, and at second hand through the organization of guerrillas. After the Japanese occupation special operations became virtually impossible, and much of SOE's effort was devoted to intelligence-gathering, not an SOE function.

---

* See Part I, Chapter 1.        † See pp. 251–5.

The first head of SOE was Sir Frank Nelson (August 1940 to May 1942), a former member of Parliament who more recently had been British Consul in Berne. He was succeeded by Sir Charles Hambro, a merchant banker. In September 1943 Major-General C. McV. (later Sir Colin) Gubbins, a regular soldier, took over from Hambro and remained as CD until the end of hostilities. The Director in charge of Overseas Groups and Missions, who had overall responsibility for special operations in the Far East, was first Colonel Brien Clarke, succeeded in March 1942 by Colonel George Taylor, who had been Hambro's Chief of Staff. Taylor was assisted by Lieutenant-Colonels Bickham Sweet-Escott and Leslie Sheridan. There were in succession three Far Eastern Branch Heads at headquarters in London: Major Christopher Hudson from August 1941 to September 1942, when he took charge of India Mission Group B in Colombo, Lieutenant-Colonel C. A. L. Guise from September 1942 to March 1944, followed by Lieutenant-Colonel G. Egerton Mott, who remained in this post to the end of the war. Sir George Moss was adviser on Chinese affairs.

PART I

# TECHNIQUES

# 1

# Recruitment

THE engagement of staff for a secret organization, especially in wartime, is an act of faith. The jobs cannot very well be advertised in the national press. The head of the organization is chosen by the Prime Minister from personal knowledge, or perhaps on the advice of senior Ministers and the Cabinet Secretary. The subordinate posts, however, are the responsibility of the head, whose choice is limited to people he knows, or who are recommended by people whose judgement he trusts. Dalton, the first Minister for Special Operations was the product of Eton and Cambridge. So was Mr Colin Mackenzie, a director of the textile firm of J. and P. Coats Limited, who commanded SOE's India Mission throughout the war. Mackenzie was a personal friend of the Viceroy of India, the Marquess of Linlithgow, also an Etonian, whose approval was necessary for an appointment of such importance. Mr Valentine Killery, head of the ill-fated Oriental Mission, who had spent many years in the Far East with Imperial Chemical Industries Limited, had also been to Eton. That the early staff lists of SOE abound with the names of graduates of the public schools and older universities did not reflect a conspiracy on the part of the old-boy network, nor did it necessarily mean that those selected were not as well qualified as others. It was an inescapable fact of life.

The finding of staff for SOE's overseas missions had its own problems. There were three levels of recruitment: for 'management' to initiate and direct policy, administer training schools and wireless telegraph (W/T) networks, order and issue supplies, and in the case of the India Mission to plan and execute operations in Burma, Malaya, Siam, French Indo-China, Sumatra, and China; secondly, the engagement of staff to carry out these operations; and thirdly, the enlistment of guerrillas to go into action when the signal was given.

It was not too difficult to find management staff for operations in Europe. The Continent was a known quantity; and there were plenty of men familiar with conditions in the countries where SOE had to operate. In the Far East, however, there were relatively few; and their orderly recruitment – planters, engineers, miners, forest managers, business men, civil servants fluent in the languages of the East and familiar with its customs – became impossible after the Japanese invasion. Those who escaped capture were dispersed throughout the free areas of the eastern hemisphere, in the armed forces or essential war work from which it was difficult to remove them even when their whereabouts had been discovered. Commanders or employers could not be told the nature of the alternative employment offered and were therefore reluctant to give them up. When India was scoured for candidates for the India Mission's Siam Country Section in 1942, seventy who knew Siam were located, but only nine were available.

The Mission did, however, succeed in recruiting men with experience of the countries for which they became responsible. The heads of the three main Country Sections, Mr R. E. Forrester, followed by Mr Ritchie Gardiner (Burma); Mr A. C. Pointon (Siam); Mr B. R. Goodfellow, and from April 1943 Mr F. I. Tremlett (Malaya) had all spent years in the East; but like everyone else in special operations they had to learn on the job. The French Indo-China Country Section found Mr François de Langlade, a planter in Malaya. The Anglo-Dutch Country Section was headed successively by Major F. Mollinger and Colonel H. G. C. Pel who had served with the Dutch army in the East Indies, and Lieutenant C. J. Wingender of the Royal Netherlands Navy.

It was more difficult to find volunteers for service in the field. It was necessary to recruit Chinese, Malays, Siamese, Indians, Burmese from the plains and hills, and men from the races of French Indo-China. In November 1942 Mackenzie warned London: 'The crux of the matter is after all the agent or operator. For the great majority of our projects natives are essential. By and large there is little patriotism from which to recruit.' Of 300 Burmese looked at in Calcutta only four were at all possible and after further consideration even they were discarded. It was equally difficult to find Malays. None interviewed in Britain was prepared to volunteer. Some were recruited in Jeddah and sent to India but they were deemed to be unsuitable for resistance work. Paradoxically, when there was an ample supply of first-rate men for field service – young Chinese communists in Malaya on the eve of the Japanese invasion – the military and civil authorities barred their employment until it was too late; and they opposed the recruitment of Europeans on the ground that their services were required for more important purposes.

The India Mission's first oriental recruits were drawn from the hundred-odd Siamese nationals living in England when the Japanese entered their country, of whom fifty-five were students. A Free Siamese Movement in Britain was ruled out by the Foreign Secretary (Eden) because the Siamese were too few and too young; but he hoped that although they were technically enemy aliens they might be allowed to join the Pioneer Corps. The War Office agreed. Thirty-five enlisted on 7 August 1942, it being understood they would eventually have duties more in keeping with their qualifications, which were excellent. Many had taken a degree in Bangkok, and most were at university or technical college in England. Eight were engineers, five in medicine, five taking commercial courses, and four barristers or solicitors. Although the Foreign Office thought their recruitment might have political advantages their potential military contribution was more important. Twenty-three were accepted as agents – known as the White Elephants – and all were used on operations. As a group they were the India Mission's most successful agents. They were without exception dedicated to the expulsion of the Japanese, and they posed no 'colonial' problem. Towards the end of the war SOE brought a further fifty-four Siamese from Siam, including members of the police force (Operations *Influx I–IV*); but there was time to return only twenty-two before the war ended.

Most recruits were Burmese and Indians – just over 370 of each; but only thirty Indians went on operations compared with 270 Burmese, half from the plains, and half from the hills. The next biggest group was Chinese. There were many Chinese in the territories occupied by Japan, so that a large number of Chinese agents were needed. Arrangements were made with General Tai Li, head of the Chinese Secret Service, to recruit in China a succession of parties which came to India for training. In all 223 were recruited of whom 107 (known as the Dragons) spoke Malay. Forty-six went on operations and gave good service, especially the first batch recruited in Chungking by Lim Bo Seng, the Chinese industrialist who escaped from Singapore and came to India in November 1942.

The other Chinese were anything but satisfactory. The Red Elephants, twelve Siamese-speaking graduates of the Chinese Military Academy who had lived in Siam, included former merchants, students, a teacher, a bookshop owner, a jeweller, and a pawnbroker. On paper they looked promising, it being assumed that although China was not at war with Siam her nationals would gladly fight the common enemy there. When they arrived in Calcutta it was found they suffered from the 'Chungking taint' – admiration of all things American and scorn for all things British. The leader had been allowed to choose the rest of the party, and had selected only close friends which made the Red Elephants a self-contained group difficult to manage.

They were followed by the Blue Elephants, also Siamese-speaking – twenty-five men in their late twenties born in China, Hong Kong, and Indo-China, with one or two from Siam: mainly salesmen (rice, timber, paint, cloth, wines and spirits) with two goldsmiths, two photographers, and one described as an ice manufacturer. Most had friends or relations living in Siam, and most, though by no means all, were fluent in Siamese. Other groups of Chinese were recruited for service in Burma (Pandas); in Indo-China (Eagles); in Sumatra (Fairheads), and the China Coast (Pelicans). None pulled their weight, perhaps because they were under instructions from Tai Li to give priority to reporting intelligence about affairs in India, which was collated at Chinese Consulates for transmission to Chungking. There was also the danger that information about future operations involving Chinese agents would be relayed to Chungking and leaked to the Japanese.

The India Mission's French Indo-China Country Section had little success in recruiting native agents, partly because of the hostility to French colonial rule. In January 1943 they were offered a group of Annamites deported from Indo-China to Madagascar for various offences – a strange mixture of engineers, jewellers, teachers, and farmers, ranging from peasants to highly educated men who had studied in France. Nine were considered for special operations, but none was taken on by the India Mission. The Eagles destined for Indo-China were no better than the other Chinese. 'Personal interest seems to be their sole ideal'; and they became notorious for their lack of fighting spirit and indiscipline. Neither the Chinese Fairheads, nor (with one exception) the handful of natives brought out of Sumatra were used on operations there.

The India Mission sent greater numbers of British into the countries of South Asia as the war progressed – 450 in all. At first they were agents in the accepted sense, concerned in theory with sabotage and in practice with recruiting resistance groups. Later, when Allied offensive operations were imminent the numbers greatly increased and their role became more paramilitary. Men with experience of special operations in Europe and the Middle East were transferred to the India Mission towards the end of 1944 and played a big part in the highly successful paramilitary operations in Burma.

Recruitment at the third level – of resistance groups and guerrillas in the field – was also an act of faith. It was necessary to rely heavily on the judgement of native leaders, who could make mistakes and allow the recruitment of men who might be in the pay of the Japanese. It was easy for a traitor to detach himself from a guerrilla group and inform the nearest Japanese outpost where to find it. Traitors got short shrift when discovered but much damage could be done before they were dealt with. Men recruited in the field were carefully listed, with their father's name, their village, police station, date of engagement, rate of pay, and weapons issued. There were two sorts: static levies to guard dumps and dropping-zones, who operated offensively up to ten miles from their village, and who were not fed by Force 136; and mobile levies under British officers, who operated wherever the army wanted them, and had their rations provided.

# 2

# Training

SOE set up an irregular warfare school on an isolated peninsula near Singapore in July 1941. It was commanded by Major J. M. L. Gavin from the Special Training Centre at Lochailort in the Scottish Highlands, being known successively as Scapula, the School of Demolitions, and No. 101 Special Training School (101 STS).* The curriculum included demolitions, sabotage, use of weapons, un-armed combat, simple navigation, communications, and diet. The courses were attended by French, American, Danish, Swedish, and Portuguese civilians in addition to British; and by officers and NCOs from the British forces in Malaya, Burma, and Hong Kong.

After the fall of Singapore most of the instructors joined the India Mission, but as it had as yet no Training School they were loaned for the time being to the army. In July 1942 the Mission opened the 'Guerrilla Training Unit' at Kharakvasla, near Poona on the shores of Lake Fife; and in the next nine months 150 communist students were trained here for post-occupational activities.

When the threat to India diminished attention was turned to offensive training. The Guerrilla Training Unit became the Eastern Warfare School (India) (EWS(I)) with a filter course to test trainees on the model of the Students' Assessment Board in Britain. This gave men a taste of weapon-training, map-reading, and fieldcraft. Because of language difficulties intelligence tests were kept simple, and personality was judged subjectively. Survivors of the filter went on to four- or eight-week courses at EWS(I) proper, the shorter course being intended for men who would be 'instruments', and the longer for 'organizers in the field'. Both covered jungle living, including cooking, Japanese tactics, the use of bamboo for booby- and animal-traps, first aid, and hygiene. There were marine courses on Lake Fife – the handling of small boats, and beach-landing – and courses in industrial sabotage. There was also a rehabilitation centre for agents returned from the field.

The School for Eastern Interpreters (SEI), at Alam Bazaar on the

---

* The preparatory mission was known as *Puma*.

River Hooghli near Calcutta, opened in May 1943 to provide agent- and propaganda-training on the lines of SOE's school at Beaulieu in England. It ran a six-week course dealing with security, surveillance, agent management, and the planning of subversive organizations. There was instruction in the reconnaissance of docks and airfields, enemy identification, and intelligence-reporting. Students were taught ciphers and codes suitable for their own language. Propaganda courses included the improvisation of printing presses and the distribution of subversive literature.

From January 1943 parachute-training was carried out at Chaklala near Rawalpindi through the Air Landing School run by the RAF; but in January 1944 it was transferred to Jessore so that SOE's special needs – instruction in dropping to reception parties, and receiving agents and stores – could be looked after. Forty men a week – from all the South East Asia Command (SEAC) clandestine organizations – were trained at Jessore.

The fourth main training establishment was the Advanced Operations School on an island near Trincomalee in Ceylon. It had much the same syllabus as EWS(I); but it was also used to instruct men destined to be infiltrated by submarines based at Trincomalee. When Taylor inspected this school in 1944 he found that relations between instructors who had been long in the East and those newly arrived from Europe were strained, one reason being that the ferry connecting the island with the mainland did not run in the evening. 'It is not to be expected that a staff can live contentedly on sandy waste backed by jungle, perpetually in their own company.' The problem was solved by transferring men to other schools and bringing in new blood.

Signals instruction was the responsibility of the Chief Signals Officer (Lieutenant-Colonel J. A. C. Knott). At first courses were held in Meerut about forty miles north-east of Delhi; but later, training wings were set up at the Advanced Operations School, and EWS(I), where basic courses lasting three to four months were given, after which the pupil went to Meerut for a month of operational training.

The difficulty of dealing with oriental trainees is illustrated by the history of the Siamese-speaking Chinese brought from China. Captain Peter Lindsay recorded that they came through their preliminary training with flying colours. They were intelligent, hard-working, and well-disciplined. When they went on to Trincomalee reports were less enthusiastic. 'They have intentionally been allowed a lot of free time, which they spend almost entirely in sleeping and playing Mah-jong, rather than in boating, swimming, exercise, or revision.' They disliked marching, camping out, and going on short rations – all vital to their future work. They found the course at SEI more to their liking, probably because it contained practical exercises, in one of which they were required to collect intelligence. 'Results were good. They found out more from brothels than previous students had obtained by purer methods of investigation.'

The conflicting assessment of the students was carried into their final reports. The Chief Instructor said they had been so thoroughly spoilt, having been treated like schoolgirls ('and schoolgirls from Heathfield rather than Roedean') that the damage could never be repaired. The Commandant did not agree. He admitted that they had been unduly pampered, but 'this attitude passed off as the course progressed'.

The conflicting assessments of the Canadian Chinese trained towards the end of the war inspired the comment: 'One is almost led to believe that the similarity of one Chinese to another in unaccustomed eyes may perhaps have led to some confusion between the Board and its President. But granted there is no confusion, one's faith in the accuracy of the findings is inevitably rather shaken.' Samples of the reports which gave rise to this observation are:

| *Filter Board Findings* | *Board President's Findings* |
|---|---|
| A negative personality which is too fogged and dull to develop satisfactorily. | Good personality . . . completely trustworthy. Very good sense of humour. |

and again:

| | |
|---|---|
| Lacks the moral fibre to do much more than drift. Very unsure of himself. Personality is weak, colourless. Not suitable for this organization. | Shrewd and intelligent. Confident of himself. Forceful nature and mature. Able to take responsibility. Has personality and character. Very self reliant. |

There were other difficulties peculiar to the Far East. It was believed that all Asiatics disliked losing face and would never admit they had not understood something. Another problem was how to convince trainees already familiar with jungle conditions that they had anything to learn from European instructors. Fieldcraft as taught by SOE made little impression on the Kachins who were unwilling to take the most obvious precautions. It was said that not even six months' training would make them alter their habits.

A major change was introduced in November 1944 when the Trincomalee School became the main training and dispatch centre for paramilitary groups. The Commandant was given command of the men during training, while they awaited dispatch, and when they returned from operations. This was resented by the India Mission Country Sections as it meant 'a considerable but very necessary corralling' of their activities. The advantage was that agents would no longer be sent on operations undertrained because of the Country Sections' impatience to get them into the field. Members of operational groups now trained together as a unit, whereas teams had formerly been made up at the eleventh hour from men who happened to be available.

As it was impossible to produce trained men at exactly the rate required, holding camps were provided where they could live until they were called in. In January 1944 three bungalows were acquired at Avisawella in Ceylon for men destined for Malaya. A holding camp for Burma was established south-east of Calcutta – an unfortunate choice. 'The area was riddled with malaria, crude encampments close to villages in which splenetic infection in children was over 80 per cent, 100 miles from the nearest large town, subject to constant heavy rain, training was quite impossible and rehabilitation a miserable farce.' The whole of the first group to occupy this camp went down with fever and spent six weeks in hospital. It was condemned and replaced with a camp at Horana in Ceylon.

At first most trainees were Asiatics. In all 1,500 passed through the various schools. Most of the 450 British officers and NCOs were trained at the end of 1944 and the beginning of 1945 for operations in Burma and Malaya. Four hundred French officers and NCOs were trained for paramilitary operations in Indo-China but only a quarter of them got there before the Japanese took complete control of the country in March 1945.

There was criticism, perhaps not all justified, of training in general, and in particular of the failure to tailor courses to the type of operation to be carried out. At first much time was devoted to training in demolitions and ambushes, when it was envisaged that SOE's task would be to organize guerrilla activities and sabotage against enemy lines of communication; but in Burma the initial task was intelligence-gathering, for which many felt they were in-adequately trained. A typical comment came from a group leader in the Shan States: 'Half our lengthy and extensive training was wasted. We could have done with more W/T and intelligence training.' Another leader in the same area said that his group had been trained to attack the enemy without the support of guerrillas, yet all they were required to do was supply intelligence. The training of the 'Special Groups' for service in Burma illustrates the discrepancy between preparation and role. These patrols of twenty to twenty-five men were trained for offensive action, but initially found themselves engaged on intelligence work for which they were far too big. It was believed that three-men teams would have done an equally good job with much less danger of detection.

There was criticism from teams in the Karen Hills. 'Training . . . was entirely inadequate and did not cover the right subjects.' Another leader there claimed that instructors did not have enough operational experience. 'A full conception of what we would have to do in the field did not appear to have dawned on anyone. Well-meaning and hard-working instructors did their best to instruct in subjects of which they had no practical experience.' The only course that came in for universal praise was the parachute-jumping course at Jessore.

The failure to provide courses of instruction which fitted groups for their exact role in the field may be attributed to some extent to SEAC's chronic uncertainty about future operational plans; but the fact remains that long before SOE was required to play a major role in Burma it was obvious that its intelligence function was to be of great importance. There was time enough to reorganize the Training Schools to take account of this, but it was not done for the Burma campaign. Although a preliminary study of SOE's role in Malaya put intelligence at the top of the priority list there is no sign that there was to be a corresponding change in the balance of the training courses.

In one respect, however, SOE's changing role was matched by a rearrangement of the training facilities. As agent operations became less important, and were replaced by paramilitary, the provision of agent training was reduced. SEI continued to function but merely as a 'time filler and insurance'; and from the beginning of 1945 the school was used only for the training of agents assigned to a specific task, of whom there were very few.

# 3

# Planning; briefing;
# operational control

THE Oriental Mission found it impossible to make effective plans, for two main reasons. In the first place it was not given the resources needed to cover the vast territories with which it was saddled; and in the second it failed to establish the close liaison with the military which was essential if its plans were to achieve their objective of furthering military operations. Planning was more successful in the early days of the India Mission, partly because Mackenzie grasped the importance of keeping in step with the military, and partly because he was forced to make defensive plans to meet the threats of a German descent from the north and a Japanese invasion of India through Burma.

With the establishment of SEAC in September 1943 responsibility for the India Mission was transferred from India Command to the Supreme Allied Commander, Admiral Lord Louis Mountbatten. On 18 December 1943 he issued a directive that no subversive operation should take place without the approval of P Division, set up to co-ordinate the plans of the clandestine bodies under his command.[1] P Division now became the focal point for planning, an important step since the clandestine organizations, in particular SOE, the Inter-Services Liaison Department (ISLD – the Far Eastern manifestation of the Secret Intelligence Service), and the United States Office of Strategic Services (OSS, which combined the functions of SOE and ISLD) were competing for the same scarce resources – linguists, submarine and air transport, for example. Plans also had to be co-ordinated to ensure that two organizations did not operate in the same Japanese-controlled areas, thereby possibly compromising each other.

However, a new difficulty emerged. Many aspects of special operations had to be catered for well in advance, for example the training of W/T operators and of agents with knowledge of a certain territory; but these long-term plans were at the mercy of SEAC's strategic planning. Thus, when it seemed likely that Operation

*Culverin* – the Allied invasion of Sumatra, which Churchill passion-ately favoured – would go ahead, the India Mission made elaborate plans and preparations for its own contribution; and when *Culverin* was called off a great deal of effort was wasted.

This problem was very much in Gubbins's mind when he visited the Far East in March/April 1944. He was surprised to find that SEAC had no overall plan for future operations, and that there was no attempt to link the operations of Admiral Nimitz, in command of the Central Pacific Forces, and of General MacArthur, in command of the South West Pacific Forces, with those of Mountbatten. He suggested that SEAC should simplify SOE's task by issuing operational directives within which the objectives of the India Mission would be clearly defined; and recommended that these objectives should include the fostering of Kachin and Karen resistance in Burma, the organization of sabotage in Burma from both within and without, and the organization of Chinese communists in Malaya.

However, it was one thing to say what should be done and quite another to ensure that it happened. When the India Mission assumed that there would be major military operations in Southern Burma before the end of 1944 they planned to raise guerrillas behind the Japanese lines, and to recruit and train *coup de main* parties to attack targets that could not be dealt with by guerrillas or aerial bombardment. In the event the Allies did not have the resources to carry out the operations in question; and once again much planning effort was wasted. It was of course inevitable that SOE's planning should take second place to the Command's strategical intentions, but towards the end of hostilities, when it was accepted that SOE could make an important paramilitary contribution, they were kept much more closely in touch with military planning.

Briefing – through which the intentions of the planners were conveyed to the operatives, and through which the latter were warned about problems in the field – was usually carried out at the end of training. It varied according to the nature of the operation. The needs of an agent party differed from those of a paramilitary group. There was much criticism of those in charge of briefing, and only occasional praise. One officer withdrew from an operation in the Shan States at the eleventh hour 'owing partly to the light beginning to dawn on the real strength of the intelligence briefing' founded 'on reports dating to the period before the Japanese invasion'. Another felt let down by 'the rather vague promises of the "Q" side of the briefing concerning our supply in the field . . . it was realized that the brief on this question was more wishful thinking with a view to encouraging the party before entering the field'. Groups in the Karen Hills were almost unanimously critical. 'Briefing was entirely inadequate and amateurish.' 'It is a pity that the briefing staff were not honest enough to admit they knew nothing and were too damned lazy to find out. Briefing was done from an out-of-date Baedeker to Burma.' 'Briefing. I hardly know where to begin. Several hours of verbose nothingness left us with the impression that those responsible had not the courage to admit that they had no knowledge of our area or tasks and that they were too lazy to make the necessary effort.'

It is difficult to decide how far these criticisms were justified. Many were made by men who had been on operations in Europe where headquarters were in much closer touch with the field, from which agents were regularly returning with up-to-date information, and they were wrong to expect European standards. On the other hand, the briefing officers should have been more frank about the limited state of their knowledge. One who did give a realistic briefing earned the gratitude of the team he briefed. He was 'exceedingly frank about the lack of information concerning the area, and therefore we went into the field realizing that we had to feel our way forward, and find out local conditions as we went along'.

Briefing for agent work or sabotage was quite different. It had to define precisely what the agent was expected to do, often in very simple terms. For example, the Indian agent (*Mahout*) who parachuted into Burma in June 1943 was told that his chief duty was to start an anti-Japanese rumour campaign, thinking out his rumours very carefully, and making sure that they could not be traced back to him. He should assemble a team of no more than five who would go around asking if people had met the man who said so-and-so . . . He was even provided with a sign to be used between the group, 'an "O" made with the left hand forefinger and thumb', which may seem to be too obvious to make a good secret sign. He was also given a series of twelve 'Don'ts', including: 'Don't speak till spoken to; Don't appear intelligent; Don't reply too quickly—it means a rehearsed story; Don't reply too slowly—it means you're thinking up a plausible reply.' His cover story was quite simple. If he was picked up on landing he was to say he had come from Rangoon and was now

looking for employment. If this was not accepted and 'the questioning becomes too severe – pretend that you have become mentally
deranged by the hardships you have undergone. The Burmese (and I
am told the Japanese) are afraid of lunatics and always treat them
with a fair amount of respect.'

Briefing of agents was sometimes unrealistically demanding. The
first team to enter Siam was told that no member must be captured
alive. One did contemplate using his suicide pill when he was taken
prisoner, but thought better of it. The *Jaywick* group,* who
successfully destroyed shipping in Singapore Harbour, were told that
if capture was inevitable they must jettison their stores and shoot
themselves. If one was wounded another must shoot him before
shooting himself. Instructions to the American members of the joint
*Sugarloaf II* operation to Sumatra in May 1944 laid down: 'Don't be
captured alive. You will wish you were dead soon after you are
captured . . .'.

On some occasions most elaborate arrangements were made to
enable agents to contact colleagues in occupied countries. A Chinese
who was to operate between Pegu and Rangoon in October 1944
(Operation *Wakering*) was told:

The contact will be wearing horizontally striped faded cotton longyi with an
oil stain about a foot long on the back; a navy blue sports shirt (Aertex) with
a white darn above left breast pocket. He will be carrying a khaki overcoat
over his left arm, with a white pocket handkerchief protruding from a torn
pocket. He is a Burman aged 19, height about 5 feet 2 inches.

A password was also provided. The agent would say, 'Have you got a
match?' to which the other would reply, 'No, I have dropped them on
the way' to which the response was, 'Doesn't matter. Have a
cigarette.' Agents were also provided with detailed cover stories
which must have been even more difficult to memorize than the
sartorial peculiarities of the *Wakering* contact.

Although there may have been a case, as Dalton argued, for keeping
SOE separate from the military, it was essential that operational
control of the guerrillas they raised should be vested in the army. Too
many commanders produce greater disasters than too many cooks.
There was no problem while the India Mission was still on the

* See pp. 96–8.

defensive and was largely concerned with 'pure' special operations, but in June 1942 the War Office sensed that a bétter definition of the relationship between the military and SOE in India was needed. Special activities must be related to military plans 'both in the general layout and for particular operations'. Overall control of SOE's paramilitary activities must be vested in C-in-C, who would define the special-operations role. The India Mission would select personnel, and provide equipment, transport, and means of communication. They would restrict their sabotage activities to areas beyond the reach of the other irregular forces and guerrillas; and they must not poach on the preserves of these bodies. However, there was no restriction on the dissemination of propaganda. When this package was put to Wavell he at once accepted it.[2]

The problem of operational control was aggravated by the large number of irregular bodies, which had both a strategical and tactical role. The former raised few difficulties since strategical activities were long-range and long-term – for example, the preparation for guerrilla operations behind enemy lines at a future date – and could be co-ordinated by P Division; but the day-to-day tactical operations of the clandestine bodies, which were reluctant to show their hand to each other, posed a real problem. In April 1944 it was decided that all their tactical functions must come under the operational control of the local Force Commanders. Staff Officers familiar with the capabilities of the irregular bodies were attached to Fourteenth Army headquarters and subordinate formations 'to prevent collisions in the field' and to assist the Army Commander in his operational control of the clandestine organizations. These Liaison Officers, who were forbidden to take part in running the guerrilla groups, were also saddled with the delicate task of deciding what was strategy (which SOE had to accept) and what was tactics (where SOE had a free hand).

Operational control of SOE in the field was now in theory in the hands of GOC-in-C, Fourteenth Army, although direct command of the guerrillas remained with SOE. It was not until the beginning of October 1944, however, that a Staff Officer joined Fourteenth Army headquarters from SOE. Slim claimed that if the appointment had been made three months earlier he would have had much better intelligence about Japanese movements.[3] By November 1944 SOE parties were fully co-ordinated with military operations; and their planning became intimately connected with military plans. The Fourteenth Army and XV Corps in discussion with SOE Liaison

Officers indicated the contribution SOE should make in support of forthcoming operations; and then formally requested that SOE groups should be deployed accordingly.

Although the theory of operational control became well established in the course of the Burma campaign, the practice was less than perfect. Some SOE groups found that the army were unaware of their presence, so that they could not be fully effective. One claimed that the India Mission 'were not in possession of information required best to fight the guerrilla forces . . . They were not fully aware of the policies and intentions of the forces on whose front we were operating or of the exact position in the field at any one time.'

These problems may be regarded as teething troubles which would have been eliminated had the invasion of Malaya gone ahead. The India Mission provided eleven teams to work with the military formations in the field in Malaya, and to evolve plans for communications, the transmission of intelligence, and the control of guerrilla operations. SOE undertook to provide intelligence, recruit guides for the army, protect key points, and raise guerrilla forces. Before D-Day SOE teams in the field would be directed by the army through the India Mission, although army commanders were given the right 'to advise their requirements from the resistance forces direct to the field'. After D-Day the guerrillas would come under the direct command of the army. The India Mission would be responsible for supplying them, but would have no say in the control of operations. There seems to be little doubt that if the invasion of Malaya had gone ahead this much greater subordination of SOE to the army command would have paid off.

# 4

# Equipment

THE range of sophisticated devices used in the Far East was comparatively limited. There was less scope for ingenuity in the jungle than there was in the industrialized countries of the west. Few 'toys', to use the code-name, were specially made for the Far Eastern theatre, and fewer still were supplied. The items on offer included a replica of a Chinese stone lantern (the original weighed half a ton) made of wood and covered with plaster to imitate stone. It had five compartments filled with explosive, and fitted with delayed-action fuses. Another line was Balinese carvings moulded in high explosive, and finished to simulate wood, sandstone, or porcelain. These were intended to be sold to Japanese troops as souvenirs by native agents posing as hawkers, in the hope that they would be taken on board troopships to explode after a suitable interval. There is no record that this device met with any success. The only other things specially prepared for the Far East, apart from Japanese matchboxes and kindred items for the use of agents, were tins of Soya sauce and kerosene with Japanese labels, designed to explode when opened.

The acquisition, storage, inspection, and issue of stores was the responsibility of Quartermaster, Operations (QOps). The main stocks were held at Poona and Jabalpur, with smaller quantities at Delhi, Calcutta, Bombay, and in Ceylon. QOps was responsible for the Special Forces Development Centre (SFDC) set up at Poona in 1944 to develop special stores and demolition equipment. The Centre also designed and manufactured containers for food and other stores dropped to parties in the jungle.

The arms carried by India Mission parties and issued to the guerrillas differed little from those supplied to the European resistance movements – rifles, carbines (rifles with short barrels), Sten guns, and hand-grenades. A typical drop for a party of 100 men included fifty-four carbines, forty-two Sten guns, and 240 hand-grenades. There would probably also be two PIATs (Projectile, Infantry, Anti-Tank), four Bren guns, a two-inch mortar, and a

Welrod, the eight-shot silent pistol developed by SOE.* Weapons
issued to the guerrillas had to be returned at the end of hostilities and
the men were paid only when they had surrendered them. The
quantities recovered varied. Many weapons had been inherited from
the retreating British forces in 1941/2, and from the routed Japanese,
so that the numbers held by the resistance forces exceeded the
number issued. In Malaya 690 more rifles were recovered than were
issued; twenty-eight more Thompson sub-machine guns; and over a
thousand more twelve-bore shotguns. On the other side of the
account SOE failed to recover 371 Sten guns; 333 pistols and
revolvers; and 317 carbines. Deliveries of arms to the field in
Burma, Malaya, French Indo-China, and Siam during the whole war
were 25,000 small arms; 1,300 Bren guns, PIATs and mortars; and
60,000 grenades. Nearly thirty tons of explosive were sent in.

The devices supplied were mainly intended for booby-trapping, for
ambushes, and for the demolition of bridges and railway lines. A
favourite ploy was to mine bivouacs when the troops were away on
patrol. Charges were laid under the shelters and connected by lengths
of cordtex – a plastic tube containing high explosive, the whole
length of which could be fired instantaneously. One man hid in the
jungle to activate the timing mechanism when the troops returned in
the evening so that the charges would go off in the small hours when
all were asleep. An effective ambush weapon was the 'grenade
necklace' – hand-grenades strung together on cordtex and buried
along a jungle track. When fired by means of a trip-wire or pressure
switch the necklace exploded the length of the marching column.
Railway lines were attacked with blocks of plastic explosive strapped
to the rails. Plastic explosive buried in a jungle track and covered by a
pile of stones, or packed in food tins filled with scrap metal, had a
devastating fragmentation effect.

Charges were set off by pull, pressure, and release switches. The
first was operated by a cord or wire which meant that the operator
might find himself dangerously near the explosion, and liable to be
hunted down by survivors. The pressure switch was concealed under
a floorboard or buried on a road to be activated by the pressure of an

---

* This was used with a two-handed grip, one hand holding the magazine, the other
the barrel of the silencer. At fifty yards the shot was not recognizable as that of a
firearm. The weapon's effective range was ten yards. It was one of a series of 'Wel'
products, which included the Welman, a single-seater underwater craft, and the
Welbike, a miniature motor cycle for use in the field.

enemy foot, or passing vehicle. The release switch was set by placing an object on top of it. When the object was removed the booby-trap exploded. The 'time pencil' was a device popular in Europe which did not find much favour in the Far East. It looked like a pencil, but contained a phial of acid which could be released several hours ahead to detonate the charge. Much of the demolition in the Far East was 'instant' and there was little need for delayed action.

The complexity of the equipment dropped with agents is illustrated by the contents of the containers provided for the first India Mission parties entering Siam. They included two W/T sets, batteries, acid for the batteries, a generator, blankets and groundsheet, knives, Sten gun and ammunition, torches, string, quinine, socks, shoe-laces, pencils, hussifs, spades for burying their parachutes – every conceivable thing to support life in the jungle. In all 2,000 pounds in weight were dropped – all of which, as it happened, found their way into the hands of lucky villagers.

In general, parties in the field were satisfied with the clothing issued, although tastes differed, and there were occasional complaints about quality. Shirts, socks, jungle caps, and lightweight blankets all found favour, but woollen underpants were written off as hopeless by many who made their own from parachute silk. Trousers were sometimes badly finished. Boots came in for more comment than anything else. There was much praise for the 'jungle boot' with rubber soles and canvas uppers. It was 'very good indeed, being light, comfortable, silent, and absolutely leech-proof'. However, one party in Burma deemed the jungle boot to be 'a veritable death trap' when used on wet jungle tracks. Another disadvantage was that the distinctive sole pattern left a print which the enemy could not fail to recognize. There were regular complaints about the size of boots supplied which often failed to match the order. It took four months to get a pair of size twelve to one group leader. 'Fortunately parachute cord was always in good supply', so he was able to keep his soles tied on. 'That sums up the inefficiency of a department who either considered the officer in the field a fool who did not know what to ask for, or perhaps his messages were not read. The officer's request should be treated as an indent. He should not ask, he should order.'*

---

* The delivery of the wrong size of boot was not the only problem. In *A War of Shadows* (Boardman, 1958), pp. 171–2, W. Stanley Moss records that when he was in the field in Siam headquarters omitted to pack a W/T set, provided an unserviceable generator, jungle boots for right feet only, and bullets of the wrong calibre for their pistols.

Watches – essential for operations, supply drops, and for keeping W/T schedules – were less than perfect. According to one team none of the watches issued was reliable and most were completely useless. Another reported: 'The biggest crib reference equipment is watches. In a group of 15 only one lasted longer than the first month, and that gained anything up to 6 hours a day.' This team echoed the sentiments of the leader with outsize feet: 'It would appear that our friends in Calcutta were far more competent to decide what were our requirements than we, who were on the spot. It does not seem to have occurred to anyone that the standard containers used in Europe were not quite what was required out here.'

Paranaval special equipment did not play a great part in the Far East. In 1944 the India Mission ordered twelve 'chariots', the torpedo-shaped underwater craft manned by two frogmen sitting astride, nine 'Welmans', a one-man submarine designed for beach reconnaissance and attacks on shipping, twenty-four 'Welfreighters', a two-man submarine that carried a ton of stores, and forty-eight 'Sleeping Beauties' (SBs), an all-metal single-seater canoe that could be flooded and dived. Only the last was delivered. It was twelve feet long with a twenty-eight-inch beam and a draught of sixteen inches, and had a range of forty miles at four-and-a-half knots on the surface and three-and-a-half submerged, but was difficult to handle because of a tendency to 'porpoise'. Near the surface the driver, who wore a diving-suit, could camouflage his head as a shark's fin – surely a precaution of doubtful value.[1] This was the craft that Captain Ivan Lyon took to attack Japanese shipping in Singapore Harbour – Operation *Rimau*, which ended in disaster.*

Specialized equipment was made to order for particular operations. Thus for Operation *Rimau* there were provided stockinette masks, rubber skull-caps to be garnished with seaweed, collapsible observation posts disguised with imitation grass, black hair-dye, an agent to crinkle hair, and body-dye to simulate Malay colouring, deemed to be 'light chocolate'. The *Rimau* party duly availed themselves of the last.

---

* See pp. 98–100. In the later chariots the crew were enclosed within the craft. The first chariot operation in the Far East was carried out by naval personnel. On 27 October 1944 two chariots based on HM Submarine *Trenchant* sank two 5,000-ton ships in Phuket harbour in Siam. It was then recorded: 'It is improbable that the remaining chariots will be used for similar operational work since, although targets exist, they do not afford that reasonable prospect of escape for charioteers which is essential when dealing with an unhuman enemy.' (ADM 199 1884, f. 16.)

It was said in evidence at their trial that 'all members applied on them so-called commando or demouflage dying-stuff, and dyed into brown the exposed part of their skin such as face, arms and legs'.*

Twelve Mobile Floating Units (MFU) were ordered by the India Mission. These were cylinders four feet in diameter and forty feet long, round which a conventional hull was built. The craft travelled on the surface to its destination, where it would be submerged while its crew of frogmen carried out an operation. It resurfaced automatically at a given time, to enable the saboteurs to make their escape. Six of these craft were completed but the war ended before any could reach the Far East.

* See p. 99.

# Dispatch and reception

ONLY Burma (from India and China) and French Indo-China (from China) could be infiltrated overland; but it was virtually impossible because of the length of the journey and the danger of attack by bandits. The alternatives were dispatch by submarine or aircraft. However, the Royal Navy considered that submarines were best used to attack shipping, and while they did land many agents, the operations were almost invariably fitted into routine patrols. Equally, the RAF gave priority to their own operations.

In May 1942 the India Air Landing School at Dinjan in Assam dropped two agents into Siam, and in the next twelve months carried out ten more agent sorties, six successful. In June 1943 No. 1576 (Special Duties (SD)) Flight was formed at Chaklala with Hudsons, and for the first time SOE and the other clandestine services had exclusive use of RAF aircraft. The Flight was re-formed in February 1944 as No. 357 (SD) Squadron (commanded by Squadron Leader J. R. Moore, succeeded in December 1944 by Wing Commander L. M. (later Sir Lewis) Hodges. The Squadron's A Flight (Dakotas, Hudsons, and Liberators) was based initially at Digri in Bengal, and from September 1944 at Jessore. B Flight – Catalina flying boats – was at Redhills Lake in Madras. From April 1945 No. 357 (SD) Squadron operated a Lysander Flight from Meiktila in Burma, using jungle airstrips to deliver and pick up agents. The Flight moved south to Mingaladon in May after the liberation of Rangoon. It carried out more than 350 sorties, taking in 142 men and bringing out 282. The clandestine operations Liberator fleet was augmented in November 1944 by the formation of No. 358 (SD) Squadron (commanded by Wing Commander P. G. D. Farr).

No. 628 (SD) Squadron, formed in April 1944 (commanded by Squadron Leader F. L. Godber) and disbanded in October of that year, operated Catalinas from Redhills Lake, as did No. 240 Squadron from December 1944 (Wing Commander B. A. C. Wood*). No. 160

* Succeeded by Squadron Leader J. C. Parry and Wing Commander C. B. G. Robinson.

Squadron (Liberators)* was transferred to special duties in January 1945 and from April operated full time from Kankesanturai and Minneriya in Ceylon dropping agents and supplies in Malaya and Sumatra.[1]

When Liberators became available it was possible to cover from India or Ceylon almost the whole of the SEAC operational area. In January 1945 a Liberator Mark VI of No. 357 (SD) Squadron, captained by Flying Officer J. Churchill DFC, carried stores for an SOE party in South Johore to a dropping-zone surrounded by tall trees and visible only from directly overhead. The aircraft was airborne for twenty-one hours fifty-five minutes and on the homeward journey had to land at Chittagong as its fuel was nearly exhausted. This feat was exceeded on 31 July/1 August 1945 when a Liberator Mark Vc of No. 160 Squadron (captain Flight Lieutenant J. A. Muir) flew from Minneriya to South Johore, being airborne for twenty-four hours ten minutes, and spending eighty-five minutes over the target area at Kota Tinggi, where alas no reception party was seen.[2]

For these long flights 16,000 pounds of fuel were needed to carry a payload of 2,000 pounds; and the aircraft had to take off at well above the official safe weight. The crews, many on their first operational tour, were under great strain, having from May to October to battle against the atrocious weather of the south-west monsoon, to navigate across mountainous jungle country where the only helpful landmark was the occasional river, and to pinpoint dropping-zones of necessity hidden in the most unlikely places, difficult to identify even on the clearest moonlit night. The weather was by far the greatest danger and accounted for many special-duties aircraft. Of the twenty-seven lost by Nos. 357 and 358 (SD) Squadrons only one was shot down by enemy fighters, over Siam on a daylight flight. Six of the crew, two of the OSS agents on board, and their conducting officer, escaped with their lives. Four of the crew were interned by the Siamese, but two including the captain and the three OSS men were rescued by the party to which they had been delivering stores. A Dakota of No. 357 (SD) Squadron later brought out the survivors.[3]

The skill and daring of the Lysander pilots won the admiration of

* Commanded successively by Wing Commander J. N. Stacey, DFC, DSO; Squadron Leader S. H. Trotter; Wing Commander G. McKenzie; and Wing Commander R. D. Williams.

the SOE parties they served. They used makeshift jungle airstrips, usually with a surface at the mercy of the monsoon rains, although some were more elaborate. At Mewaing in Burma a six-hundred-yard all-weather strip was constructed from split bamboo; and in Siam two semi-permanent strips were laid down with the help of village labour. One of these was 1,000 yards long, and consisted of nine inches of rock covered by gravel and earth in which grass was sown. Catalinas, which could carry agents to within a few miles of their landing-beaches, made it possible to dispense with submarines.

Parties could be dropped 'blind', that is to say into an area where there was no one to receive them; or they could drop to a 'reception committee'. In the more hazardous blind drop the leader jumped in the middle of the group so that he would be well placed to marshal them on landing. When all had landed they flashed their torches to provide an aiming point for the aircraft to drop their stores. When all containers had arrived torches were extinguished, or covered with a blue filter, and the collection of stores began. Reception committees and aircraft crews sometimes failed to appreciate each other's difficulties. In May 1945 Wing Commander Hugh Verity made a compilation of reception committee comments and the related pilots' reports which 'showed how both sides do their damndest to make operations a success, and how difficult it is for the man on the ground to assess the aircrew's difficulties', in the hope that each side would become more tolerant of the other.[4]

Blind dropping was very much hit or miss. Information about the dropping-zone might be out of date; and even an area that looks safe from aerial reconnaissance could have changed, for example, through the planting of 'panjis', *chevaux de frise* of sharpened bamboo waiting to impale the agent as he landed. Seven Kachins dropped in the Shan States in Burma had a lucky escape from this defensive weapon. They overshot their intended dropping–zone, and later discovered that the whole area had been panjied. Another group in the Shan States was equally lucky. They landed in the only place for miles around 'which was not staked against glider attack and sown with panjis against parachute landings'. Even slight panji wounds were liable to turn septic.

It was safer to go in to a reception committee whether by day or by night. The dropping-zone was delineated by pre-arranged signal fires, or torches, perhaps in the form of a 'T', with a torch flashing a letter in Morse code. At night fires could be seen a long way off, but in daylight pilots had to rely on smoke which might be dispersed by the wind or masked by the jungle. There was also the danger of confusion with ordinary village fires, and from time to time villagers received unsolicited gifts of foodstuffs and highly sophisticated explosive devices.

The reception committee could communicate with an aircraft in daylight by means of a visual code using three white panels. A single panel, looking like the figure 'I' from the air, was a request for a W/T set, 'II' for a W/T operator, 'III' for a doctor, and so on. Two panels making an arrowhead directed the aircraft towards a bombing target, other panels, each representing 1,000 yards, indicating the distance. Towards the end of the war in the Far East visual methods of communication were being replaced by the *Rebecca/Eureka* system which used radar in the aircraft (*Rebecca*) to help the navigator to locate a ground party equipped with the matching *Eureka*. An alternative was the *S-phone* through which the ground operator could talk to the aircraft, using a silent microphone which allowed him to speak in little more than a whisper. Some parties were equipped with these devices but neither had much success in the Far East.

Many agents – 'Joes', as they were termed in the aircraft captains' reports – appeared to make light of the considerable ordeal of a parachute jump. One, dropping into French Indo-China, 'went out calmly chewing a sandwich'. However, Major R. A. Rubinstein's account of his drop into Burma in January 1945 probably epitomizes the feelings of most. Although he was a twenty-four-year-old veteran who had served with the Maquis the parachute jump was still a challenge.

Felt rotten all the afternoon and very frightened. Thought I would never face another op. after this, and was very annoyed at the offhand manner of the non-op types who kept saying 'Don't worry, old boy, the chute won't open anyway', all very funny . . . When the take-off came I felt much better . . . Was quite easy during the run and didn't feel too bad on the slide . . . Felt much better when I heard the engine note change, and I went . . . The moon was very bright and even colours showed up . . . A grand reception, all fear gone and glad to have arrived. One never notices the fear going, it just does!

There were few fatal parachute casualties. One occurred when a man's weight proved to be more than his parachute could cope with. There was a bizarre accident when a Liberator's crew had to bale out over Burma. The radio operator could not find his parachute and was taken on the back of the second pilot, an Australian; but when the parachute opened the man lost his hold and fell to his death.[5] Minor mishaps were not uncommon – bones could be broken, especially when men jumped from a low height. A whole party dropped into Malaya in February 1945 found themselves hung up on trees, and one member narrowly escaped strangulation. Another, carrying the W/T battery on his back suffered severe burns from leaking acid. The failure rate of parachutes carrying stores was much higher – round about 5 per cent.

There was an art in camouflaging the arrival of agents in enemy territory. Sorties could be synchronized with bombing raids to divert attention from them. Flares could be used to give the impression that photo-reconnaissance was the sole object of the mission. Leaflets could be scattered on the flight to and from the dropping-zone to make the enemy believe that the aircraft was flying a routine propaganda sortie. These methods were surprisingly effective. One dropping-zone in Burma no more than two miles from a Japanese outpost was regularly supplied for five months before the enemy became aware of it.

Before SOE could call on special-duties aircraft it had to rely on submarines for long-range operations. The Royal Navy approved these missions but usually only as part of their own routine patrols, a compromise that neither side liked. Submarine commanders' reports are often scathing about SOE's performance and are regularly endorsed: 'Yet another wasted mission.' In July 1943 Mackenzie asked for a submarine force for his exclusive use

so as the present procedure whereby SOE operations must of necessity be secondary to submarine renders any precision of execution almost out of the question and has proved to react most unfavourably on SOE personnel whose despatch has frequently to be postponed at the last minute and who have to remain under conditions detrimental to their physique for longer periods than would be needful if they were allowed to proceed direct to their operational area.

Nothing came of this breathless sentence; but the need for a special submarine fleet disappeared when longer-range aircraft became available.

Collapsible canoes known as 'folboats' were carried in the

submarine to be launched as near inshore as practicable. Later, outboard motors were provided – a mixed blessing. The humidity in the submarine affected the ignition so that it was difficult to start them, even when they had been stowed in a waterproof covering with a desiccating chemical. In the larger submarine-borne operations the landing party was accompanied by a ferry party and a beach party, the last being responsible for security while the landing party established itself. The earlier folboats were gradually replaced by heavier craft, but there was of course a limit on the size of canoe that a submarine could carry. One of the more successful – the Mark VII – only just went through the forehatch and almost invariably suffered some damage when it was launched or recovered.[6]

The problems of the ferry party are well illustrated by an operation of which the submarine commander wrote: 'It is hard to imagine any operation more simple and elementary than this: merely one man to be landed with his stores. Reasonable weather, no enemy opposition, bright moonlight.' Yet the operation took three nights instead of one, and very nearly failed simply because the 'boat-keeper' had no watch. He had to hold on to the canoe until 0300 hours when the beach party was due to return, standing up to his neck in the sea. He knew that the moon set at 0200 hours, so that he must remain at his watery post for sixty minutes; but his estimate of sixty turned out to be a mere twenty and he returned to the submarine alone. The stranded beach party were rescued later. Occasionally enemy action made it impossible to recover a ferry party, which meant that it had to join forces with the main operation.[7]

In some of the earlier Malayan operations a friendly junk was used as a staging post. The junk crew were briefed by an earlier party about the rendezvous date, on which they would display a pre-arranged signal, perhaps a length of cloth of a certain colour, as if it were hanging out to dry. When the junk had been positively identified through the submarine's periscope, the submarine withdrew to a safe distance and returned under cover of darkness to put the agents on board the junk, where they could lie low before choosing the best moment to go ashore. Surface craft were never used to infiltrate agents, mainly thanks to the ineptitude of the India Mission's paranaval section.*

The dispatching officer was essential for all operations whether by

* See pp. 100–2.

air, land, or sea. He provided moral support for the agents, ensured that all their needs were taken care of, and that they carried no compromising papers or articles. On his return to headquarters he reported the results of the operation. The job called for special qualities and experience and was more important than it might appear on paper.

# 6

# Communications

EFFICIENT radio communication is vital for any clandestine service. It was particularly important in the Far East where agents operated far from their base and where it was virtually impossible to send messages by other means. On the rare occasions when a message went by hand – as a rule on microfilm – it could take months, and the courier had to run the gauntlet of enemy patrols and bandits.

The India Mission had four main radio stations. Two at Calcutta, one linked with agents in Burma, Siam, and Indo-China (India Mission Group A), and the other providing a separate service for its Psychological Warfare Branch. A station in Colombo communicated with agents in Malaya and Sumatra (India Mission Group B). At Chungking, in China, a fourth provided a service for the *Remorse* economic-warfare activities,* and for the prisoner-of-war escape organization, the British Army Aid Group (BAAG). There were also 'Guard' stations at Colombo and Calcutta. If an agent failed to get in touch with base through his normal channel he could transmit to the Guard station which remained open twenty-four hours a day.

The first W/T equipment available in the Far East was designed for temperate climates and mains electricity. It was bulky and was not proofed against the rough treatment, high humidity, and heavy rains of jungle operations. Further, it had to be run off batteries. They in turn needed their own portable generator. The total weight of the equipment could exceed 400 pounds, and might have to be carried by only two agents.

These unwieldy sets were replaced by the B I at the end of 1942. It was much more portable, but the transmitter, receiver, and power unit were a single entity, which meant that if one element became unserviceable the whole set was useless. It was replaced by the B II in which the three elements were separate and could be individually replaced. However, the set was not yet tropicalized, although some survived submersion. One set was twice covered by flood water 'and suffered multitudinous indignities, but never failed, provided that

* See pp. 216–20.

during the monsoon it is put in front of a fire for half an hour daily'. Knott, in charge of signals, designed a set to stand up to rough handling, humidity, and even immersion in water – the B III.

There was no attempt to disguise the equipment, which caused caustic comment. One agent praised the performance of the B I, but pointed out that it weighed fifty-five pounds and caught the eye of the casual observer. 'After all, a Kachin carrying a new wooden suitcase in the hills is just as conspicuous as a European agent in the streets of Berlin carrying a Kachin basket.' He suggested that the set should be assembled in two parts each of which could be hidden in a native basket. The weight of the equipment still came in for criticism in 1944. The commander of HM Submarine *Trespasser* wrote:

It seems incredible to me that men who have to land in enemy country and walk miles under considerable duress should not have been provided with easily-portable W/T equipment. It is comparable to a submarine going to sea with 18-inch torpedoes and finding when she reaches her area that she is fitted with 21-inch tubes![1]

Many attempts were made to solve the problem of battery charging. Hand generators were easy to set up but had to be cranked for hours on end. The fibre gear wheels soon disintegrated, and that was that. One hand model had no 'cut-out' so that if it was not cranked fast enough current from the battery escaped back into the generating apparatus. The pedal generator was easier to work, and like the hand generator had the virtue of silence. However, it was easily damaged, the pedals tended to break, and the bicycle frames were designed for longer legs than the guerrillas were endowed with. The motor generator needed petrol, which added to the weight to be carried, and it was noisy and therefore a security risk. The steam generator – a portable boiler driving a small steam-engine which drove the generator – was designed to run on any combustible material not excluding cow-dung, and like the petrol model was noisy. Moreover the flames tended to play on the rubber washer fitted to the boiler headcover, and made it perish very quickly.

The Signals Plan set out call signs, transmission times, the ciphers to be used, and transmission and reception frequencies. It was carried by the W/T operator, a duplicate being held by the leader of the party and of course by the base station. The frequencies were determined by the crystals used, of which the agent might carry three. They were wafer-thin quartz discs about the size of a monocle, designed to operate on a single given frequency. This meant that the home station could get in touch with the field very quickly, and that the operator in the field did not have to 'tune' his set.

Another time-saving device was the 'crack signal', a word or number which could be transmitted in a matter of seconds without risk to security, the meaning of which had been agreed in advance. For example, the crack signals of a mission to Siam in 1944 were '696' meaning 'We are safe and are establishing a hideout'; and '572' meaning 'We cannot stay here because it is unsafe, and are therefore moving.' In fact, this party was attacked before it had time to set up its W/T, two members being killed and the other taken prisoner.

The volume of traffic from base stations naturally increased markedly in the weeks before the military operations which SOE were called on to support. To prevent the enemy from deducing from this increased activity that an attack was being mounted the stations were loaded with dummy traffic for a long period ahead, which was tapered off as the genuine traffic increased.

The danger that the enemy monitoring services might happen on the frequency being used was minimized by keeping messages short, by transmitting at agreed irregular intervals, and by ringing the changes on the crystals. The identity of the transmitting station was hidden by using the call signs of international shipping, and radio 'hams'. Essential operating instructions, for example to make initial contact, were signalled in 'Q', the merchant shipping international code. 'QSL' meant 'I acknowledge receipt . . .' and 'QSU 1200 hours' meant 'Call me at 1200 hours.' Agent stations were identified by the code-name of their operation; and in larger operations related field stations were given secondary names – flowers, animals, colours, vegetables, Disney characters, and so on. Operation *Humour* in Negri Sembilan in Malaya in 1945 had a main station *Reed* with five related stations, *Reed Blue, Green, Brown, Orange* and *Slate*. Field stations were not allowed to communicate with each other direct, but sent all messages through the base stations in Calcutta or Colombo. The enemy's radio direction finders had a better chance of tracking down two field stations talking to each other than if they communicated through base, although of course it doubled the work of transmission.

Messages were invariably transmitted in cipher. Until 1943 the system normally used was known as 'LMT 2', a high-grade cipher in which each message had a different key based on a page and line number in a book of which one copy was held by the base station and another by the agent. The page and line selected were indicated at the beginning of the message. This system was simple and effective but had the disadvantage that the agent's copy of the book, usually a paperback, tended to disintegrate in jungle conditions. It was superseded by the 'one time pad' which as the name suggests was a pad on the pages of which were printed a random series of letters which were used to transpose messages, and then destroyed. Duplicate pads were held by base station and agent. The one time pad was simple and efficient but the paper was not waterproof and sometimes the pages stuck together making the printed letters illegible. Later the paper was replaced by silk which was much more durable. In Burma some stations were given too few pads so that they had to use the same pages more than once – a serious breach of security. Others ran short of paper to draft and encipher messages. One party was forced to do this complicated job on split and flattened bamboo.

Security checks, an essential part of the Signals Plan, were memorized by the operator. Their purpose was to ensure that if he fell into the hands of the enemy and was put under pressure to act as a double agent he could warn the home station of the fact without alerting his captors. The most important check was the deliberate mistake – the regular insertion of a wrong letter at a pre-arranged point in every message. By omitting the mistake the operator revealed that he had been captured and was transmitting under duress. Another device was a question asked by the home station to which there were alternative answers, one meaning that all was well, the other that it was not.

'Fingerprinting' was an important security check. The agent's manipulation of the key transmitting the dots and dashes of the Morse code was as distinctive as his handwriting. Operators consistently prolonged or shortened a dash in a certain letter, or prolonged a dot, not deliberately but simply because of the way their reflexes worked, and headquarters, familiar with individual styles, would quickly spot a strange fingerprint. At the end of training each operator's transmission style was recorded and filed for future comparison. Agents were encouraged to reveal the secret of fingerprinting if they were captured to discourage the enemy from using a substitute operator. Ordinary fingerprinting was used as a security measure. Fingerprints taken before an agent went on operation would confirm his identity on his return.

There is a good deal of pointed criticism of the signals arrangements in the 'funding of experience' reports which group leaders were required to write at the end of hostilities. One leader in Karenni in Burma wrote: 'If the dumbhead responsible for issuing us with Mark II wireless sets for intercom. in the field had managed to tear himself away from his club long enough to test them he might have discovered that they would be absolutely bloody, and useless to us.' If this was an isolated comment it might be set aside as the contribution of someone with a chip on his shoulder, but a leader in a different area reported in the same vein. He had been assured that the W/T sets had been tried out and were equal to the work they would have to do.

This was either a deliberate misstatement or gross incompetence . . . the B 2 was excellent at long ranges and at short ranges up to 15 miles; but that was no help to me when the majority of my out-stations were between 30 and 40 miles away . . . I must draw attention to the fact that the emergency link to Calcutta functioned only so long as the operator remained awake. Speaking from memory I do not remember a single occasion when we succeeded in getting through between the hours of 10 pm and 7 am.

Another, in a different country – Malaya – said that operators in the home station frequently failed to keep skeds, or closed down before the scheduled time, which was claimed to be inexcusable bearing in mind the conditions in which the home operators worked.

· Not every comment was adverse, however. *Mouse*'s W/T briefing was considered to be full and concise. 'The plan was excellent and worked perfectly. Home station operators were very good, and I am very grateful for their patience and excellent operating.' *Wolf*, in north-east Burma for more than a year, recorded that communications worked extremely well both from outposts and base, except during monsoon periods when there was a good deal of interference. The longest period they were out of touch with base was four days, and they found that the emergency channel worked well. *Dilwyn* in the Shan States said 'the W/T briefing for this party was very good and the operators were never in doubt as to the plan or procedure or coding'.

· It may be said in defence of the signals arrangements that those suffering the discomforts of active service in the jungle may well have exaggerated any shortcomings of their fellows at headquarters far from the battlefront. Again, an occasional failure to get through to the home station might be due to atmospheric conditions, or it could be the fault of the operator in the field. Further, it is natural that weaknesses in the signals system should loom larger than the successes since the purpose of these reports was to make things better in the future. The field officers, taking it for granted that everything should go like clockwork, would as a rule not trouble to record that it had. The day-to-day records, which would throw light on the allegations about failing to keep skeds, no longer survive, so the evidence cannot be tested. All that can be said is that when all these factors are brought into the account many of the field parties in Burma seem to have been less well served in the vital area of communications than they were entitled to be.

*Character/Hyena* – in Burma – provided a more restrained and fundamental criticism of the signals arrangements. The overall plan worked very well for clandestine activities when security was paramount, but it was totally unsuitable for military operations. Normal army procedures designed for rapid communication when it mattered little if the enemy did read the signals would have been much more satisfactory.

The very stringent security regulations, far from being a safeguard, became a definite danger to the security of our troops in that they precluded any rapid exchange of messages . . . the correct solution would have been to recognize clearly the sharp distinction between clandestine and purely military operations and to arrange a complete change to ordinary army procedures after the assumption of offensive action . . .

It was also suggested that the simplified code for ordering stores developed in the Chindit operations would have greatly speeded up the ordering of stores for the field.

In the early days of the India Mission a few women, both locally recruited and posted from Britain, served as secretaries, typists, and cipher clerks. For example, his wife Clodagh, whom Mackenzie had recently married in England, joined the Mission in October 1941 as one of the first 'cipherettes'. She later became Head of the Records Department – a difficult job in an organization where the secrecy of papers was of paramount importance. The change over to offensive operations after the establishment of South East Asia Command and the increased need for W/T operators and cipher clerks made it necessary to recruit women in larger numbers. The employment of members of the First Aid Nursing Yeomanry (FANY) (a volunteer force formed in 1907, which drove ambulances and manned field hospitals in World War I) was approved after Commander Gamwell visited the Far East at the end of 1943. The first group of FANYs (who in 1936 had become the Women's Transport Service (FANY) were posted to SEAC in April 1944 as confidential secretaries. Most served with Force 136, although a few were in other branches of SEAC headquarters. In the course of 1944 Force 136 FANY sections were formed at Meerut (April); Colombo (July); Poona (August); Kunming (September); Calcutta (November); and Kandy (December). Detachments were sent to Bombay and Trincomalee in March and April 1945; and to Rangoon in July 1945. Commander Merriman took up her duties as FANY Staff Officer on 8 May 1944.

The FANY complement eventually increased to over 600, of whom 400 were engaged in signals work, including 130 on ciphers, 126 on W/T operation, and six fingerprint experts – the last being responsible for recording the idiosyncracies of individual agents' transmission styles before they went on operations. Most were at the main radio stations in Colombo (234) and Calcutta (135). Kunming was the most sought after post. 'The departure of the first FANY over the Hump [the Himalayas] gave the China station a glamour that never faded ... from then on there was always a long waiting-list for postings to China.'

By the end of 1945 all FANY Sections except Meerut and Poona had closed; and the last contingent left India at the end of April 1946.

# 7

# Survival

SURVIVAL in the jungle, regardless of any Japanese threat, was itself a challenge. Conditions were new to most European officers and other ranks who were warned in an official manual to 'treat jungles with respect, even with fear'. Everything would be unusual to them. 'Humidity is high in jungles which steam under the heat of the sun. The dense foliage overhead acts as the lid on a cooking pot, keeping the air heavy with moisture. The sun's rays cannot penetrate the heavy foliage so the air is never dry. The jungle nearly always appears steaming wet especially at night and in the early hours of the morning when the moisture is like light rain dripping from leaf to leaf.'

This exposition may have caused as much alarm and despondency as the jungle at its most hostile. The newcomer will at once feel shut in. All sounds are strange and will have a marked depressing effect. It is easy to get lost. Inexperienced men lose their bearings a few yards from camp. While it is easy to move through rain forest where there is no scrub, in secondary forest you may have to cut through every yard. Worst of all are the swamps. Vegetation is matted, roots hamper all movement, the ground is often under water, hot and foetid. In coastal areas where mangrove and nipah abound the black mud is poisonous. Leeches are the worst jungle pest. Don't pull them off as the bleeding will last for hours. In swamps mites may attack the feet. Ticks embedded in the skin are to be removed by applying near-scalding water. The jungle has many snakes. Most are harmless – except for the King Cobra, which may attack unprovoked, the black cobra, the krait, a few vipers and adders, and most of the sea and water snakes. There are many poisonous trees, plants, grasses, and thorns. Every scratch must be instantly treated with disinfectant. Sleep is important – lack of it 'makes cowards of us all'.

However, there is no need to go hungry. Monkey, flying fox, and crocodile tail are palatable. Bamboo shoots make excellent eating, provided their leathery sheaths are removed. The roots and seeds of the lotus are edible. Tapioca roots are excellent but must be well boiled and the water thrown away, as some varieties contain prussic acid. Empty kerosene tins can be used for cooking. Split in two they make satisfactory dishes.

The ten jungle commandments are:

*Thou shalt not*

Stay in wet clothes
Disregard scratches
Sit on bare earth
Eat fruit
Scratch leech bites
Sit up late talking

*Thou shalt*

Look after your feet
Keep your boots oiled
Carry citronella oil
Keep a teaspoonful of salt in your water bottle

All this was good advice, but anyone who took it too seriously may have had a vision of himself partaking of his kerosene-flavoured crocodile tail, worrying as to when a King Cobra would launch itself from the steaming outer darkness. In practice there was of course a great deal of discomfort in jungle living, and operatives occasionally succumbed to disease, their resistance lowered by long spells of privation. All six members of the *Sugarloaf II* operation which crossed Simalur Island off Sumatra went down with leptospiral fever, due to walking in rat-infested pools with abrasions on their feet. However, the great majority survived the hazards of the jungle more easily than the author of the vade-mecum quoted above might have expected.[1]

The case history provided by Lieutenant-Colonel Steven Cumming, who became the India Mission's Operations Officer, and Lieutenant-Colonel Peter Lindsay of the Oriental Mission (who also joined the India Mission) during their epic walk from Fort Hertz in Burma to Margherita in north-eastern Assam in May and June 1942 confirms much of the official handbook. They found bamboo shoots and a vine leaf 'not unlike spinach' in a few places, but saw no game. It was essential in this wilderness to carry basic rations. Sandflies and bamboo ticks were very troublesome and poisoned their hands and legs. Some members of the party were seriously weakened by the attentions of innumerable leeches. Gravel rash was another problem – fine gravel caused foot sores which were infected by poisonous water. Others who made the same remarkable journey (on which there was only one fatal casualty – Corporal Sawyer was drowned when he fell in a river) were Gardiner, who became head of the India Mission's Burma Country Section, and Lieutenant-Colonel Eric Battersby. They gained first-hand experience of the things needed for jungle survival. Each member of the party must have a jungle knife – the traditional Burmese 'dah' being by far the best. Also an axe was needed for felling trees to bridge rivers, and a block and tackle would help to position the trees when felled. The official ration bag was not waterproof, a serious weakness. A sandfly net thick enough to be used as a blanket would help; and if porters were employed a supply of opium for them should be carried.

An analysis of the reports at the end of the Burma campaign reveals the successes and failures of QOps, the branch of the India Mission responsible for keeping agents in the field supplied with the necessities of life. There was a good deal of criticism of the delivery of stores and equipment. Paper bags used for tea, sugar, powdered milk, and salt often burst on landing. One mission found that when oil was packed with sugar and tea the tins of oil burst and everything was ruined. It was suggested that cloth bags would be better. Another mission claimed that 75 per cent of their rice bags burst. As a result they were strengthened, so that only half burst. The popularity of the various ration packs varied according to the taste of the customer. Operation *Bison* thought that the right solution of the food problem had not been found. Some rations had to be 'non-cooking' for use on patrol. The cooking rations for base *must* include rice; but there had to be separate meals for British and native troops. The crying need was for meat 'but we could not shoot for a variety of reasons, the chief being that the Mossberg [the silent American rifle issued for the provision of game] when discharged drowned the noise of the bombing of Mandalay'. An administrative problem was created by 'the multiplicity of rations' – British, Australian, and American types – which made it difficult to calculate how many days' rations there were at any given moment.

On the whole the scale of rations was adequate, but some found it difficult to satisfy their hunger, especially in colder areas. At first it was a problem for Europeans to eat the large quantities of rice needed, but this came with practice. Food supplied by base could be supplemented by local purchase, especially of pigs, chickens, vegetables, fruit (in spite of the fourth commandment), and oil for cooking; but in Burma the quantities of food available varied greatly from district to district. *Walrus Red* decided they could live off the country at a time when they were desperately short of ammunition. In spite of a plea that only ammunition should be sent, subsequent drops were devoted exclusively to ration packs and rice. This

jeopardised the operation, and incidentally our lives, but I presume we are expendable. Something had to be done to arouse Calcutta so a message was sent in clear: 'Want ammo., not food'. As expected this brought a first class rocket about security and bringing the Force into disrepute; but it did not stop a message in the same sked 'Sending two Daks. rice tomorrow'. We are still alive! No thanks to the Calcutta office, but to luck, to the courage of the hill peoples, the guts of the RAF, and the whole-hearted co-operation of Tac. HQ when they took over certain supply commitments.

Parties which had been a long time in the field with little action to occupy them were critical of headquarters' efforts to cater for their amenities. *Bison* complained in February 1945 that they had only once received newspapers, which were very welcome in spite of the fact that they were several months old; and they had only once received mail, which was uncensored and openly addressed to Force 136. This breach of security was reported to base and whether or not as a result no more mail was sent in to *Bison*, who considered that an effort should be made to send mail with every drop. They had all the soap they needed, but were short of toothbrushes and toothpaste. Another mission had an overabundance of toothbrushes, but no toothpaste. *Character*, hypercritical of almost everything done and left undone by headquarters, listed the faults of QOps including the omission of items specially asked for, on the ground that they were not really necessary ('unforgiveable, and in any case should never be done without first consulting the field'); 'the inclusion of items neither ordered nor required . . . It was infuriating to receive luxuries and special rations at that stage in excess of the amounts ordered. They were an encumbrance and a liability'; lack of information about what would be omitted, especially specials. 'Personnel travelled long distances and waited days at DZs to receive these special items. They were almost invariably disappointed.' *Character* estimated that if aircraft had been loaded in accordance with orders from the field the number of sorties could have been reduced by 25 per cent. Even those missions which praised the efforts of QOps to keep them supplied with the means of survival qualified their enthusiasm.

One which recorded 'Taken as a whole "Q" was very generous and considerate' found it necessary to add, 'but they tended to ignore specific requests and to drop what they thought was best for us, but they did not always know.' *Walrus/White* missed the personal touch. 'The men would have appreciated the odd note "Sorry, no paraffin, boys. Trying to get it in the next drop. Happy birthday! Paddy."'

The health of the India Mission teams and the guerrillas depended to a great extent on the ready availability of the appropriate medicines, and also on adequate supplies of equipment generally. For example, Operation *Wolf* in Kengtung suffered badly from jungle sores which they believed would have been avoided by a more generous supply of footwear; and from scabies due to a shortage of soap. In general, however, *Wolf* were well satisfied with the supply of medicines although they suggested that ordering could have been much simplified by the use of a code. Quoting long and complicated medical names in signals led to mistakes and delays. *Wolf*, who were in the field for over a year before a doctor was sent to them, thought that all large parties should have their own doctor, or at least a good medical orderly; and that all personnel should have a course in first aid. *Walrus/Red* saw the British officer in the field as 'guide, comforter, friend, be all and end all to the native. He is considered omniscient, qualified to explain any weapon in the country, to heal obscure diseases and straightforward wounds i.e. physician, surgeon and what have you.' The rapid exploration of medicine at ME 25 [the Trincomalee Training School] left him more in a haze, and did not qualify him for the demand made on him.

Of all the remarkable case histories of survival in the jungle one stands out. When a Hudson of No. 357 (SD) Squadron crashed delivering stores to operation *Spiers* in Kokang on the Burma/China frontier in March 1944, four of the crew were killed. The Squadron's Medical officer, Flight Lieutenant G. D. Graham, who had never made a parachute jump, at once volunteered to go to the aid of the two survivors. He dropped, accompanied by Flight Sergeant T. E. White, a parachute instructor, on 17 March to find that one had died. The other, Flying Officer W. Prosser, had severe injuries, including a fractured skull, which meant that for two weeks he could not be moved. Then twelve coolies were hired to carry him on a litter into China, which they reached after two days' heavy going. After two more days the coolies refused to go further lest they be conscripted into the Chinese army; but an offer of higher pay, rum, and aspirins induced them to go on. On 5 April they reached an American outpost where the Americans hired – and paid in advance – a new set of coolies, who immediately absconded. The party rested while replacements were found, and Prosser became rational for the first time since the crash. Eventually, after struggling in atrocious weather across several passes, on 11 April they reached the jeep road and travelled in greater comfort to Yunnanni airfield where the Americans promised to fly them to India. On 16 April they took off in an aircraft whose landing gear failed to retract; and they returned to base. Next day the flight went according to plan. Prosser was admitted to hospital in good condition, and eventually made a full recovery.[2]

# PART II

# SPECIAL OPERATIONS

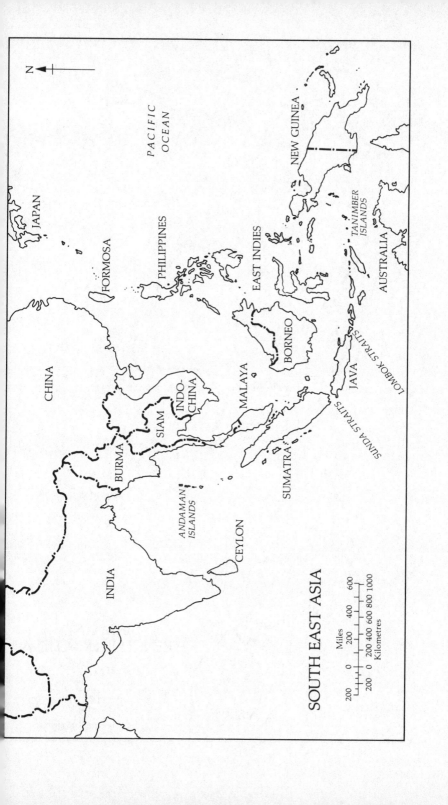

SOUTH EAST ASIA

CHINA

TONKIN

Lao Kay
Red River
Black River
Langson
Hanoi

BURMA

R. Nam Tha

LAOS

Paksane

Sakon Nakon • Tong

Hue

SIAM

R. Mekong

FRENCH

INDO-CHINA

Kanchanaburi
• BANGKOK

Hua Hin

Phnom
Penh

SAIGON

Cap St. Jacques

Chumphon

Ranong

COCHIN
CHINA

N

Nasan

• Ronpibon

Huey Yot

Phuket Island • Trang

KRA ISTHMUS

SIAM AND
FRENCH INDO-CHINA

Miles

100        0        100        200
|          |        |          |
100    0    100   200   300
Kilometres

Land above 1000 metres

MALAYA

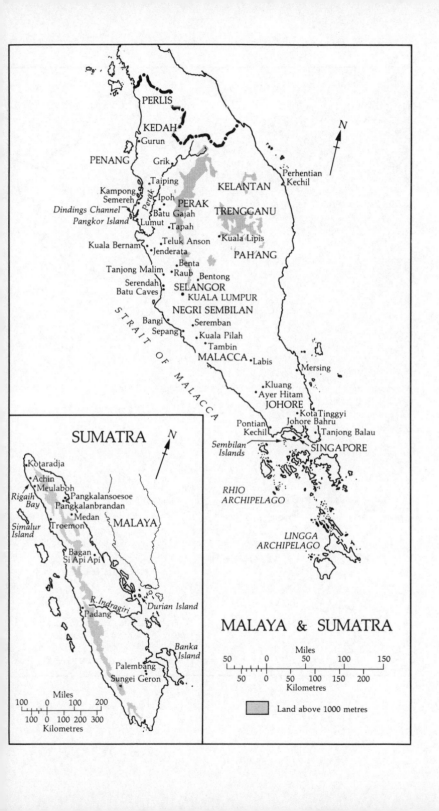

USSR

MONGOLIA

MANCHURIA

KOREA

PEKING
Tientsin

CHINA

Sian

Hankow    R. Yangtze    Shanghai

Chungking    Ningpo

N

YUNNAN
Ping Kwei    KWANGTUNG
Kunming    Kweilin    Amoy
Mengtze    Lipuhsien    Waichow    Kowloon
Hokow    KWANGSI    Canton    Swatow
Kengtung    Bias Bay    FORMOSA
Macao    HONG
Haiphong    KONG

HAINAN

SIAM    CHINA

INDO-CHINA

Red River

Kilometres
200  0    200  400  600  800  1000
100  0   100 200 300 400 500 600
Miles

Land above 1000 metres

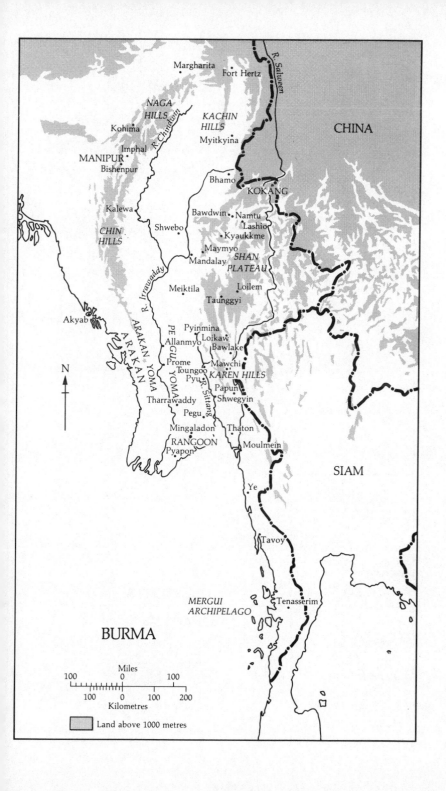

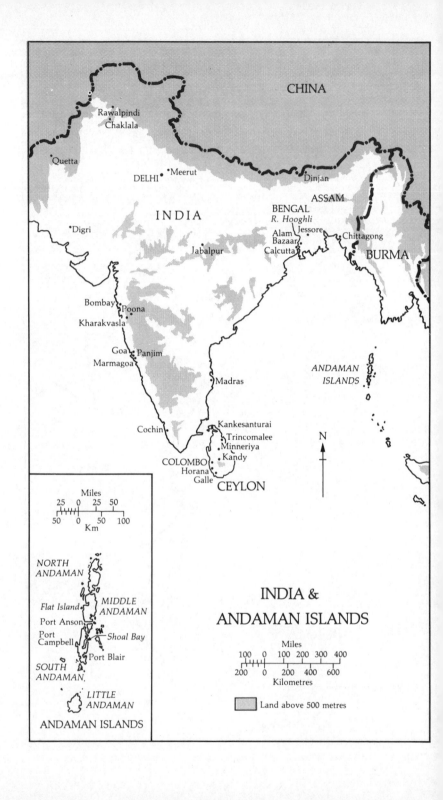

CHINA

Rawalpindi
Chaklala

Quetta

DELHI •Meerut
Dinjan

ASSAM

•Digri

INDIA

BENGAL
R. Hooghli
Jessore
Alam Chittagong
Bazaar
Calcutta
BURMA

Jabalpur

Bombay
Poona
Kharakvasla

Goa
Panjim
Marmagoa

Madras

ANDAMAN
ISLANDS

Cochin

Kankesanturai
Trincomalee
Minneriya
Kandy
COLOMBO
Horana
Galle CEYLON

N

Miles
25  0  25  50
50  0  50  100
Km

NORTH
ANDAMAN

Flat Island
MIDDLE
ANDAMAN
Port Anson
Port
Campbell
Shoal Bay
Port Blair
SOUTH
ANDAMAN
LITTLE
ANDAMAN
ANDAMAN ISLANDS

INDIA &
ANDAMAN ISLANDS

Miles
100  0  100  200  300  400
200  0  200  400  600
Kilometres

Land above 500 metres

# 1

# The Oriental Mission

VALENTINE KILLERY arrived in Singapore on 7 May 1941 to establish the headquarters of OM, ostensibly the Far Eastern office of the Ministry of Economic Warfare (MEW). He estimated that it would take a year for the organization to become fully operational on the reasonable assumption that he would have the willing co-operation of the military and civil authorities; but that co-operation was not forthcoming and in the seven months before the Japanese invasion very little progress was made. There were three phases in the life of OM. In the first it was virtually impossible to accomplish anything in any of its territories, mainly thanks to the attitude of the military in Singapore. In the second, immediately before and after the arrival of the Japanese, the Mission was allowed to go into action when it was far too late to be effective. In the third, when the fall of Singapore was seen to be inevitable, the Mission used its resources to set up an escape route through Sumatra.

Colonel A. G. Warren, formerly with MI R, had been sent by the War Office to study the scope for special operations in the Far East before Killery's arrival. His previous experience, ability to get on with people, and the fact that he was a professional soldier, well qualified him to head the Mission; but, perhaps in deference to Dalton's views, London had chosen a civilian.

Killery planned to divide Malaya into six zones each controlled by a local European with two or three 'gangs of tough and reliable natives' led by an Asiatic Police Inspector. These men would be trained at 101 STS,* then return to their district to hide weapons and explosives ready for use when the invaders arrived. Unfortunately he did not discuss these plans with GOC, Malaya (Lieutenant-General A. E. Percival), who took umbrage when he became aware of them accidentally. Percival, 'a completely negative person with no vigour, no colour, and no conviction',[1] protested to Brooke-Popham about the proposed activities of the new organization within his Command; and on 1 October 1941 C-in-C sent Killery a curt minute: 'Last night I

* See p. 16.

discussed with the GOC the question of "left-behind parties" in Malaya. As a result of this conversation I have decided not to proceed with this project.'

Killery appealed against this abrupt decision, and on 23 October he and Percival met the Governor, Sir Shenton Thomas. GOC stated his objections to left-behind parties: Europeans could not move freely in an occupied Malaya; the scheme would absorb scarce manpower; and any hint of an impending Japanese invasion would damage morale. Killery left the meeting convinced that neither Governor nor GOC would agree to special operations at any price. He thought their apprehension about morale was simply a ploy, and he had no doubt about the real reason for their opposition. 'The GOC is obviously suffering from pique owing to the fact that he was not consulted in the first place.'

There seemed to be nothing for it but to resign and Killery now wrote to Brooke-Popham saying he could not do his job without the support of C-in-C and all British representatives in the Far East. If his competence was suspect he would return to Britain where his services might be of more use. There is no record of C-in-C's response, but he must have been shaken by this tough line, realizing that the War Office would not take kindly to actions on his part frustrating the operations of the new organization. Killery was induced to hold his hand, however, when on 11 November Percival devised his own version of a special-operations scheme. This was acknowledged in a provocative letter (from a colleague, Killery being away at the time) which claimed that Percival's plan was exactly what OM had proposed, and added that it was a pity valuable time had been lost.

Percival replied angrily that his scheme differed in two respects. Special operations would come under military control; and they would be allowed only at the frontier. He omitted a third difference – the Mission would do no more than collect intelligence. He concluded: 'I would suggest that the loss of valuable time was due primarily to the problem being tackled from the wrong angle. Had I been consulted at the very start the loss of time in producing a faulty scheme would have been avoided . . .'. This childish bickering ended when the Japanese landed and it was realized – far too late – that OM might have a contribution to make.

The Mission's second phase began when planters, miners, engineers, and civil servants were given a crash course at 101 STS to train them for left-behind activities. By the end of January 1942 eight parties totalling forty-five men (including two Chinese and one Malay) were in position. Ideally they would have been established all over the country but the Japanese were now in control in the north and it was impossible to get the parties through the Japanese lines. The whole operation was commanded by Captain Frederick Spencer Chapman, who had succeeded Gavin as commandant of 101 STS, and who was supposed to lead one of the parties (at Tanjong Malim in North Selangor) but was at first prevented by illness. The other parties were south-east of Benta in Pahang (led by W. H. Stubbington, a peacetime surveyor); ten miles out of Bentong, also in Pahang (J. P. Garden, a tin miner); and near Seremban in Negri Sembilan (A. J. Wynne, an irrigation engineer). There were four parties in Johore: nine miles south-east of Labis (T. M. Smyllie, a civil servant); near Kluang (J. Reid, a timber engineer); off the road from Kluang to Mersing (T. D. Mackay, a planter); and sixteen miles north-east of Johore Bahru (D. S. Matthews, also a planter).* All these parties were located near communications bottle-necks where there was good jungle cover.

There was a ninth European party led by the acting manager of the Kuala Reman rubber estate in Pahang, Mr J. M. Cotterill, which included Mr B. F. Tyson, Mr J. W. Smith, a Chinese W/T operator, and an Indian. When the Japanese reached their neighbourhood they destroyed the estate machinery and rubber stocks, distributed rifles to their employees, and established a camp in the jungle from which they sent intelligence for a few days. At the end of January 1942 they were ordered to Johore but were penned up for months by the Japanese; and only in June could they join a guerrilla group.

When it was accepted that the Chinese might play their part, and the Communist Party agreed to co-operate (on 19 December 1941) Gavin prepared left-behind parties from the Chinese who passed through 101 STS. Mr John Davis of the Police Force and Mr Richard Broome, a senior civil servant, arranged to put them on the ground in areas where Party membership was strong. By 30 January 1942 they had set up seven arms and food dumps, to which 163 trained men were taken: fifteen to Serendah in Selangor, thirty to Tampin, and sixty to Tenang in Negri Sembilan; fifty-eight were shared between

---

* The leaders were commissioned as Lieutenants, the team members as Second Lieutenants. Reid was a Second Lieutenant, the leader and other members of his party not having been appointed.

dumps at Ayer Hitem in Negri Sembilan, and Pontian Kechil, Kluang, and Kota Tinggi in Johore.

The men were well equipped. Each had a revolver or automatic, a fighting knife, a jack knife, a parang for cutting through the jungle, a compass, and a steel helmet; and for every three men there was a sub-machine gun and a rifle. Each party had large quantities of explosives and ancillary equipment. They were self sufficient in food for three months, their rations including cheese, butter, jam, milk, tinned salmon and instant coffee, in addition to rice and army biscuits. Perishable food was packed in tins, hermetically sealed against insects and weather. Canned foods were dipped in wax to make the cans rustproof. There was a generous allowance of clothing and camping equipment.*

All parties were on the ground by the end of January. They travelled as far as possible by road, but then had to manhandle stores and equipment to a secure base in the jungle. It was reckoned it would take two weeks to become self-supporting but the swift advance of the Japanese denied the parties any real chance of establishing an effective guerrilla effort. Nevertheless Spencer Chapman's party did much damage to road and rail communications and inflicted between 500 and 1,000 casualties before they were forced to retreat into the hills. Spencer Chapman later wrote:

If only we had been vouchsafed a small measure of support by Malaya Command and had been allowed to start preparations even a few weeks earlier, there would have been a large number of British officers, backed by hundreds of trained Chinese, Malays and Indians, operating under ideal circumstances; and it is reasonable to argue . . . that had such a force been in operation from the very time the enemy set foot in Malaya, the advance of the Japanese would have been delayed sufficiently to allow the 18th Division – which had landed at Singapore just in time to be interned – and the 9th Australian Division – which only reached Java on its way to Malaya – to go into action . . .[2]

The British parties were supported by a Dutch special force which was sent from Sumatra in response to an appeal by Warren. It was led by Captain T. J. Supheert and comprised eighty troops, nine demol-

---

* The administrative effort needed at short notice may be gathered from the lists of stores provided. There were forty-three separate items of arms and equipment; fifty-four of explosives, incendiaries, and other devices; twenty-five of camping equipment; and thirty-two of food – 154 in all.

ition experts, a small medical unit, with forty native convicts (described as 'non-volunteers') to carry their baggage, and arrived in Singapore on 17 January 1942. Three days later they were taken to Johore where for the next two months they carried on a highly successful guerrilla campaign.

A third of their 'non-volunteer' convicts deserted, but not before they had betrayed many of the Chinese who had helped them. The regular troops showed what well-trained and disciplined men could accomplish against heavy odds. For the loss of five killed they accounted for 200 Japanese, twenty-five cars and trucks, several stores and dumps, bridges, telephone lines, and the airstrip at Labis. One group dressed as natives were hired by the Japanese to repair a railway. They killed twelve of the guard and set fire to a warehouse full of oil and petrol drums.

When they fell in with the British left-behind party No. 8 led by Matthews they worked with them as long as their ammunition and explosives lasted. Then 'after many interesting and unhealthy experiences we agreed with the British volunteers to stop action and try to retreat to Sumatra'. At first the British elected to remain in Malaya because they thought '*Shonan* would become Singapore again within six months'; but in the event they went to Sumatra where they were taken prisoner. The Dutch left from Kampong Semereh in a boat with a 'masquietonet'* for a sail, at one point going straight through the middle of a Japanese convoy. Supheert was captured in Sumatra at the end of March 1942 and spent the rest of the war in a prisoner-of-war camp.

There was now no hope of carrying on special operations based in Malaya, and OM entered the third phase of its brief and unhappy existence, in which it strove to get to safety as many of its own members and the British forces as possible. Three of Spencer Chapman's left-behind party – Frank Vanrenan, Richard Graham, and Boris Hembry escaped by fishing boat to Sumatra and flew back to Singapore to report that many British troops were still at large in Selangor and Negri Sembilan, sheltered by the Chinese. Warren, Vanrenan, Graham, Davis, Broome, and ten Chinese sailed from Singapore in the *Hin Lee* on 3 February to establish a base at Bagan Si Api Api on the east coast of Sumatra, hoping to rescue some of these

* Captain Supheert's interesting spelling.

troops. On 16 February Davis and Broome crossed to Sepang in Selangor in a fishing junk to find out how their Chinese parties were faring, but a Japanese order forbidding the movement of shipping forced them to return to Sumatra almost immediately. They did, however, hear reports of guerrilla activity in Northern Malaya, and in Selangor and Negri Sembilan, where camps had been set up in the jungle.

Kuala Pilah police station in Selangor had been attacked and some Australian prisoners of war rescued in an action in which there were thirty Japanese casualties. Eleven of the guerrillas responsible were executed at Seremban. Several bridges had been blown and the railway line between Kuala Lumpur and Seremban had as a result been declared a prohibited area where trespassers would be shot at sight. The demolition of a bridge at Bangi had led to the massacre of several hundred Chinese.

Vanrenan and Graham also crossed to Selangor, hoping to get in touch with Spencer Chapman, of whom nothing had been heard. When they did not return it was presumed they had succeeded, but in fact they were captured on 15 March and imprisoned at Kuala Lumpur. They escaped, but were recaptured at Bentong on 2 September and executed sixteen days later.

As the fall of Singapore came near, OM planned an escape route through the many islands of the Rhio Archipelago. On 3 February 1942 Captain Ivan Lyon and Major H. A. Campbell with some men from 101 STS left in the *Hongchuan*, a small vessel loaded with food, to establish dumps on Durian Island and at Prigi Rajah near the main mouth of the Indragiri River in Sumatra. A third was later set up by B. R. Goodfellow, again using the *Hongchuan*, on the small but conspicuous island of Pulo Salu, ten miles south west of Singapore. Only a few were expected to use the escape route, but ten days before the city fell – before the troops were officially told about the route – it was used by large numbers, including many 'without doubt deserters, military and civilian'. As the days passed the numbers increased. They used every conceivable form of water transport, ranging from the Singapore Rowing Club's shells to baulks of timber paddled by hand. 'Some of these men, who arrived tired, often with no food or water, and with no certainty of their next move, speak of the discovery of an organization to help them as something of a miracle.' Lyon provided a ferry service from Durian Island to the Indragiri River for those whose craft were not equal to the final passage. Campbell rounded up the new arrivals and took them to a rest camp near Padang on the west coast.

Between 18 February and 8 March 1942 ten ships evacuated nearly 2,600 from Padang on the west coast of Sumatra, mostly to Colombo. All reached their destination, except the *Rosebloem*, which was sunk with 200 troops. Warren, as senior British officer in Sumatra, aimed to see all the troops safely away, and he would probably have succeeded had the *Chilka* not been delayed for a week in Calcutta. She could still have reached Padang several days before the Japanese, but was sunk *en route*, and the last chance of escape disappeared.

On 8 March 1942 Warren ordered eighteen key men, including five from OM – Campbell, Lyon, Broome, Davis, and Lieutenant Passmore – to leave on the *Sederhana Djohannes*, a Malay prahu acquired for the purpose. Although there were several naval men in the party, Warren ordered Broome to take command. Lyon – 'the type of well-informed officer who is always fit, always cheerful, always planning adventures in which it is essential he plays a part' – was navigator. After ten days they were becalmed. Twice they were machine-gunned by Japanese planes, but miraculously no one was hit. Lyon feared they would be driven back by the south-west monsoon, but it came late, and westerly winds took them to Ceylon after thirty-five days without fresh food and little water. They were taken on board the *Anglo-Canadian* bound for Bombay, and the *Sederhana Djohannes* was sunk by gunfire lest she become a danger to navigation. Warren and the British troops left in Sumatra became prisoners of war.

At the end of January it was decided to transfer 101 STS to Rangoon because of the worsening military situation in Malaya. Instructors and students loaded stores and equipment, and food to be dumped in the neighbouring islands for the benefit of escapers, on to a four-hundred-ton coastal steamer, the *Krian*, which left Singapore on 5 February 1942. At Batavia, where they watered and coaled, they were joined by Gavin, stranded *en route* for Chungking. He had just married Barbara Murray, who had been on war work in Singapore – in a Dutch Register Office, as they had failed to persuade the captain of the flying boat bringing them to Batavia to tie the knot in the aircraft. In view of the growing threat to Burma the *Krian* made for Colombo, where she docked on 28 February 1942.

The 101 STS signals establishment left for Rangoon at the

beginning of January. Knott's deputy, Captain A. B. Butler, went ahead by air on the 6th, being followed by Knott and Sergeant Shufflebotham on a tramp steamer with their equipment. They overhauled the Rangoon station, which had been operational for some weeks, and were almost immediately instructed by Singapore to move north to Lashio, where the operator from Phuket in Siam (Sergeant Misselbrook) had already been sent. They went by truck to Lashio, which they found 'rather like a goldrush mining town, not much semblance of law and order'. They established contact with Rangoon, and continued the game of leap-frog to Kunming in China, where they set up a station in the grounds of the British Consulate. Then on to Chungking to erect a station in the now-vacant German Embassy. Knott found the Chinese unhelpful. They 'did not give the impression of being very co-operative – evasive and tepid, though of course extremely polite'. Finally they came to rest in Calcutta where they established a station in the suburbs to communicate with those of the links they had scattered across South East Asia which did not fall into Japanese hands.

*Burma*

Killery visited Rangoon in August 1941 to agree a charter with the Governor of Burma (Sir Reginald Dorman-Smith). Unhappily Dorman-Smith delegated responsibility for the detailed arrangements to GOC, Burma (Lieutenant-General D. K. McLeod) who did not 'fully appreciate the purpose of our Mission'. This made it easier for Brooke-Popham, when he went to Burma in September, to reduce SOE's role to virtually nothing, as he had done in Malaya; but when it became obvious that the Japanese must invade Burma it was conceded that SOE could help. Left-behind parties would be drawn from the police force. The Defence Council approved a plan, but the Home Minister (U Aye) insisted that a Burmese should operate it. When Killery objected the Governor claimed that senior Burmese must be entrusted with this sort of activity so that he could count on their co-operation generally. In the event the scheme never got off the ground; and a plan to link up with OM agents in Siam was no more successful. Mr W. D. Reeve, Killery's representative in Burma, posted three Europeans and some Chinese near the Siamese border to recruit refugees as agents; but the speed of the Japanese advance killed off the enterprise before it began.

Some months before Killery visited Rangoon Mr H. N. C. Stevenson of the Burma Frontier Service* had begun to train guerrillas in the hills, and even to manufacture arms for them. 'Our *pièce de résistance* was an anti-tank mine made out of a 500-cigarette tin, three torch batteries, two sticks of gelignite, and a detonator. The contacts were held apart by springs of bamboo.' In December 1941 the Governor appointed him 'Commandant, Burma Levies' to organize recruitment in the Karen Hills, but when he asked for a few officers who knew the hill tribes the army refused to release them. The position changed when Lindsay of OM joined him. 'He had the money, some backing, and some arms, but no knowledge of the country, and no clear notion of what was possible. I had the plans and the knowledge, but no money and no arms . . . Our meeting was like putting a match to petrol.'[3]

They put their plan to General Alexander, now GOC, Burma. Forest officers would be sent to the hills to raise morale, restore Britain's prestige, and report intelligence to army headquarters. Alexander at once agreed, leaving it to Lieutenant-General Hutton to discuss the detail. 'Then the fight began, and lasted forty-eight hours! The plan was agreed, but only on condition the army took it over.' Lindsay commented bitterly: 'No-one considers the general war effort, but only his own position . . .'. Nevertheless the fact that the Burma levies had been accepted even under different management was considered to be a victory.

Stevenson was put in command, with the rank of Lieutenant-Colonel, and succeeded in raising over 2,000 Karens. They fought with distinction and delayed the advance of the Japanese into the Shan States for a critical two days. They also provided intelligence and protected the left flank of British troops retreating up the Sittang Valley. When it was clear that they must be overrun, they were ordered to hide their arms and await the eventual return of the British. Levies raised in the Kachin Hills covered the withdrawal of the last elements of the army from north-west Burma, at times operating more than forty miles behind the retreating troops, destroying bridges on the main roads. Most important, they prevented the enemy from constructing a fighter strip in the Fort Hertz plain which would have threatened the last air link between India and China. They also evacuated women and children. On one

---

* The Burma Frontier Service administered the hill country – about half the total area of the country.

occasion Stevenson's jeep carried to safety three women and eighteen
children.[4]

Elsewhere in Burma OM did little. In Tenasserim their leader
undertook to remain behind with fifty men of his mining company to
destroy military objectives, put tin mines out of action, and attack
Japanese lines of communication; but in Reeve's view he was 'a talker
rather than a doer . . . His demands for finance, and still more finance
were fantastic.' A party of Australians which offered to help in the
area withdrew their offer as soon as they met him. He did lead out
some troops cut off by the enemy – for which he was commended by
the army – but SOE believed that he should have remained in the
jungle to receive reinforcements. Seven men asked to destroy native
boats at Ye landed from a naval launch which was to pick them up
fifty miles away, but then decided the operation was too dangerous.
They simply marched through the jungle to the rendezvous, having
attempted nothing. The Namtu silver and lead smelter which
serviced the nearby Bawdwin mines was scheduled for destruction,
but the army refused to allow OM to go into action until it was too
late. There was time only to deal with the generators. The Mawchi
wolfram mine was reprieved when the Governor accepted 'the more
or less specious arguments of the management' that immobilization
was enough. This surprised SOE London, but given the pace of events
there was nothing they could do about it.

### Siam

In April 1941 Brooke-Popham proposed that a Japanese threat to
attack Malaya through Siam should be met by moving troops into the
Tenasserim peninsula. He was told to make the necessary plans
'bearing in mind that it is our policy to avoid provocative action'.[5]
Churchill added the rider: 'We must not tie up a lot of troops in these
regions which we can so readily and rapidly reinforce from India.'[6]
On 7 May 1941 Sir Josiah Crosby, British Minister in Bangkok,
complained about Japanese infiltration to the Siamese Prime Minister
(Luang Pibul) who admitted that many Japanese visitors were
military officers. Some had been arrested for taking photographs in
restricted areas but none had been brought to trial. He suggested that
Britain should follow Japan's example and send in 'officers disguised
as civilians'. The War Office agreed, and on 28 May 1941 Brooke-
Popham reported that the infiltration of officers in plain clothes had
begun.[7]

In the next two months large-scale infiltration was leisurely discussed. The War Office asked the Judge Advocate General if a whole unit in mufti could be ordered into Siam. His opinion was passed to Brooke-Popham on 30 August 1941. It was doubtful whether a soldier could be ordered to undertake unlawful acts in a neutral country, but if there were substantial military advantages he was free to use volunteers in this way.[8] Should the infiltrators come from SOE or the independent companies – the forerunners of the Commandos? Brooke-Popham suggested that SOE should draw on the independent companies, but it was pointed out that this might blow OM's cover. It was finally decided not to send in whole companies. Sabotage and subversion would be left to SOE. Intelligence must be a military responsibility.[9]

From the start there was friction with the British Minister. He accused Killery of putting out an anti-Japanese pamphlet, claiming that if this 'foolish and pernicious activity' continued, he (Crosby) could not do his job. Killery angrily disclaimed responsibility, adding that the Minister was doing everything he could to frustrate SOE. Crosby replied that this was 'somewhat intemperate . . . I do not propose to retaliate . . . it is better for us all to keep our tempers'. He did retaliate, however, in a disparaging memorandum which he circulated at the highest level to prove that SOE could not succeed in Siam. He also said that the man he had found to represent OM thought the job too risky. Crosby had advised him that he had a duty to family and firm, and that he must judge where his allegiance lay. (A marginal note added in London asks where allegiance to country came in Crosby's batting order.)

On 17 November 1941 Killery told London he proposed to operate behind Crosby's back. He sent his message in a two-part telegram, saying in the first part that he was sending George Windred, an Australian, to investigate the recruitment of orientals in Bangkok – bypassing both Minister and his own man 'who appears to have cold feet'. Before they saw the second part of the telegram London warned him that Dalton had just assured Eden that SOE would do nothing without the Legation's approval. If Crosby found out what was going on he would raise hell. 'We trust therefore that you will be most careful regarding the instructions you give to Windred.'

Killery assumed that London had seen the second part of his telegram which asked authority to *recruit* oriental agents. So

Windred went off to Bangkok, ostensibly a Fleet Street journalist, armed with 'discreetly-forged correspondence' on his supposed employer's notepaper and, perhaps as a gesture to Crosby, also on Foreign Office notepaper, to carry out a secret recruiting campaign. London now realized that they had unwittingly approved recruitment behind the Minister's back; but decided with misgiving that the approval should stand. However, the transaction found its way to Dalton who insisted that Crosby must be put in the picture.

The telegraphic exchange was now completely out of phase. On the same day that Killery was instructed to come clean with the Minister he thanked London for agreeing to his ploy. Then the proposed use of forged letters set off a belated explosion in Whitehall. A Most Immediate telegram commanded that on no account was Windred to use them – but he was now in Bangkok incommunicado. The comedy of asynchronous telegrams ended on 6 December 1941 when Killery confessed he could not stop Windred. He added peevishly: 'It is quite hopeless to attempt to extract the bee from Crosby's bonnet . . . You no doubt realize that so long as you insist on his prior approval a Bangkok organization is definitely impossible.' A colleague confirmed this verdict. It had been madness to consult the Minister. 'One might as well expect a Chief of Police to sponsor a Guild of Housebreakers.'

Two days later the arrival of the Japanese made all this academic.

SOE made a reasonable start in Southern Siam in spite of Crosby. Windred placed at key points twenty-four operatives, most of them trained at 101 STS. (Another twelve were still in Malaya when the Japanese landed.) They were to support British troops entering Siam if Operation *Matador* (the plan to forestall a Japanese attack) was launched. The chosen agents, familiar with the country, were well equipped with arms and explosives smuggled in from Malaya. They would attack railways, commandeer transport, prepare bridges for demolition, seize the airfield at Phuket, and recruit Europeans to form a guerrilla force. Civilians were to be alerted four days before danger threatened, by the broadcast of 'Abide with Me' over Singapore Radio. 'Keep the home fires burning' would warn them to leave the country immediately. The 'Alert' to SOE operatives would be passed from Radio Singapore through a numerical code, and transmitted to the SOE W/T stations at Phuket and Ronpibon at the same time as the military standby order 'Awake' was given in Malaya.

In the event 'Keep the home fires burning' was not broadcast until 11 a.m. on 8 December, ten hours after the Japanese had landed; and although the military 'Awake' was ordered in Malaya on 29 November, ten days before the invasion, Brooke-Popham refused to allow the SOE 'Alert' to go out as arranged, leaving those in the field in Siam believing that there was no immediate danger. As late as midnight on 7/8 December he confirmed this refusal, which may seem extraordinary since the 'Alert' committed no one to anything irrevocable. It was only when European civilians were instructed to get out of Siam in the forenoon of 8 December that SOE's agents were told to go into action.

The experience of Mr J. W. Omay in the Huey Yot area twenty miles north of Trang shows how difficult it was to do anything at all. He heard the warning announcement from Singapore Radio on Saturday evening 6 December, and next morning instructed his colleague Mr R. G. Sarrell to start dismantling their tin dredge. He then went by train to Nasan to inspect the bridge they were to destroy. Early on Monday 8 December he learned that Singapore had been bombed, and ordered Sarrell to speed up dismantling the dredge – which proved impossible as workers and a Siamese CID officer were watching. Between 11 a.m. and noon the radio news was interrupted and the numerical code message which Omay had been waiting for came through at last. However, he found that the Nasan bridge was now guarded by armed men; and when he suggested to the District Officer that it might be in their mutual interest to destroy it received a curt refusal. As he had volunteered for special operations on the assumption that Siam would be fighting alongside Britain he felt under no obligation to do anything more. Therefore he and two colleagues made for Phuket Island hoping to find a boat for Penang; but they were arrested by the Siamese police, and taken to Bangkok where they were interned.

The only achievements of OM in Siam were the occupation of Phuket airfield for two days and the cutting of some telephone lines. Tin denial was carried out at only three of the thirty-four mines. All 111 Europeans on the west coast were safety evacuated, but on the east coast only seven out of seventy-six got away. Ten of SOE's operatives in the south were killed and the rest captured. Their ten agents in the Bangkok area who were not ready to go into action were interned.

OM's report on Siam concludes: 'The organization was ready to function. It merely required the pressing of a button' – but thanks to the army the button was pressed too late. However, as the Siamese made no real attempt to resist the invaders, there might have been little scope for special operations even if there had been plenty of time to make preparations.

## French Indo-China

In French Indo-China OM was up against an agreement that Britain would not support the Free French there so long as French warships refrained from hostile action in the China Seas.[10] It followed that SOE must not operate in Indo-China; and their long-term plans had to rely on second-hand information about the country. Civilians, especially government servants, were said to be corrupt, indolent, interested only in their pensions. Opium smoking was widespread. The navy resented the Allied attack on the French fleet at Oran; but the army resented the Japanese who had been made welcome by the Vichy Government. There were rumours of a resistance movement among the European population.

Baron François de Langlade, a French estate manager with Gaullist sympathies, volunteered to find out about the resistance movement. As he could not get a visa from the Vichy French Consulate in Singapore he was impersonated and his photograph substituted after the passport had been stamped. On his return a month later he confirmed the existence of a resistance movement; and reported to OM that he had arranged for a party to stand by near Cap St. Jacques to receive a consignment of explosives and arms, and also an SOE W/T operator and a demolitions expert.

Because of the undertaking not to support the Free French and because Indo-China was technically neutral a naval vessel could not be used, so a 250-ton Yangtse River steamer, the *Wan Yuen*, was hired for the operation, which was kept secret from her captain and crew. The party, which was led by Spencer Chapman, included Knott, Shufflebotham as ship's W/T operator, and Professor Meyer May, formerly on the staff of the College of Medicine at Hanoi, who had been organizing Free French propaganda in Singapore. May was to go ashore at Cap St. Jacques to confer with the resistance leaders, and hand over the explosives and a W/T set, hidden under coal in the hold. The agent and the demolitions expert* (both trained at 101 STS) would go ashore with him.

The *Wan Yuen* sailed from 101 STS on 19 October 1941; and three days later OM received a telegram from the resistance: 'Market very

* He was M. Pierre Boulle, author of *The Bridge on the River Kwai*.

dangerous. Cancel order.' When the *Wan Yuen* party did not acknowledge an order to return to Singapore a Catalina flying boat was sent to warn them that they were running into a trap, but it failed to locate the ship. They *had* picked up the signal, however, and got safely back to Singapore on 29 October 1941. A second attempt was ruled out as the captain of the *Wan Yuen* now knew what was going on.

Goodfellow, ostensibly on a business trip, went to Saigon on 4 November 1941 to find out what had gone wrong. He discovered that the authorities knew all about the subversive organization, but were leaving it alone until it became a serious threat. Although the leader seemed afraid to do anything, he had been totally reckless in the matter of security, so that the proposal to bring in explosives and agents had been freely discussed as far afield as Shanghai. The Japanese had set up a new gun emplacement on the chosen beach at Cap St. Jacques to deal with the expedition. Goodfellow returned to Singapore dejected. He had no doubt that all SOE's contacts in Indo-China were unreliable and that OM must start again from scratch. The only bright spot was that the agent whom the *Wan Yuen* expedition had failed to put in travelled with Goodfellow on an ordinary passenger steamer, pretending to want to join his fellow-countrymen, and was admitted without difficulty.

*Hong Kong*

In July 1939 – before war was declared in Europe – General Grasett, GOC, Hong Kong, asked Mr F. W. Kendall, who had spent some years in charge of refugee camps, to form a unit code-named 'Z Force' to engage in covert operations should the Colony ever be occupied. He enlisted Major D. R. Holmes (later Sir Ronald), Squadron Leader R. G. K. (later Sir Robert) Thompson, Lieutenant E. B. Teesdale, Captain H. B. Williamson, and Captain C. M. McEwan. Later four civilians joined. Six food and ammunition dumps were prepared in the New Territories, one in a disused mine shaft, and the largest in two caves a mile to the south east of Taimoshan Mountain, which were enlarged by the Royal Engineers to accommodate seven men. This hide-out was well camouflaged and so inaccessible that it was unlikely that an enemy would stumble on it.

Kendall attended a course at 101 STS in July 1941. In October Gavin visited Hong Kong to give Z Force, now renamed the Reconnaissance Unit, the benefit of his experience and arrange for the supply of operational stores from Singapore. A secret telephone line was run from the caves to Brigade headquarters in Kowloon. Plans were made for Kendall to carry out underground activities in Canton, Amoy, Swatow, and Hainan. He recruited a number of Chinese to act as saboteurs, for whom a Training Centre was provided in the New Territories; but the Japanese arrived before it opened. The Reconnaissance Unit moved to the Taimoshan caves, except for Williamson, who was in Singapore at 101 STS. When their telephone line failed Kendall and McEwan went to Kowloon to have it put right, and were prevented by the Japanese advance from returning to the Unit.

Kendall, accompanied by Mr Monia Talan, a civilian member of the Unit, twice rowed out in a sampan to attack ships which the Japanese were using as observation posts. They sank one and severely damaged another. On the last day of the siege Kendall organized the escape of seventy-five men, whom he led to Waichow on the Chinese mainland, where he remained to organize further escapes from Hong Kong.

Meanwhile the other members of the Reconnaissance Unit had been overrrun by the Japanese. They were able to observe enemy positions, but when they tried to telephone information to Brigade headquarters, the line having been repaired, they heard a Japanese voice at the other end. In the next fortnight they destroyed several lorries, mined a road, and killed two sentries. When Hong Kong fell some members of the Unit surrendered, but Teesdale, Holmes, and Thompson decided to attempt the journey to Chungking, which they reached without difficulty.

### Shanghai

In Shanghai OM had a team of six under Mr W. J. Gande. None of them was trained, and they had no equipment; but in any case the Foreign Office had ruled that nothing was to be done against neutral or enemy property in Shanghai. In September 1941, however, the group, with the agreement of C-in-C, Far East, proposed to attack the Italian sloop *Eritrea* off the International Settlement. The Embassy at once killed off the project by telling the Foreign Office that it would damage property, arouse anti-British feeling, and perhaps lead the Japanese to occupy the Settlement. SOE were furious at what they regarded as a stab in the back. Killery claimed that they had no intention of doing anything without the Ambassador's blessing.

Although the Shanghai team accomplished nothing, the Japanese knew of their existence, probably through someone in Gande's office. On 17 December 1941 Mr H. G. Clarke, who had been associated with them, and later the others, were arrested and confronted with copies of telegrams exchanged with OM in Singapore. They were kept in cages twenty-seven feet by twelve – 'thirty of both sexes and all nationalities, all packed in so tightly that it was impossible for everyone to lie down' – and brutally treated. They were transferred to military headquarters ten miles out of Shanghai, where conditions were better, their wives being allowed to bring them food. On 29 April 1942 a military court convicted them after a farcical trial, but they had to wait a month to hear their sentences. Gande was given four years and the others from twelve to eighteen months. When the trial was reported the men were described as ringleaders of a secret society conducting anti-Axis espionage, propaganda, and sabotage under instructions from Singapore.

In the Ward Road Gaol to which they were finally transferred they were reasonably treated by the Gendarmerie, including a colonel – 'the smallest Japanese officer I have ever seen . . . the ever-present sword just cleared the floor, with the hilt reposing somewhere in the neighbourhood of his shoulderblade'. In August it was rumoured that they were to be repatriated, which they dismissed as a trick; but in fact five were released in an exchange of prisoners. Two remained, including Gande, who served his full sentence.

## China

In March 1941 Brooke-Popham proposed a British-led *corps d'élite* of Chinese guerrillas for occupied China. He envisaged groups of fifteen British or Indian other ranks to carry out demolitions in five areas; but London vetoed this before Britain was at war with Japan. The War Office pointed out that OM was authorized to organize guerrillas led by non-British Europeans; and in August 1941 the British Ambassador to China (Sir Alexander Clark Kerr) suggested to Chiang Kai-Shek that a group of Danes posing as employees of an industrial firm should set up training schools and carry out sabotage. The men, who knew China well, were recruited in Malaya, and christened the China Commando Group.

Their leader, Mr Erik Nyholm, went to Chungking in October 1941 to get Chinese approval for the project but there was no response until

Killery visited Chungking in January 1942.* Then Chiang Kai-Shek agreed that the Group should become a self-contained unit within the Chinese Special Operations Section which was responsible for secret activities behind enemy lines. Killery was delighted: for the first time his Mission could make a real contribution. He reported that the Commander of the Special Operations Section, General Chow Wei-Lung 'makes a most favourable impression. He is practical, thorough, determined, and experienced.' The Commando Group would train partisans at three centres and operate in nine sectors in enemy-occupied territory. Everyone was enthusiastic. The Ambassador was 'enthusiastic ... that we should work for and with the Chinese within their own army, and there is no doubt that General Chiang Kai-Shek feels the same'. The first school opened near Chungking in March 1942 and in April 'the first bunch of enthusiastic Chinese youths graduated'.

Enthusiasm quickly evaporated. Chow addressed a letter to Mr J. (later Sir John) Keswick, who looked after OM's interests in China – 'the Honourable Representative of the British Side'. Oriental politeness gave way to a series of commands. Since the Commando Group would be part of the Chinese army, it must drop its name. Radio stations set up to support it must close. Its demolition materials, trucks, petrol, and stores must be handed over to the Chinese. Its offices, storehouses, and living quarters must be built by the Chinese. Finally, Chow enclosed a long list of things required by the Special Operations Section ranging from plastic explosive to assorted disguises including 'wigs, artificial eyes and teeth'.

In reply Keswick expressed his deep admiration for Chow's great valour, and then said bluntly he was breaking an agreement approved by Chiang Kai-Shek. The Commando Group must remain independent. Without trucks it would be immobile. No Chinese could handle its sophisticated explosives. He would appeal to the Generalissimo. However, Chiang Kai-Shek refused to see him and simply sent a curt message to the Ambassador demanding the immediate withdrawal of the Group, ostensibly because it had been improperly dealing direct with Provincial Governors. One explan-

---

* Second in command was to be Vladimir Petropavlovsky, who was taken prisoner in Hong Kong in December 1941. He escaped in February 1942 and reached Chungking only to find that the Commando Group had been liquidated. He transferred to SOE in the Balkans, and later returned to Force 136 as Adviser on Chinese Affairs. A Russian by birth, he became a naturalized British citizen in 1945.

ation of this volte-face was that the Chinese feared that the stalemate on their front (due partly to the withdrawal of seventeen Japanese divisions after Pearl Harbor) would be broken if an Allied commando force went into action. Alternatively, but less likely, the Chinese, having seen Britain lose so much face in the Far East had no real desire for British-sponsored help.

The Danes were bitterly disappointed. Nyholm wrote to Keswick: '. . . when so much could have been achieved, the political situation transformed the usual oriental inertia and negative resistance into an active opposition . . .'. Keswick replied: 'Our failure has been due to the trend of this world war and in particular the attitude of the Chinese towards it, and towards the British. Over and above this I am afraid that our original estimate of General Chow was wrong. He is a little man and will always remain so.'

*Dutch East Indies*

Although the Dutch East Indies were in OM's territory virtually nothing was done there. Brooke-Popham refused to approach the Dutch on behalf of the Mission, which meant that Killery could not put agents into Sumatra or Java. The British Consul General did invite a member of the Mission to Java for informal talks, but before they could lead to anything war had broken out.

When General Sir Archibald Wavell became commander of the American-British-Dutch-Australian (ABDA) forces in January 1942 Killery was even more critical of him than he had been of Brooke-Popham. He believed that the latter's opposition was based on local considerations, but Wavell made no attempt to conceal his distrust of SOE based on his experience in the Middle East. Killery, who made his way to Java, did have some dealings with the Dutch, having been instructed by London to recruit agents, guides, saboteurs, and pilots suitable for post-occupational work some of whom would be withdrawn to be trained for their eventual return; but the main contribution was made by Captain (later Sir Laurens) van der Post, the South African whom General Wavell had recommended for guerrilla work in the Far East because of his experience in Ethiopia. When van der Post arrived at Wavell's headquarters in Java three days after the fall of Singapore, he was ordered to form No. 43 Special Mission to bring out units still at liberty in Malaya, but by the time he had recruited a team including four Europeans it was too late to mount a rescue operation. He was therefore instructed to plan for the

escape of Wavell and his staff. He spent three days mapping a route to
Pemangpeuk on the south coast, but meantime C-in-C had left from
the port of Tjilatjap. It was now agreed that he should establish a left-
behind group on the pattern of the Malayan parties, although he
insisted that it be a purely military operation, unconnected with SOE.
None the less, OM provided seven W/T sets to enable them to
communicate with Ceylon or Australia, and also money for their
support. In co-operation with the Dutch they planned a headquarters
in the jungle on the south-west coast of Java from which escapers
would be sent by motor boat to Sumatra and there transferred to
native craft to take them to Ceylon. The voyage to Australia was
considered to be impracticable.

The Dutch were shocked by the sudden collapse of the British in
Malaya, which had left them vulnerable to a Japanese invasion. Van
der Post recorded later that they

were understandably very bitter about us and very defeatist, and for the first
time I began myself to fear that the Dutch resistance when the Japanese
landed would have very little heart in it. What was more disquieting still was
the change I noticed in the attitude of the natives. Overnight they had
thrown away the traditional headdress of their country and had all donned
the newfangled black fez of the extreme native nationalist and anti-Dutch
movement. As the success of our mission was going to depend a great deal on
the goodwill of the natives this evidence of their adhesion to Dutch authority
was a very bad sign.

As in Malaya there was not enough time to give a left-behind
party a real chance of survival; and in any case Japanese reprisals
would almost certainly have made the party's activities counter-
productive. They were assembled round about 24 February 1942.
The Japanese landed on Sunday 1 March. On 8 March Java
capitulated. By 28 March van der Post had gathered together a group
nearly 100 strong, in the most difficult conditions.

Everywhere on the roads one met Dutch planters fleeing for their lives from
the natives who had been their servants for 100 years or more. Everywhere
one saw houses which had been completely deserted and I myself smashed
many locked doors to let out thirsty dogs that had been left behind by their
Dutch masters in the general panic.

The group, which had only one W/T operator (Lieutenant Cooper,
RNVR), made many attempts to get in touch with Colombo, but
although they transmitted – from the top of a mountain – and
listened during the scheduled hours, they got no response. It was a

matter of time before they were tracked down by the invaders. Van der Post himself was captured at the end of June; and the rest of the group, including Cooper, were forced to surrender in September when the Japanese threatened to destroy ten villages if they did not give themselves up.[11]

In November 1941 Major A. B. O'Dwyer was sent from London to report on OM. He concluded that up to the time of his visit it had achieved virtually nothing. Its charter was unworkable. Killery had tried to make the best of a bad job, but had made no attempt to plan subversive operations. The organization suffered from the lack of a military staff branch, which in O'Dwyer's view was essential.

Sir Frank Nelson, head of SOE, in submitting Killery's final report to Dalton, said he had done his damndest against impossible odds, but had been wrong to suffer in silence. He should have kept London better informed about his difficulties with the diplomats and the military, and he should have concentrated on the more fruitful parts of his territory. 'It is most tantalising to see in the report how His Majesty's Representatives have vetoed any preparatory work, cried for help from SOE the moment trouble started, and then complained if we did not deliver the goods. This is life . . .'. Dalton said he did not understand the report, and made the curious suggestion: 'The story ought to be written at length like a novel and printed for private circulation.'

Sir George Moss, SOE's adviser on Chinese affairs, wrote:

It is clear that the British Colonial administration, British officialdom in the Far East, and the British Secret Service had failed to make adequate preparation in time of peace for internal organization in time of war e.g. Fifth Column activities in enemy territory, communications, and intelligence on anything approaching the scale accomplished by Japan . . . Sir Josiah Crosby virtually expelled his [Killery's] Mission from Thailand two weeks before war was declared, the Frée French organization in Indo-China proved a broken reed . . . The military failed to give orders for demolition in time, and crowning misfortune, failed to hold Singapore long enough to enable his left behind parties to operate in favourable circumstances . . . It is a story of military ineptitude.

It may be said in Crosby's defence that he was merely implementing policy; and he cannot be blamed if the policy was misguided. However, the correspondence leaves the impression that, having spent the greater part of his career in the Far East, he believed he knew all the answers, and was moved as much by a desire to oppose the intruding Killery as a wish to further British policy.

OM was certainly hamstrung by Brooke-Popham's ineptitude and the singular small-mindedness of Percival. In August 1941 the Governor of Burma said the time had come to replace Brooke-Popham. COS loyally claimed he had shown energy, resource, and vision; and asked that judgement be suspended until Mr Duff Cooper (later Lord Norwich), Minister Resident in Singapore, had a chance of saying what he thought. Without knowing this, Duff Cooper recommended that C-in-C should be replaced. When Mr Leo Amery, Secretary of State for India, drew Churchill's attention to these independent recommendations he said both might be wrong, but it is hardly likely that two experienced men would make the same error of judgement.[12] Duff Cooper dismissed Percival as a man who lacked the qualities of a commander, 'namely personality, vision, power of rapid decision and grip'.[13]

In his final dispatch Brooke-Popham describes SOE's contribution:

An attempt was made to organize left-behind parties in Northern Malaya with the object of obtaining information and carrying out sabotage of all sorts in the enemy's rear. This duty was entrusted to the OM Section of the Ministry of Economic Warfare under Mr Killery. It was, however, started too late and there was no time to organize it thoroughly. This was in no way the fault of the OM but was due to factors mentioned . . . above. [Killery and his staff were] keen and capable, but they had no experience and very little knowledge of how to set about their work . . . In consequence of this, but through no fault of Mr Killery and his staff the OM activities never got functioning properly by the time war with Japan broke out. There was also a curious reluctance on the part of many people to have anything to do with these activities or to help on the work.[14]

Perhaps when he wrote these words Brooke-Popham had in mind C-in-C, Far East, and GOC, Malaya.

The latter also referred to SOE in his final dispatch:

In the summer of 1941 Branch of the Ministry of Economic Warfare was started in Singapore. It suffered from an excess of secrecy and from a lack of knowledge on the part of the gentlemen responsible as to how to set about the work. At the request of the Governor I arranged for every facility to be given to these gentlemen to enable them to carry out very secret work in Malaya. It was only some two months later that it came to my knowledge that this work consisted of organizing 'left-behind' parties which should obviously have been part of the military plan. Thus valuable time was lost. Later, however, some very useful work was done by this organization'.[15]

Good drafting can save a multitude of reputations.

# 2

# The India Mission

SOE's India Mission was set up through the initiative of the Secretary of State for India, who sent Colonel Joyce of the Indian Political Service to Singapore in May 1941 for discussions with Killery. Joyce was quickly convinced of the need for a special-operations organization in India and the Viceroy equally quickly agreed. Mackenzie, who had lost a leg in the Great War, was appointed to command the Mission, first designated GSI(k) (ostensibly a branch of GHQ, India) and after 16 March 1944, Force 136.*

Mackenzie was given singularly vague terms of reference. He would proceed to India with his deputy, Major Gavin Stewart, to be attached to the Viceroy as head of a special-operations Mission. It was uncertain where he would operate. He would be wholly responsible for Afghanistan and Tibet, and possibly Persia, where an SOE Mission was then controlled from the Middle East. He might be asked to operate into Russia and China. Burma was looked after by OM, but circumstances might require him to take over that country. How prophetic!

It was admitted there would be little scope for normal special operations – subversive political activity, sabotage, and subversive propaganda. Pre-occupational demolitions would presumably be carried out by the military, and post-occupational sabotage by existing organizations. However, it was conceivable that there would be some scope for subversive propaganda. 'This subversion would of course be the subversion by us of subversive forces in India' – a daunting intellectual exercise.

These instructions were revised after the Japanese invasion of Malaya and Burma brought India into the war zone. Mackenzie's new directive in August 1942 was again in general terms since his remoteness from London and vast territory made it difficult for SOE headquarters to be precise. He was to perform tasks of a political or operational nature outside the scope or capacity of other secret or

---

* In fact Mackenzie adopted the new designation only after his headquarters moved from Meerut in India to Kandy in Ceylon on 16 December 1944 (WO 203 4331 (14.12.44); WO 203 5748 (16.12.44)).

overt organizations, but only on the orders of the Viceroy or C-in-C, India. His sphere of operation was the area in which the writ of the Viceroy and C-in-C ran, with the addition of Eastern Persia (the rest of Persia being left to SOE Cairo), Afghanistan, and Tibet, where he would carry out subversive political activities aimed at forwarding the policies of the British Government. He would also seek to reduce the influence of enemy powers by underground means not available to diplomatic missions or the military, prepare pre-occupational and post-occupational sabotage, and disseminate subversive propaganda.

In India, in addition to assisting the Viceroy and C-in-C, he was authorized to raise guerrillas, including communists 'of hitherto blemished or (less likely) unblemished reputations'. In Burma he would help the army by providing communications and supporting anti-Japanese elements. Siam, French Indo-China, Malaya, the Dutch East Indies, and the Pacific Islands were, at least for the time being, defined as no man's land for special operations, which meant that the India Mission, the American OSS, and Special Operations, Australia (SOA) were free to operate there provided they kept each other fully informed about their activities.

So long as the threat of a Japanese invasion of India and a German descent through the Caucasus existed, the India Mission was compelled to remain on the defensive. If the Japanese advance was unchecked it was expected that three areas might become the scene of military operations – Assam, Madras, and Calcutta; and it was on these that Mackenzie focused his attention. The enemy might also try to capture the naval base at Trincomalee in Ceylon; but Mackenzie had been warned in his revised directive not to take on too much (as OM had done) and he wisely left Ceylon out of his calculations. In any case the C-in-C, Ceylon had indicated that he did not want any post-occupational activities there.

It was planned to organize parties among the hill tribes in Assam for post-occupational work under British officers, especially in the neighbourhood of the Manipur-Imphal road, which would be a key line of communication. This scheme was approved by GHQ India, which then expanded it and took it over. It was hoped to raise 10,000 men, but they could not be armed for a long time as the supply of rifles to India was barely enough for the recruits entering the regular Indian army. The India Mission did, however, recruit men for post-occupational work along the road. They were briefed to join repair gangs engaged by the Japanese so that repairs carried out during the day might be balanced by sabotage conducted at night. Demolition stores for their use had been hidden at convenient points.

The India Mission established a small Training Centre at Kohima to instruct men of the Assam Rifles. These were later to form 'V' Force, and to be administered by SOE's military representative. This alliance with the military was blessed by C-in-C, India, but the new Chief of Staff (Major General T. J. W. Winterton) had the decision reversed. All guerrillas would become the responsibility of the army, except that SOE would be allowed to control those operating behind enemy lines. Mackenzie deprecated the decision since he believed that the new V Force would provide an ideal spring-board to launch agents overland into Japanese occupied territory at a time when air transport could not be spared.

In Calcutta the India Mission shared in the pre-occupational demolition scheme managed by Eastern Command, being given responsibility for the destruction of the power-stations (Operation *Dogleg*). SOE prepared the demolitions, but they were to be carried out by members of the Calcutta Scottish who had been specially trained for the operation. The Calcutta docks were also to be dealt with by the India Mission. Another defensive activity was the setting up of an Indian group in Eastern Bengal organized by an Indian member of the Indian Civil Service. So that the Japanese would regard him as an ally he was supposed to have quarrelled with the Government of India. The movement had some success, but when the India Mission suggested that its members should join V Force the army refused to have them, as they were unsure of their military ability. They did, however, agree to use them as a screen against the infiltration of enemy agents. The scheme happened to become exclusively Muslim and was liquidated in February 1943 when the danger of invasion had virtually disappeared.

In Madras the India Mission was forced to fall back on the Communist Party of India. The Secretary of the Party, P. C. Joshi, put forward candidates for sabotage training who would become leaders of cells at key points along the east coast of India. Three regional heads were appointed with headquarters just outside the areas likely to be taken over by the Japanese to direct operations within these areas. In all 150 men were trained, in spite of the misgivings of the Madras police; but just as arms dumps were about to be set up, the war situation improved, and with relief the India Mission ended the scheme. Joshi asked that members of the Party throughout India should continue to be trained lest it became necessary to deal with Fifth Columnists and collaborators. SOE agreed to modified training courses, partly out of gratitude for the communists' co-operation, although Mackenzie had no doubt that if it had suited their book to help the Japanese they would not have hesitated for an instant.

It was also necessary to look to the dangers in Eastern Persia and Afghanistan. In March 1942 Wavell instructed the India Mission to organize irregular forces from the local tribesmen to defend the East Persia Road and to interfere with any enemy lines of communication established there. Two SOE agents already in Eastern Persia were told to recruit 100 men who would be required if the occasion arose to levy a force of 1,000. Some of the first recruits would be sent to India for training. Arms accumulated at Quetta were specially packed for burial in Persia, and preliminary contact was made with suitable tribesmen, although none were actually recruited. When the threat to Persia disappeared in March 1943 the scheme was wound up.

The India Mission was authorized to operate in Afghanistan if there seemed to be real danger that the Germans would occupy the country. It was assumed that the Afghan Government would not oppose the entry of German troops. The attitude of the hill tribes was uncertain, but one view was that 'their dislike of foreign intrusion or domination should offer us an excellent field for exploitation by subversive political means'. On the other hand it was argued that they might be unwilling to co-operate unless the German occupation was very oppressive and there was some sign that Britain was winning the war. So after occupation the Mission would foster antagonism to the Germans, encourage guerrilla warfare, and destroy communications, although they were so poor that there was little to destroy. Indeed, if the Germans were to establish themselves permanently they would have to make massive improvements.

A further problem was that Afghanistan kept foreigners under close surveillance, and India was anxious that nothing should be done to impair relations with their neighbour. Nevertheless, an agent was sent to Afghanistan to spy out the land. A forecast was made of the tribes' attitude along the line of a German advance: one would fiercely resent occupation, but might not relish the danger and discomfort of a guerrilla war; another was comparatively civilized and had lost its martial qualities; a third had the toughest and best fighters in the country, but now lived in permanent villages, susceptible to blockade. As it turned out none of the dozen tribes examined was required to go into action.

During this period Mackenzie had serious misgivings about the India Mission's contribution. When his first reports were studied in London he was politely congratulated, but reminded 'we must never forget the "O" in Special Operations Executive. I know it is hard to put this into effect . . .'. A few months later the same point was made: 'SOE is an *operational* and not an intelligence organization.' The India Mission did not make its position easier by using the branch cover symbol GSI(k) in which the 'I' (for Intelligence) aggravated the problem of 'O' (for Operations) by leading many, for example those in charge of the issue of operational stores, to believe that the secret organization *was* concerned with intelligence. The real point was that SOE headquarters in London were slow to recognize the limited scope for 'European-type' special operations in the Far East: they continued to expect the impossible.

Mackenzie was disconcerted by the ambitious plans which, apparently under the impression that to draft a plan was to guarantee its accomplishment, London provided. He warned London that the Mission's reputation did not stand high. SOE was considered to be a substantial and expensive failure in the Middle East where Wavell, now C-in-C, India, had firsthand experience of the organization. Everyone suspected the India Mission and was unwilling to give it any responsibility, or to provide staff. The Viceroy had done what he could to help, but 'I cannot emphasize too much that SOE is suspect on the ground that there are too many plans, much talk, but little performance, and such performance as there is at exorbitant cost; and by cost I do not refer by any means entirely to money but also to the numbers and calibre of those employed . . .'. Since the oriental mind tended to side with the apparent winner in a war there was in the face of the Japanese success no hope of effective co-operation from the indigenous population. Nor was there any point in asking Europeans to organize resistance. They would simply be slaughtered.

In August 1942 the fortunes of the India Mission were at their lowest ebb. Mackenzie wrote to London: 'Gavin Stewart and I have now been in this country for 10 months and it must be admitted that to date we have very little to show for it. Excuses are rightly of little avail in wartime . . .'.

It was only in the second quarter of 1943, when the threats of Japanese invasion and a German breakthrough in the north had been removed that the India Mission began to think about positive action in the countries now included in its charter: Siam, French Indo-China, Sumatra, the Andaman and Nicobar Islands, China, Burma, and Malaya.

By now the Mission had settled broadly into the shape it retained for the rest of the war. Mackenzie ran it on the lines of a business, with himself as Chairman, and his first Deputy Mr Gavin Stewart* and the Controllers (as they were originally designated) of the four Divisions – Finance and Administration, Operations and Training, Political Warfare, and the Country Sections – as Directors. Mr Walter Fletcher, in charge of Operation *Mickleham*,† was nominally independent but looked to Mackenzie for political guidance, and in practice worked closely with the Mission, making a sixth Director.

In addition to Mission headquarters at Meerut there was an office in Delhi which kept in touch with the Viceroy's staff, and an office in Bombay to receive new arrivals in India; a sub-mission at Calcutta (Group A – the Burma, Siam, and French Indo-China Country Sections); a sub-mission at Colombo (Group B – the Malaya, Anglo-Dutch, and Islands Country Sections); and sub-missions in China at Chungking and Kunming which later became Group C.

The main organizational change in the lifetime of the India Mission came after the establishment of SEAC in November 1943 when arrangements were made to co-ordinate the work of the clandestine bodies operating in the Command – in addition to SOE, the American OSS, ISLD, SEAC's own Political Warfare Division, and the group concerned with deception planning (D Division) – all competing for the same resources. From this time India Mission plans had to be submitted to the new P Division, headed by Captain Garnons-Williams RN, for discussion before going to the Supreme Allied Commander for approval; and it was through P Division that the Mission was told what was required of it by the military.

The difficulty of running the India Mission was increased by the wide dispersal of its establishments. When Colonel George Taylor, the headquarters Director in charge of overseas missions, made a tour of inspection at the beginning of 1944, visiting most, but not all of the

---

* Stewart was succeeded by Brigadier D. R. Guinness (formerly SOE Director of Plans in London) in December 1943. He was in turn succeeded by Lieutenant-Colonel J. (later Sir John) Anstey in November 1944.

† See Part II, Chapter 9.

establishments, he travelled 10,000 miles by air and 3,000 by rail. He wrote: 'When the internal distances between one establishment and another, combined with wartime transport deficiencies, are taken into account it seems almost as if the administrative difficulties behind the lines equalled in complexity and demand for clear leadership those of the men operating in the jungle against the Japanese.' It took a day and a half by air from Delhi to Colombo, and five days by train. Delhi to Calcutta took six hours by air, and thirty by train. It was a day's flight from Calcutta to Kunming over 'the Hump' – the Himalayas – weather and the Japanese air force permitting.

Given these timings, and the need for agents to move round the area during training, it is hardly surprising that the gestation period for an operation could be more than a year, something which those in the comparative efficiency of headquarters in London found difficult to understand. In February 1944 Guinness illustrated the problem by sending home a map of India superimposed on Europe. He also set out a rail and air timetable for the region in which the Mission operated, adding that a letter from Delhi to Colombo could take ten days, so that it might be three weeks before a reply was received. The dispatch of stores by rail from Jabalpur or Poona to Calcutta or Colombo took as long as it would have done to send them from Britain to an Indian port. If SOE London's operational area was on the same scale it would stretch as far as Moscow and Teheran. London was not impressed. His letter was simply endorsed: 'Bobby Guinness says India is rather big.'

The pressure from London to do something – almost *anything* – led the India Mission to plan Operation *Creek* (later *Longshanks*) very soon after it had been established. This was some form of action against four Axis merchant ships which had taken refuge in neutral Goa when war was declared.* The plan was on and off during most of 1942 before it was finally adopted in December. One of the Axis ships – which it was suspected might be relaying intelligence gathered in India to German submarines in the Arabian Sea – would be removed and taken to Calcutta.

An early version of the plan was mind-boggling. The Governor General (Colonel José Cabral) would be induced 'by financial

---

* The German *Ehrenfels*, *Braunfels*, and *Drachenfels*, and the Italian *Anfora*.

considerations' to throw a party for the captains and crews of the four
ships, at which 'plenty of drink would be provided for the men, but
not too much for the officers, because their suspicions might be
aroused'. There would be a dance to keep the men on shore as long as
possible. Meantime a party of handpicked SOE men disguised as
German and Italian sailors would board the undermanned vessels,
shoot any of the skeleton crews who opposed them, and await the
return of the revellers. 'As they came on board they would be clubbed
and captured, or shot as necessary.' The new crews would sail out
their prize at leisure. However, to bring the operation within the law,
or almost, 'arrangements would have to be made to complete any
formalities and pay any harbour dues'.

On 26 December 1942 the Foreign Office, always fearful of the
damage SOE might do to relations with neutral countries, agreed that
the India Mission should try to get hold of one of the ships, but only on
the strict understanding that it was done through 'bribery pure and
simple and nothing else'. There must be no act of violence in
Portuguese territorial waters.

In November Stewart had made a preliminary reconnaissance;
and on 17 December Lieutenant-Colonel Lewis Pugh and another
SOE agent drove to Goa to collect further information about the ships,
and inquire into the activities of Robert Koch, a Nazi agent living in
Panjim, capital of Goa. They discussed these matters with the British
Consul (Lieutenant-Colonel C. E. U. Bremner) without discussing
their real purpose. Next day they reconnoitred Koch's house while he
was away; and 'in view of the necessity of causing no embarrassment to the Portuguese Government by creating a breach of the
peace, it was decided to effect entry to Robert Koch's house on the
plea of discussing business'. This ploy, thus recorded in language of
which any village constable might be proud, succeeded. After a brief
discussion, Koch and his 'wife', whom the SOE men had not expected
to find, were persuaded to accompany them to British India, driving
openly through Portuguese and British Customs.

SOE now made contact through intermediaries with the Germans,
including Captain Rofels of the *Ehrenfels*. The intermediaries reported
that the sailors were a mixture of Nazis and communists, seriously
depressed after years of living in uncomfortable conditions, and at
loggerheads with each other. When Rofels was told he would be paid
a large sum to hand over his ship outside territorial waters he seemed
to welcome the proposition. This rather flimsy evidence satisfied the

India Mission that he would co-operate; and on 13 February 1943 the operation order for *Longshanks* was issued.

The personnel for the expedition, commanded by Pugh, were drawn from the India Mission, supplemented by men from the Calcutta Light Horse and the Calcutta Scottish. A plan to sail the *Ehrenfels* from the harbour was abandoned when it was reported that she could not move under her own power. Instead she would have to be towed. Neither the Ministry of War Transport nor the Royal Indian Navy would provide a vessel for the job, but the India Mission prevailed on the Calcutta Port Commissioners to charter Hopper Barge No. 5. With some difficulty the Bengali crew were persuaded to sail the barge from the Hooghli River to Cochin – ostensibly for a combined training exercise.

Every precaution was taken to conceal the true purpose of the enterprise. The operation orders were written as if the destination was Persia. The members of the expedition had no idea what was required of them, but were simply told to report to Cochin by 4 March 1943. Nevertheless, security was less than perfect. When the SOE members of the party, coming by rail from Kharakvasla, had to change trains there was in their baggage a box labelled 'Grenades' for all to see. It was only when their craft was twelve hours out of Cochin that the true objective was revealed. Training was carried out on board – revolver, Sten, and Bren guns, silent killing and self protection, knotting and lashing ropes, and knife fighting. The men exercised at night to become thoroughly familiar with their surroundings and equipment. Half of the operational group were housed aft and half forward and during the outward voyage they were not allowed to meet.

A Bren gun was mounted on the bridge to command the deck of the *Ehrenfels* lest the plan to tow her out without a struggle misfired. The bridge was protected with sandbags; and drawbridges were erected on either side of the forecastle to make it possible to board the German ship without delay from either port or starboard. Hopper Barge No. 5 entered Marmagoa harbour after midnight on 9 March 1943, and having rounded *Braunfels* approached the *Ehrenfels* from starboard. She was immediately challenged in English by Germans standing on the engine-room superstructure. The plan *had* misfired.

However, the barge held her course. The lowered drawbridge fouled the *Ehrenfels*'s main mast but was extricated without difficulty; and at 0225 hours the order to board was given. In spite of the steep incline due to the difference in the vessels' height the main boarding party scrambled up and moved to their pre-arranged positions. The Germans at once opened fire, but their resistance was quickly overcome without casualties to the assault party. The ship's siren was sounded until the operator was shot. It had been assumed that in the event the German captain might not co-operate and that he might try to scuttle the ship by opening the seacocks; and two men (Major J. A. Hislop and Captain C. McEwan) were deputed to close them. Although demolition charges were already being detonated and it was clear that there was no hope of moving the ship with or without the help of the crew, Hislop and McEwan who had boarded by means of a rope net thrown over the side of the *Ehrenfels* descended interminable ladders in the hope that they might close the seacocks but found the task impossible. There were now many fierce fires and the order to withdraw was given. Within a few minutes the *Ehrenfels*, a mass of flame, settled on the harbour bottom. Almost simultaneously the other German ships were fired and scuttled; and two hours after Hopper Barge No. 5 had withdrawn – taking with her three prisoners – the Italian *Anfora* also scuttled herself. There were no British casualties in the brief engagement, but five of the *Ehrenfels* crew had been killed.

There were three inquests into Operation *Longshanks*: in the India Mission to find out why the operation had failed; in Whitehall, to determine why SOE had ignored the Foreign Office condition that there must be no violence; and by the British Consul in Goa, who was in duty bound to report on unusual occurrences in his territory.

The India Mission had completely misjudged the situation. It had been wrong to accept the advice that there were communists among the Axis crews who would willingly collaborate against the Nazis. Since Captain Rofels and his officers were lying in wait for the boarding party it was obvious that they had no intention of accepting a bribe. The Axis ships were blacked out when Hopper Barge No. 5 arrived, which was unusual – they had been fully lit when Stewart and Pugh had made their reconnaissances. The barge was challenged in English. The demolition charges were detonated almost before the drawbridge was lowered on to *Ehrenfels'* deck; and almost simultaneously the other two German ships were scuttled. It was obvious that the whole Axis group had known exactly what was going to happen, and were ready and waiting.

The India Mission inquest found that before the barge had left

Cochin there were rumours that she was going to carry an armed party to an Indian Ocean island to seize a submarine, or that she was taking a force to Goa as part of a military operation to secure Portuguese India in response to a German invasion of Spain. However, the captain of the *Ehrenfels* did not have to rely on rumours. The India Mission had already told him what was going to happen.

The most interesting thing about the first hare-brained plan which was wisely not adopted is that it laid down that although the Axis crews might be homesick after years cooped up in a foreign port 'their morale is far too good to make possible any sort of plan which involved removing them by bribes and promises'; and in rejecting this earlier plan the India Mission also put out of its mind the fundamental fact which doomed *Longshanks* to failure.

The main contributor to the Whitehall inquest was Taylor. His specially commissioned report is a masterpiece of special pleading, which seeks to prove that the India Mission's disregard of orders was due to forgivable misunderstandings. The Minister – Selborne – was not impressed. He told Gubbins that SOE's pledge to the Foreign Office, *his* pledge, that there would be no act of violence, had been shamefully violated. He took a most serious view and considered that those responsible should be recalled. What on earth had Mackenzie been about? If SOE officers did not obey instructions there might be another Jameson raid at any minute. Meantime Mackenzie had offered his resignation, which Gubbins refused to accept. When Selborne saw Taylor's report he still thought that the chief blame rested on Mackenzie, but since he had honourably offered to resign he contented himself with sending the head of the India Mission a stiff reprimand, in which he made much of the complete disregard of instructions from London. To sugar the pill he added that he did not wish to detract from the personal gallantry of those who had taken part in the operation.

The British Consul, whom SOE had not taken into their confidence, unwittingly came to their rescue. His own detective work led him to conclude that the Axis crews had mutinied; and fearing that the Gestapo would hold it against them after the war, had invented the story of an attack by a small vessel which disgorged masked and helmeted men. He put this explanation to the Governor-General of Goa in conversation, who accepted it. He also argued that the presence of fifteen partly-used fire extinguishers on the *Ehrenfels* (which the India Mission party had carried with them to nip in the bud any fires started by the Germans) proved that some of the crew had tried to prevent the scuttling of the ship. When Selborne saw the Consul's report he minuted: 'This is the most amazing piece of luck SOE has ever had.'

The captains of the Axis vessels – except of course for Rofels, one of the five killed – were found guilty by the Goanese courts of 'disturbing the tranquillity of the port'. Their defence that they had been attacked by a strange vessel was dismissed as lacking all foundation. The captain of the Italian *Anfora* was unable to explain why his vessel was fired so long after the German ships.

At the end of 1942 it was planned to establish a base in the Japanese-occupied Andaman Islands – part of the Indian Empire 1,000 miles south-east of Calcutta – to observe enemy naval, air, and army dispositions, and possibly to foster resistance. It was hoped to install a radio station to relay messages from Siam, Malaya, and Indo-China since the contemporary agents' W/T sets were not powerful enough to operate from these countries to Calcutta or Colombo. A base in the Andamans could also be used to refuel surface craft ferrying agents to Malaya and Sumatra, and as a point for collecting rubber under the *Mickleham* scheme.*

Major D. McCarthy, formerly Commandant of the Andamans Police, with a party of five, landed from the Dutch submarine O 24 (Lieutenant-Commander W. J. de Vries RNN) on the west coast of Middle Andaman on 19 January 1943 (Operation *Bunkum*).[1] They were to be joined eight weeks later by two more agents with enough stores and ammunition to maintain the enlarged party for seven months, and to equip any volunteers they found among the local population.

McCarthy, Jemadar Habib Shah, a Viceroy's Commissioned Officer (VCO), and Havildar Joseph Baxla left their base camp on 1 February 1943 and, moving mainly by night, passed through the Andaman Strait and down the east coast of South Andaman to Shoal Bay. They had to avoid many defence posts and to hide not only from Japanese troops but also from the Jarawas, aboriginals extremely hostile to strangers, who in fact made an unsuccessful attack on the base camp while the reconnaissance was in progress. At Shoal Bay the party hid their folboat and continued overland through dense jungle and

* See Part II, Chapter 9.

mangrove swamps to the neighbourhood of the capital, Port Blair, where they made a thorough study of the defences. They also made contact with a man who seemed well qualified to lead a resistance movement. By the time they got back to base on 4 March 1943 they had covered 130 miles in the most difficult conditions; and their journey was all the more remarkable as McCarthy was seriously ill during the whole thirty-two days they were moving in enemy territory. On the way back Habib Shah fell into a dry riverbed and was killed when his Sten gun went off accidentally.

*Bunkum* confirmed that the Andamans could be a fertile ground for subversion. 'Japanese brutality, which consists of public beating and limb-breaking at the smallest provocation' had induced many to take refuge in the jungle. They, and loyalists who had so far escaped imprisonment, including members of the police and the Forest Service, would help to found a resistance movement. *Baldhead II,** led by Colonel Beyts, used O 24 to rendezvous with McCarthy's party on 21 March 1943. Because of McCarthy's illness, however, and the loss of his second in command it was decided that it would be foolhardy to carry on with the longer-term plan, and both parties returned to Ceylon. The large quantities of stores and rations brought by *Baldhead II* were buried for future use, having to be carried 250 yards over a coral reef where the breakers were rolling with great force. The W/T equipment, which had been used to prove the feasibility of communication with Calcutta, was brought off the islands, and all traces of the expedition were removed. On his return Beyts recommended that the *Baldhead* operations should not be resumed until October 1943.

In fact, *Baldhead III* did not set out until December 1943. The party was led by Major Greig with Captain Falconar, two Indian officers, two British Signals Sergeants, and ten Indian other ranks. They travelled in HM Submarine *Taurus* (Lieutenant-Commander M. R. G. Wingfield).[2] A small advance party landed at a point which McCarthy had recommended, on 19 December 1943, but they lost contact with the submarine. It was not until two days later that they were able to signal the all-clear for the rest of the party to follow. The original plan had been to find a base as part of the groundwork for a general assault on the Andamans, but as soon as *Baldhead III* sailed they were told by headquarters to abandon this plan. Instead, they

---

* The code-name *Bunkum* was compromised and had to be changed.

were to survey strategically important areas, to collect intelligence to help an attacking force, and to identify inlets where motor launches could be concealed.

*Baldhead IV* (again using *Taurus*)[3] arrived on 23 January 1943 when its leader Major Croley took over command of the combined parties and carried out four separate reconnaissances. He himself took over the Port Campbell area. His deputy, Major Duncan, mapped creeks and bays between Breakfast Bay and Ike Bay. Greig studied a land route to the Wilitang area on the east coast. Falconar covered the west coast as far as the approaches to Port Anson. All four parties accomplished their tasks without mishap.

There were no enemy outposts at Port Campbell or on the west coast, although it was learned that a month earlier patrols had operated in this area. The Jarawas were not actively hostile, but simply kept out of the way. In the Wilitang area much forestry work was in progress, and the important Forest Canal was in good working order. The mapping of the sector Breakfast Bay to Ike Bay was successfully carried out. Here too there was no sign of enemy activity. The investigation of Port Blair was more hazardous. Croley and Duncan supported by two Indian other ranks went as near as they dared, but were spotted and withdrew to the hills. When they found that their trail was being systematically followed they decided to return to the base camp. The information collected by the *Baldhead* teams would have been of great value to any force invading the Andamans; but their efforts, like so much that the India Mission did, were fated to show no dividend. *Taurus* picked up the two parties on the night of 24/5 March 1944 and they reached Trincomalee without incident on 27 March 1944.[4]

The India Mission's most successful single operation was *Jaywick*. It was conceived by Ivan Lyon who knew intimately the waters of the Rhio and Lingga Archipelagos near Singapore.* The operation was based on Australia, partly because of poor security in India and the greater vigilance of the Japanese in the region west of Singapore. The only difficulty foreseen was Australian hostility towards the British after the loss of Singapore; but it was hoped that SOE would get some credit for helping Australian troops to escape. The seventy-foot MV *Krait*, a Japanese vessel seized in Singapore in 1941 and used to ferry

---

* His part in organizing the escape route from Singapore is described in Part II, Chapter 1.

refugees to the neighbouring islands, was shipped as deck cargo to Darwin to be fitted out for the operation.

Although the project was put to London by the India Mission in June 1942 and was approved a month later, it was not until 2 September 1943 that the *Krait* sailed from Exmouth Gulf at the north-west corner of Australia with Lyon as commander and Lieutenant H. E. Carse RN as navigator. Most of the twelve other members of the party were Australian. The few vessels they encountered took the *Krait* for the fishing vessel she used to be. About midnight on 17 September 1943 they reached the Island of Panjang in the Rhio Archipelago; and next afternoon the shore party of six landed with their three folboats. Lyon had intended to keep the *Krait* in the neighbourhood to pick them up but decided it would be safer to rendezvous further south at Pompong Island in the Lingga Archipelago, which added fifty miles to the return journey.

That everything had gone perfectly was due to sound planning, rigorous training at Z Experimental Station at Cairns in North Queensland, to Lyon's leadership, and to good luck, or rather the absence of bad luck, a condition of success in every military operation. With the departure of the *Krait* the enterprise entered a critical phase. The six members of the assault party must have pondered their last orders – that in no circumstances were they to be taken alive.

The climax of the operation is best told in the unemotional official reports. Lyon's second in command, Lieutenant-Commander D. M. N. Davidson RNVR, in Canoe No. 2 with Able Seaman W. G. Falls, Royal Australian Navy, wrote:

The approach was uneventful, with the exception of a searchlight on Blakang Mati, which searched the sky every now and then. Heavy rip tides enabled us to keep to the water boat channel and soon the tripod pylons of Keppel Harbour boom were visible. A big steam ferry, a tug burning navigation lights, and bound to the south of Blakang Mati, nearly ran us down, but we were not sighted. We found the boom gate (at the Tanjong Pagar end) open, with no boom vessel in attendance.

Inside the boom against the east wharf were 2 ships but they were too small to be worthy of attack. No shipping was seen at the main wharf, and that in the Empire Docks was too brilliantly lit up and too small to warrant attack. We turned back and crossed over the boom again, heading for the roads. Here there were many excellent targets and we selected three of the largest cargo vessels . . . .

Each ship was attacked on the port side, away from Singapore's lights. We timed ourselves by a chiming clock (probably on Victoria Hall) that told us the quarter hours.

At 0115 hours 27th September we left the roads and headed for the Rhio Straits. We halted at a point of land 6 miles west of Nongsa and left again at 1900 hours proceeding in the direction of Tanjong Sau. Here we landed shortly before 0430 hours on 29th and left again at 1900 hours, passing to the north of Lepang to Tanjong Piayu, thence to Anak Mati and down the channel between Rempang and Setoko. Off Tanjong Klinking we encountered the patrol boat and had to hug the bay. Just after we landed on Panjang at Otter's Bay a violent storm arose, bringing with it a deluge of rain, thunder, and lightning and lashing the sea into a fury. We kept the bows of the canoe into the wind and sea and were tossed about for two hours, when the storm abated. We landed on Abang Besar and left again at 1900 hours on 30th September. Pompong, our rendezvous with *Krait* was reached at 0100 hours 1st October. *Krait* appeared at 0015 on the morning of the 2nd October.

The success of *Jaywick*, which disposed of 50,000 tons of enemy shipping, suggested that native craft could be safely employed in the China Sea if they had a base inside the perimeter of Japanese-occupied islands. The India Mission asked SOA to put a party into Eastern Malaya, which was easier from Australia than from Calcutta or Trincomalee; and to this SOA, just as capable of thinking big as the India Mission, added an extensive programme to cover the whole of 1944. It included the provision of an operational base on Natuna Island – little known, sparsely populated, and strategically situated 300 miles north-east of Singapore. In March 1944 five officers and two natives would reonnoitre it from a submarine. In September 1944 six replicas of Japanese motor sampans would carry stores and equipment from Exmouth Gulf to Natuna – eventually as many as sixty of these craft might be needed. The sampans would attack shipping in Bangkok and Saigon and locate coast-watching positions in the neighbouring islands. By the end of December the coast-watching system would be complete, food dumps established, and a permanent base found in the North China Sea. The programme was extended to include the insertion of parties into Malaya, Siam, and French Indo-China to build up resistance there. Agents would be put into the Rhio Archipelago ready to move to Singapore on the eve of an Allied attack. Groups would prepare for landings on the China Coast to circumvent Chiang Kai-Shek's ban on overland parties in China.

This ambitious plan was whittled down, and the timing changed, partly because a strike delayed the completion of the first six sampans. The original operation, code-named *Hornbill*, was divided into *Rimau*, an attack on shipping in Singapore from a base on the Rhio Archipelago, using a captured junk to get within striking distance; *Kookaburra*, a reconnaissance of Natuna Island, and the provisioning of a base there; and *Tuckshop*, the balance of the original *Hornbill*.

The twenty-three-strong *Rimau* party,* led by Lyon with Davidson again as second in command and Major R. N. Ingleton as SEAC observer, left Fremantle in the mine-laying submarine HMS *Porpoise* (Lieutenant-Commander H. A. L. Marsham) on 11 September 1944.[5] *Jaywick* had relied on folboats to carry their limpet mines, but *Rimau* planned to use fifteen SBs based on the captured junk to carry out simultaneous attacks on six different areas of Singapore harbour. Ten of the miniature submarines would then return to the junk, and the other five make for the hides used by *Jaywick* where their crews would be picked up. All SBs would be scuttled.

*Porpoise* reached Merapas Island on 23 September. Reconnaissance showed that it had good cover and water, and would make an excellent long-term base. Next day the stores were taken ashore on folboats, Lieutenant W. G. Carey being left to guard them. The junk had now to be captured. On 28 September *Porpoise* encountered the *Mustika* which was boarded by a party of seven including Lyon and Davidson. Submarine and junk made independently for Pajantan Island where on 30 September the SBs and other equipment were transferred to the junk. *Porpoise* left for Fremantle which she reached on 11 October. She intended to return to Merapas to pick up the operational party on 8 November or at any time in the ensuing four weeks, but had engine trouble and was laid up, being replaced by *Tantalus*, whose commander (Lieutenant-Commander H. S. Mackenzie) considered that his first priority was to hunt and attack enemy shipping so long as his torpedoes lasted.[6] So it was not until 21 November 1944 that *Tantalus* made the rendezvous at Merapas. No trace was found of the operational party or of the stores left on the island.

The fate of the expedition was pieced together after the war. *Mustika* had returned to Merapas Island where three men were left to support Carey. She then made for Singapore, but in the afternoon of

* Fourteen of the party were Australians, nine from the United Kingdom.

10 October, when anchored in the Rhio Straits, was challenged by a
Malay police launch. Lyon, believing that the game was up, gave the
order to open fire, and all on board the launch were killed. *Mustika*
with her precious cargo of fifteen SBs was scuttled and the party took
to their folboats, hoping to paddle to the rendezvous at Merapas
Island. All Japanese troops in the region were put on the alert – the
enemy would do everything in their power to prevent a second
*Jaywick*.

On 16 October 1944 some of the party were spotted on Asore
Island near Merapas, and in a two-day engagement Lyon and
another British officer and two Japanese were killed. The others
escaped and paddled from island to island, reaching Merapas in good
time for their rendezvous with the submarine; but on 4 November
1944, only four days before the first of the rendezvous dates, the
Japanese again caught up with them. Another engagement followed
in which one more of the party was killed. The others continued their
desperate odyssey south, losing nine more, mainly in clashes with the
enemy. Finally all eleven survivors were captured, the last on 28
December 1944. One died from wounds. The remaining ten were
found guilty of espionage and beheaded on 7 July 1945, a month
before the end of the Far Eastern war.*

*Jaywick*, *Baldhead*, and *Rimau* showed the scope for sea-borne special
operations in the India Mission area, and even before *Jaywick's*
outstanding success a paranaval group was formed – Section N. Its
objectives were to transport agents and equipment to enemy-
occupied countries, carry out clandestine activities there, and even to
operate in enemy (as distinct from enemy-occupied) territory, which
meant Japan itself. Virtually nothing of this ambitious programme
was accomplished.

Section N acquired a forty-foot two-masted Akyab sloop, typical of
those in use along the Arakan coast, powered by a Buick motor-car
engine; a seventy-foot lugger *Island Gold* peculiar to the Mergui
Archipelago, through which she could sail without arousing
suspicion; four 150-ton buggalows, similar to Arab dhows; and six
small craft 'no more than native lighters, which had no operational

---

* There are accounts of *Jaywick* and *Rimau* in *The Return of the Tiger* by Brian Connell
(Evans Brothers, 1960). Intercepted Japanese telegrams now in the National Archives
in Washington provide additional information about the fate of *Rimau*. There is
evidence that the party succeeded in slightly damaging a Japanese cruiser in Singapore
harbour before they had to disperse.

value of any kind'. At first SOE London was against the use of country craft because of the great distances to be covered, the poor quality of the ships, and the coastal conditions which made it essential to get agents ashore very quickly. Fast motor launches were to be preferred. After lengthy discussion, during which naval personnel were transferred to the India Mission's strength and then back again to the Royal Navy, it was agreed that SOE would operate country craft, including some to be specially built, and 'special craft' – Welmans, Welfreighters, SBs, and MFUs. A fleet of motor launches would be operated by the Royal Navy on behalf of the India Mission.

In May 1944 Section N planned a long-range operation to the Mergui Archipelago (*Prunella*) using the *Island Gold* to explore the possibility of establishing a secret base there. However, although for the last eighteen months structural alterations had been carried out and a new engine installed under the supervision of Gavin Stewart, head of the Calcutta sub-mission, when the operational party took over *Island Gold* it was found that her deck structures were unsuitable for an ocean voyage, that she had been fitted not with a marine engine but with 'a diesel salvaged from a junk heap', and that her bottom was seriously wormed. The vessel when surveyed was unhesitatingly condemned, but it was eventually agreed that she would be certified seaworthy after certain modifications, which were expected to take six weeks, although in fact they took five months. A new 150-hp engine was fitted and the vessel was equipped with rocket-launching apparatus to defend her against Japanese attacks. During the sea trials before *Prunella*, *Island Gold* leaked so badly that she had to be written off, and the operation abandoned.

After this fiasco the disbandment of the paranaval section was seriously considered; but in January 1945 it was decided to make a fresh start using two of the buggalows, which were converted to the type of nondescript schooner found in Far Eastern waters, again under the supervision of Gavin Stewart. They suffered much the same fate as *Island Gold*. 'The manner in which these two ships had been fitted out cannot be too strongly condemned' – the verdict of the India Mission's own report. The work, which could have been done efficiently by the Director General of Shipbuilding and Repairs (DGSR) at the expense of the Admiralty, was entrusted to 'incompetent and inexperienced' private enterprise. Once again the craft had to be handed over to DGSR to rectify 'major engineering and other faults'. The pair sailed to Trincomalee on 5 May 1945 to load stores urgently needed in the Cocos Islands; but before they could leave one, the *Azad Hind*,* was wrecked in Koddiyar Bay. The other, the *Anwari*, successfully completed the round trip of 3,000 miles – a small return for the effort and money invested in the paranaval section.

---

* *Free India*, the name of the traitor Subhas Chandra Bose's political party.

# 3

# Siam

WHEN the Japanese entered Siam in December 1941 they allowed the Government to remain in office, confident of their co-operation. On 25 January 1942 Siam declared war on Britain and the United States, but not on China. Britain took up the challenge. The United States merely deemed Siam to be enemy-occupied territory. In 1943 President Roosevelt and Generalissimo Chiang Kai-Shek made sympathetic declarations about Siam's future. Britain did not. The gulf was further widened when the Siamese welcomed Japan's promise of parts of Burma and Malaya after the war.

This posed a problem for SOE. They had to find a resistance group in an enemy country whose Government seemed to have the support of the people, and persuade them that Britain would not penalize Siam for her alliance with Japan. This would be easier if it was acknowledged that the Government had acted under duress. The Foreign Office felt, however, that Siam should have done more to resist the invaders and that 'she must work her passage home'. This parrot cry ignored the reality of the situation. The country was in fact occupied by the Japanese who could not be thrown out without help from outside. Nevertheless, when Mr John Keswick of SOE complained to the Foreign Office in February 1943 about Britain's failure to offer *rapprochement*, his letter was dismissed as 'rude and rather silly'.[1]

Siam had begun to work her passage home soon after the Japanese arrived. The Finance Minister, Luang Pridi, was opposed to the Japanese, but his influence within the Government ended when the Prime Minister, Luang Pibul, appointed him one of the two Regents – the young King being in Switzerland. However, Pridi held a series of meetings with like-minded men to discuss resistance, out of which grew the *Seri Thai* (Free Thai) Movement. Chamkad Balankura, an Oxford graduate, formed his own group, *Ku Chat* (Liberation), which merged with *Seri Thai* to become 'XO Group', with Balankura as Secretary. At the end of 1942 eleven men from XO tried to go to China in search of support, but were never heard of again.

Early in 1943 Balankura himself did reach China hoping to form a Provisional Government, and in August he put his ideas to the British Ambassador in Chungking (Sir Horace Seymour). He said that Pridi regarded Siam's declaration of war as unconstitutional and that he hoped to put the clock back to 1941. Would Britain bring him and other leaders out to form a Provisional Government in India?[2] The Chinese had taken Balankura's mission seriously, but the Foreign Office did not. Sir Josiah Crosby, the former Minister in Bangkok, said he had never heard of the XO Group – which was of course formed after he left the country. Balankura's proposal was written off as 'a storm in a teacup'.*[3]

SOE, on the other hand, saw the young man at least as a source of information and sent Prince Subha Svasti, who had joined the British Army in England, to Chungking. The Chinese allowed him and Mr G. Findlay Andrew to meet Balankura, who continued to urge that Pridi should be brought out. The Siam Country Section agreed. They undertook to smuggle a message to Pridi promising to send in agents which should be acknowledged either by courier or by code words over Radio Bangkok. 'Coconut oil in fifty bottles' would mean 'Come'. 'Groundnut oil in twenty-five tins' would mean 'Don't come'. Microfilm copies of this proposal were handed to Balankura on 7 September 1943, along with 100,000 Chinese National Dollars and a diamond ring (provided by *Remorse*†) to bribe the Chinese to allow his couriers to leave.

Although the Chinese had kept Balankura under virtual house arrest, he found 'a little hideout' to meet the British. His importance diminished, however, when two more influential Siamese arrived in Chungking – Sanguan Tilurak and Deng Gunatilika – who did not like SOE's plan. They argued that the Allies should recognize Pridi as head of the Provisional Government *before* he left Siam; and that when the Provisional Government was established in India SOE should provide a W/T station in Siam to link it with the Free Siamese Movement. Further, they pointed out that there was no need for a complicated communications system involving Radio Bangkok. It

---

* When asked for an assessment of Balankura, the Master of Balliol said: 'When he was here there was a certain wistful innocence about him which I should be inclined to trust.' (FO 371 35977, ff. 59, 62.)

† See Part II, Chapter 9.

would be easier to make contact through couriers, or even by sending a commercial telegram.

SOE nevertheless insisted on sticking to their plan. Balankura sent off his messenger – a Sino-Siamese deputed by the Chinese Secret Service to keep him under surveillance, whom he thought he had won over. He now fell sick and was taken to a Chinese hospital. Major McMullen, one of SOE's men in Chungking, visited him on 18 September 'disguised as a doctor complete with the instruments of his craft' to fool the Secret Service men watching the Siamese. Having pretended to examine him he arranged for Balankura to be removed to the Canadian Mission Hospital, where a British doctor diagnosed cancer; and the young man died on 7 October. When the doctor offered to carry out a post-mortem Sanguan said it was unnecessary. SOE suspected that Balankura had been poisoned to prevent his setting up a Free Siamese Movement outside China – although this motive had disappeared when he was effectively replaced by Sanguan and Deng. The British doctor had no doubt about the cause of death, although the presence of General Tai Li, head of the Chinese Secret Service, when the body was cremated does suggest a professional interest. The only reasonable verdict at this time of day is 'not proven'.

The Siam Country Section went ahead with the plan to bring out Pridi (Operation *Prichard*) assuming that the messenger had got through. Radio Bangkok was closely monitored. 'Though the words and phrases asked for were nowhere clearly and unequivocally heard, there were grounds for thinking that an attempt had been made to send over the air from Bangkok something approximating to their sense'; and 'there was reason to believe that a messenger from Chungking had reached Pridi'.

Three White Elephants* from the group of Siamese recruited in England were selected: Captain Pratan Pramekamol (code-name Deng), who had been working for a higher science degree at Liverpool University, and was an expert W/T operator; Captain Samran Varnbriksha (Keng), a final-year student at the Royal Veterinary College; and Major Puey Ungphakorn (Khem) 'with a long string of academic successes'. They were taken by HM Submarine *Tactician* (Lieutenant-Commander A. F. Collett) to a rendezvous near Ranong on the west coast of Siam, where they arrived on 9 December 1943 –

* See p. 13.

three days late because the submarine had been delayed on another operation.* There was no sign of the recognition signals – a yellow cloth, perhaps a Buddhist priest's saffron robe, by day, and a blue lamp by night – to which the response would be the 'XO' of the resistance movement in morse. After seven days the party returned to Ceylon where the Commander of the Fourth Submarine Flotilla said some harsh things about a failed operation that kept one of his submarines in hostile waters for so long.[4]

In fact, the microfilmed plan did not reach Pridi until June 1944, six months too late. The Siam Country Section *thought* some of the code words were *possibly* heard. It is to be hoped they did not refer to the words common to both 'Come' and 'Don't come' responses – which left half a dozen words which must have been regularly used over Radio Bangkok. Perhaps *Prichard* was triggered off by a radio report on coconut-oil prices.

On 14 March 1944 Khem, Deng, and Keng made another attempt to enter Siam – to deliver a letter from Mountbatten to Pridi, to establish W/T communication with India, and to assess the potential for raising guerrillas (Operation *Appreciation I*). They dropped blind from a Liberator, having failed to locate the chosen dropping-zone on an earlier sortie. Khem suspected the navigator had got it wrong again: 'We saw many lights on the ground and were wondering if we were in the right place since we were supposed to be in the forest with the nearest houses a few kilometres away. At any rate we had neither time to make enquiry or to argue. The order came to jump, and we jumped.'[5] Khem's misgiving as he floated down through the cold moonlit night was justified when all three landed in a paddy-field which should not have been there, fifteen miles east of their destination. They recovered six of the containers dropped with them but the seventh landed in the middle of a village outside the temple. When they tried to retrieve it they were frustrated by a barking dog.

Dawn was still an hour away, but some charcoal-burners, whose lights were those they had seen from the air, happened on them. They helped to carry the stores, and then went on their way, no doubt puzzled by the strange containers. The three Whites buried the equipment and made off into the jungle hoping to warn the follow-up operation (*Appreciation II*) that they had landed in the wrong place.

---

* An unsuccessful attempt to contact ISLD agents earlier infiltrated into Malaya (*Missive II*).

They picked up Calcutta's signal but Calcutta could not hear theirs. Next day they failed to pick up anything. They made a third attempt on the following morning, while Khem stood on guard some distance away. Suddenly he was surrounded by twenty-nine men, some armed, led by a policeman 'who jumped at me in the manner seen in a *likae* [a Siamese folk opera] theatre. He did not sing, but mumbled something.' Khem found this ludicrous form of arrest amusing.

He briefly toyed with the idea of swallowing the cyanide pill issued to all agents but decided it was more important to try to get Mountbatten's letter to Pridi. Then began a royal progress which after many days took him to Bangkok. Everywhere the police exhibited him as if he were a rare animal. Sometimes he was badly treated – one man 'enjoyed himself by hitting me and talking to me in bad language' – and on the final stage of the journey he was chained to a madman who had murdered a monk.[6]

When he reached Bangkok gaol his companions were already there. The Japanese interrogated them in the presence of their fellow-countrymen, but they gave nothing away. Their prison guards told the Secretary of Thammaset University (Professor Wichet) about them, and he told Pridi. This led to a meeting at Pridi's house when Khem handed over Mountbatten's letter which said everything the Foreign Office had most objected to: namely that Pridi was accepted as leader of the Free Siamese Movement; that the British Government were about to announce that they would recognize an independent Siam after the war; that they were considering the release of frozen Siamese funds; and that they would eventually allow a Provisional Siamese Government in India.

*Appreciation II* – Captains Prem Buri (Dee), Rachit Buri (Kham), and Thana Poshyanda (Korn) – dropped blind on 4 April 1944, again fifteen miles east of target. They too were soon spotted by the police, pursued through the jungle, caught, and taken to Bangkok.

Luang Adul, Chief of Police and Deputy Prime Minister, who was gradually transferring his allegiance to the Allies, eventually accepted that the six were genuine Allied agents; and on 6 June 1944 allowed Khem to send a message by hand to Kunming which was passed to SOE Calcutta on 17 August 1944. Five days later he made radio contact with Calcutta. At the same time Pridi telegraphed news of the arrival of the *Appreciation* teams to the Siamese Legation in Berne, and the message then found its way to SOE headquarters in London. He pointed out that of the sixteen agents known to have entered Siam six had been killed,* which would not have happened had there been proper reception arrangements. He asked that another party should be sent and gave details of a safe dropping-zone and the recognition signals he would use. This message reached SOE India just before the overland message arrived. Now for the first time there was a direct line of communication with the Free Siamese Movement.

The time seemed ripe for the declaration to bring Britain more into line with the United States and China which SOE had been requesting for nearly a year. In fact, the Foreign Office had accepted after the formation of SEAC in September 1943 that a declaration was overdue, but for the next six months their efforts to get War Cabinet approval had failed, mainly because of difficulties over the wording, which led Eden to note: 'This silly business becomes an increasing bore.'[7]

The War Cabinet considered yet another draft on 10 July 1944. The official who put it up wrote: 'I submit, with some trepidation, and I hope for the last time, a further paper on the Free Siamese declaration.' When it was claimed to be unduly favourable Eden argued that Roosevelt had gone a good deal further. Then Sir Firoz Khan Noon, representing the Government of India, said parallel declarations were needed for all neighbouring territories. This was unhelpful enough, but SOE's Minister dropped a bombshell. He said that the declaration, which his own people had been desperately fighting for, would not help SOE. This killed it stone dead and left speechless its sponsors. One recorded that Khan Noon's intervention, on grounds 'which with respect do not seem to be altogether convincing', had helped to finish off the proposal; but the prime cause of death was the 'inexplicable statement of the Minister of Economic Warfare' for whose benefit the declaration had been prepared.[8]

While this transaction was in hand the Pibul Government fell and was replaced by an administration which, although outwardly prepared to co-operate with the Japanese, was well disposed towards the Allies. It seemed more than ever necessary to make it clear where Britain stood. Deng Gunatilika tried his hand at drafting a message to Pridi, now sole Regent. It stated that the British Government warmly welcomed Siam's new Cabinet, with so many proven friends in it, and promised every assistance. That Britain had made no helpful

---

* These were OSS and ISLD agents.

declaration about Siam hitherto was not due to any wish to impair her sovereignty, but to unfavourable circumstances. Deng proposed that a letter on these lines, signed by Mountbatten, should be taken in immediately.

The India Mission was also carried away. Pointon recorded that there were no sabotage materials, arms, or ammunition that the Siam Country Section would not supply on demand for use against the Japanese. In return Siam would organize reception committees, cover for agents, provide information about prisoners of war, internees, and Japanese dispositions. She would establish radio links, encourage railway sabotage, and prepare a landing-strip. When these euphoric proposals reached SOE headquarters in London they told the India Mission that there was not the slightest hope of getting Foreign Office agreement to a declaration. However, Mountbatten, in London at this time, appealed to Eden for at least a free hand to put agents into Siam. They could have real strategic importance in future.[9]

The Foreign Office thought that the change of Government would make no difference. The new Government would be equally afraid of provoking Japanese retaliation, and to make the sort of approach suggested by the India Mission would lead them to believe that they had already worked their passage home. None the less, a member of the Far Eastern Department said in conversation with SOE headquarters on 23 August 1944 that so long as they made no political commitment SOE could go ahead with their plans to send in agents. This was confirmed in writing three days later and SOE at once telegraphed the good news to India, where arrangements to send a mission to Pridi (Operation *Brillig*) had been virtually completed. The Siam Country Section had taken it upon themselves to prepare an encouraging letter addressed to the Regent, but at the instigation of Mr M. E. (later Sir Esler) Dening, Mountbatten's Chief Political Adviser,* it was replaced by a directive in Mountbatten's name addressed to no one.[10]

* The Foreign Office claimed that this post was unnecessary since Mountbatten was concerned only with military affairs. However, when he proposed to appoint John Keswick they promptly nominated Dening (who had consular experience in Japan and, more recently, had served in Washington) on the ground that if SEAC must have a Political Adviser he should be a professional. In fact politics loomed so large in most SEAC countries that the post became of crucial importance. Curiously enough, it was not until September 1944 that Dening realized that America was not at war with Siam (FO 371 41845, 22.9.44).

At this point Eden threw a spanner in the works by deciding to put to the War Cabinet Mountbatten's request for authority to send in agents, in the belief that they would turn it down. He found the proposed collaboration with Pridi

> hard for us all to swallow and British public to understand . . . I don't pretend that I understand Far Eastern affairs. But here we are having dealings with a government or creature that collaborates with the Japs as a head of the government. This don't seem to make political sense and I have a pretty clear view that the War Cabinet would feel as I do.

His Minister of State, Richard Law, was more sympathetic. It was distasteful to deal with collaborators but Mountbatten's plea of military necessity could not be overruled.[11]

The decision to discuss in the War Cabinet the infiltration of agents caused grave alarm and despondency in the Far Eastern Department, which had without Ministerial approval – let alone War Cabinet approval – authorized SOE to go ahead. They hastily asked SOE that any action taken as a result of their conversation of 23 August 1944 should be nipped in the bud; and they alerted Dening to the dangers of the situation – to which he replied that he should have been kept informed about the Department's discussions with SOE headquarters.[12] There now existed the possibility that the War Cabinet would rule that no agents should be infiltrated, which would leave the Far Eastern Department on a limb. In self-defence they begged SOE to ensure that their Minister did not shoot down his own case a second time.[13]

Happily, the War Cabinet agreed on 25 September 1944 that SOE could proceed with their plans, so long as they made it clear that Britain was concerned only about the expulsion of the Japanese and avoided any commitment about the future regime. To the great relief of all concerned the Minister of Economic Warfare strongly supported the proposal. The Far Eastern Department noted on the file: 'Fortunately no message was sent to Luang Pradit [i.e. Pridi]'[14] – a neat piece of wordmanship founded on the fact that the message taken in was addressed to no one, although it certainly found its way to the Regent.

The directive in Mountbatten's name was carried by Lieutenant Prasert Padumananda (Pau), an economist trained at the London School of Economics, who took with him as W/T operator Lieutenant Kris Tosayanonda (Kong) – both of them Whites. The directive authorized the bearer to find out how the Siamese resistance movement could work with the Allies, to promise help, and to warn against premature action against the Japanese. Pau also took in a massive questionnaire to elicit the information SEAC needed about the state of affairs within Siam, among both the Siamese and the occupying forces.

The two Whites were dropped near the southern seaside resort of Hua Hin where there were few Japanese. They had been warned to beware of the Siamese Home Guard, who were known to be on the look-out for parachutists, but in the event they were troubled neither by them nor the nine-man Japanese garrison of Hua Hin. Indeed, the drop was so accurate that Pau actually landed on the roof of a house belonging to one of the reception committee. Their onward journey by sea and rail to Bangkok was equally uneventful and the apolitical communication and questionnaire were duly handed over to Pridi.*

The communication thus begun should have developed into a regular exchange of information and ideas; and in October 1944 Pridi proposed that Direk Jainam, a former Foreign Minister and staunch supporter of the freedom movement, should visit SOE. This was agreed, but Pridi cancelled the visit on the ground that Direk could not discuss military matters. He asked instead that SOE should send a party of British officers to Bangkok. SOE, however, were not prepared to do this until Pridi had given more proof of his reliability. The Regent sent an evasive reply. He was still anxious to help the Allies; he was now organizing the police for guerrilla work and needed more time 'to tame' the Chief of Police.[15] Nevertheless, he dropped his request that SOE should send a military mission, and in January 1945 revived the idea that Direk should come out, accompanied by the Chief of Staff designate who would handle the military side of the talks. In spite of their objections to political discussions the Foreign Office agreed that Direk should come – as part of the price of military talks, and also because 'it is probably against our best interests to continue to maintain complete silence on political issues vis-à-vis Siam having regard to the more forthcoming attitude of the Americans and the Chinese'.[16] The War Cabinet approved this line, laying down that Mountbatten must stick to

---

* Kong's account of this event is printed as Appendix D in *Bangkok Top Secret* by Sir Andrew Gilchrist (Hutchinson, 1960).

purely military matters in the discussions, although he was given discretion to hold out some political hope to Siam.[17]

The Siamese party (code-name *Sequence*) arrived at Trincomalee on 22 February 1945 – Direk, General Chatr Nakrob, the Chief of Staff designate, and an official from the Foreign Ministry. The General brought a great quantity of military intelligence in response to the *Brillig* questionnaire, including elaborate statistics of Japanese dispositions, maps of airfields, Japanese military manuals, and much other material. Mountbatten later recorded that it was invaluable. In return for the information Nakrob asked for large quantities of military supplies.

Soon after their arrival Direk suggested to Andrew Gilchrist, who met the party and had been with the British Legation in 1941, that there should be political talks with 'someone like yourself'. Later he met Dening – Mountbatten thought that if *he* received the Siamese it would raise their expectations unduly – when the Chief Political Adviser closely followed the brief from the War Cabinet. Britain hoped for an independent Siam and a renewal of friendly relations, but the latter would depend on what Siam did to defeat the Japanese, on her readiness to make good damage done to Britain through her association with the Japanese, and on her guarantee of good-neighbourly relations. But for the time being, all that interested Britain was the expulsion of the Japanese.

Direk replied that Pridi had instructed him to say that the declaration of war against Britain had been engineered by a few unscrupulous people. Most Siamese were now eager to work with the Allies in driving out the Japanese and restoring normal relations with their friends. There would be no question of retaining the British territories which Japan had promised to Siam. When the Allies gave the signal, a Resistance Government would be established in an area where the Japanese were at their weakest.[18] Mountbatten acknowledged this progress in a message to Pridi. Effective assistance by the Free Siamese Movement 'would be regarded as a valuable contribution by your country to the Allied cause', which meant it was still up to the Siamese to work their passage. He hoped shortly to send a return mission to Bangkok.

While *Sequence* was still in Ceylon the Foreign Office deemed it necessary to tell the Chinese Government about the visit, because the Chinese had informed them about a Siamese political mission to China. Colin Mackenzie saw that this information could be leaked from Chungking to Bangkok and that the Japanese might be waiting to pick up the *Sequence* party when it returned. He shot off a 'Most Immediate' to London: 'Horrified to learn fantastic proposal from Foreign Office ... please do your utmost to prevent this criminal stupidity ...'. Mountbatten came to the rescue. He diplomatically accepted the need to keep the Chinese informed, but asked that he should be allowed to inform them when he next saw Chiang Kai-Shek. The Foreign Office reluctantly agreed. In the event Mountbatten decided he must do nothing – 'in view of recent evidence from a reliable source which must on no account be compromised'.[19]

The return mission was *Panicle*, led by Colonel Victor Jaques, a former resident of Siam. When he was indoctrinated at the Foreign Office Sterndale Bennett, Head of the Far Eastern Department, gave the standard hard-line briefing. There must be no political commitment to Siam. It might be unpalatable, but she still had to work her passage. When Jaques sensibly asked him what he should reply when a direct question was put to him – for example, did Britain stand by the Atlantic Charter – he was told he should say 'No comment'. Surely this would arouse suspicion, suggested Jaques. The Americans would have taken a more sympathetic line. This common sense cut no ice. Right or wrong, the War Cabinet line must be followed.[20]

Jaques was accompanied by Major A. T. Hobbs and Prince Subha Svasti. They were landed on 28 April 1945 from a Catalina, and received by Direk and Adul. They spent four days in Bangkok in an empty house belonging to Svasti's father, well hidden by trees, discussing the future of the resistance movement and the role of the Siamese army. Pridi again claimed that he had had nothing to do with the declaration of war against Britain, having been absent from Bangkok at the time. His name had been put to the proclamation without his knowledge. He realized that Jaques could not discuss political matters, but nevertheless he had to ask about the letter brought in by *Appreciation* in March 1944, promising among other things that Britain would shortly make a favourable declaration about her relationship with Siam. Jaques admitted he knew about the letter, but mindful of his briefing, said he had no idea why it had not been followed up.

According to Pridi the Free Siamese Movement was now well advanced. The army would not go into action unless the Japanese struck first; but an irregular force was being trained for independent use. The role of the police was not yet settled but they had orders to impede the Japanese at every opportunity. A chain of informers, including Siamese employed by the occupying forces, would provide advance warning of open hostilities; and when that happened all important members of the Japanese General Staff would be assassinated. There were already about 5,000 trained guerrillas in the north-west of the country, a quarter of them armed. It was difficult to communicate with them but Pridi hoped that SOE would be able to do something about it. Jaques brought back a comprehensive record of the discussions. He was accompanied by a Siamese who would act as Liaison Officer with Force 136. The ground was now prepared for SOE's real task in Siam.

Before that task is described the contribution of the Sino-Siamese agents recruited in China – the Red and Blue Elephants – whose performance in training had caused much anxiety,* must be assessed.

The Sino-Siamese, whose assigned role was trail-blazing for the native Siamese agents (the Whites), carried out four operations, all total failures. The first, *Billow*, was intended to establish a radio link with India. It would also sabotage shipping in Bangkok harbour, derail a train inside the tunnel at Ronpibon, and then blow up the tunnel – an ambitious programme for even the most resolute of agents. In May 1944 three Reds led by Captain Ngit Yin Yok, a Chinese born in Malaya, landed from a Catalina at Ranong on the west coast, where *Prichard* had waited in vain six months earlier.

Take-off from China Bay in Ceylon had been difficult because of the weight of the stores, and the petrol needed for the long flight. It took seven attempts to get the Catalina airborne, and five miles to reach a safe height. Eight hours later the landing was just as hazardous. The aircraft bounced on the surface a dozen times before it came to a halt, which did not help morale. According to the pilot the agents had been cheerful at first, but now they showed signs of nervousness. They disembarked without incident, however, in two two-seater dinghies towing a larger 'Catalina' dinghy carrying their operational stores. When last seen from the aircraft they were paddling strongly towards a good beach with good jungle cover behind.

They survived one day. The noise of the aircraft, especially on take-off, and of a second Catalina circling overhead, alerted the villagers.

* See Part I, Chapter 2.

Shoe-tracks on the beach revealed that strangers had landed, and when the four approached a village the Siamese gendarmerie were lying in wait. *Billow's* leader fired first but he and another member of the party were killed. The others were taken prisoner. The Siam Country Section had intended to bring them out by submarine in July, but when no radio signal came, and a prolonged aerial reconnaissance revealed no trace of the party, the rendezvous was cancelled.

*Blandings I* planned to make contact with the agents already in Bangkok, and send out information about suitable dropping-zones for future parties. Three Reds, armed with ample funds, left Chungking in September 1944, hoping to enter Siam overland through French Indo-China. They were dispatched from Waichow in the company of some Chinese guerrillas bound for Tunghing. It was reported in December that they had failed to cross the Indo-China border; and when nothing more was heard they were written off. They turned up, however, in Bangkok in August 1945 after the Japanese surrender and submitted an astronomic claim for expenses.

*Blandings II* was another attempt to reach Siam overland through Indo-China. Five Blues left Kunming in March 1945 in in the charge of Captain J. S. Lee, having first refused to move unless they were issued with operational watches, which had a high value in the black market. They climbed down when Lee said he would report them to the Chinese military authorities – a temporary victory, for they next refused to change their Western clothing for Chinese because their cover was that they were rich merchants. They demanded large amounts of pocket money to enable them to play their part better. Lee pointed out that the Siam Country Section was already paying them three times as much as a Chinese major-general, cancelled the operation, and sent them all back to the Chinese army.

The last of these ill-fated missions was *Rotary*. In April 1945 three Blues were dropped near Bangkok to subvert industrial and dock labour, and to carry out industrial sabotage. Their radio was never heard and in June it became known through other agents in Siam that they were too afraid of the Japanese to do anything at all. There was now overwhelming evidence that the employment of Chinese agents had been a total waste of effort, and those remaining with the Siam Country Section were sent back to China.

*Appreciation, Brillig, Sequence,* and *Panicle* had been the ceremonial dropping of visiting-cards – making contact without getting too deeply involved with the other party. But if Force 136 was to make the most effective use of the Siamese Freedom Movement, much had to be done. In particular more Siamese had to be trained as agents. The best of the Whites had already been used. The Reds and Blues had been a dead loss. Operation *Influx* was mounted to increase the supply of suitable candidates.

This was the exfiltration of young Siamese for training and eventual return to Siam. Eight police, known as the Blacks, were selected by the Chief of Police, who was now totally committed to the Allies, and taken to an island off the west coast, ostensibly in search of smugglers but in reality to rendezvous with a Catalina from the Siam Country Section. The aircraft spotted the recognition signal – a fire at the southern tip of the island – and landed smoothly. Thereafter everything went wrong. The engine of the policemen's boat broke down, wind and current kept it far from the plane, the dinghy which was to ferry the men sank. Eventually the reserve dinghy, designed to carry four and already manned by two men from the Catalina, reached the boat and took on board all eight policemen, which virtually submerged it. They got back with the greatest difficulty to the aircraft, which took off after three dangerous hours on the water and returned safely to Trincomalee. A second group (the Browns) came out when the *Sequence* party was exfiltrated, being carried in the escorting Catalina. Since these men were supposed to be away on police duty their absence was unnoticed.

When they had been trained and returned to Siam, Force 136 was able to use them for its real job – preparing for full-scale guerrilla warfare to make a diversion if the Allies invaded Malaya, or to support them if they entered Siam. These preparations included the building of landing-strips, finding dropping-zones, organizing the reception of arms and equipment, reporting bombing targets to the RAF, locating prisoner-of-war camps, and studying Japanese dispositions. All had to be done in great secrecy. If the Japanese became aware of widespread underground activity they would instantly stamp it out.

Mountbatten put his Siam plans to the Chiefs of Staff in April 1945. He believed there was little chance of successful resistance among the people at large, but the army and the police might be used in the guerrilla role – and guerrilla operations could deal with Japanese troops in Burma who were driven into Siam.[21]

From this time on there was the danger that the Japanese would sense the growth of the resistance movement and try to suppress it; and indeed for a time the movement itself seemed eager to come into the open and take on the occupying forces – in spite of the Siam Country Section's consistent advice that they should not. On 22 May 1945 Pridi told Mountbatten that he believed that if the Free Siamese Movement went into action right away it would hasten the surrender of the Japanese; and he asked whether Britain would recognize Siam's future independence if the resistance movement was given its head. The Foreign Office had no doubt that Pridi should await the go-ahead from the Supreme Commander, and the State Department, who had received a similar message, agreed. They told the Regent they could not understand his sudden proposal to unleash the guerrillas. Far better to wait until they could directly benefit Allied operations.[22]

Mackenzie speculated about the reasons behind Pridi's proposal. Was it fear that the Japanese were about to take over Siam as they had just done Indo-China; or an attempt to jump on the Allied bandwagon now that Germany was defeated; or a genuine belief that the Freedom Movement could successfully take on the Japanese without waiting for Allied help; or was it simply a ploy to put across the idea that they were working their passage home before the Allies had won the war in the Far East without any assistance from Siam? He concluded that the Siamese genuinely wanted to further the Allied cause. They had just rejected Japanese demands for a huge credit, for control of the roads and railways, for the use of a weather-station, for the creation of many 'reserved areas' for Japanese troops, and for the removal of two Siamese arsenals. They were also helping the Allies by facilitating the escape of shot-down airmen, harbouring SOE agents, supplying intelligence, and above all continuing to build up the Free Siamese Movement.

There were signs that the growing opposition to the Japanese might precipitate a crisis. They refused to send representatives to the State funeral of a Deputy Minister. A Japanese speaker at a State dinner delivered a warning about the presence of Allied agents in southern Siam. Information from various parts of the country indicated that the occupying forces were reaching the end of their tether. An incidental, but most telling reason for removing the velvet glove was an Allied deceptive plan to support the planned invasion of Malaya by leading the Japanese to believe that Siam was the Allies' true objective – an interesting example of the unpredictable side-effects of deceptive operations.[23]

The Siam Country Section now had a pool of trained Siamese leaders whose job it would be to recruit their fellow-countrymen. The main guerrilla areas organized by the British were in the north, designated *Candle* and *Coupling*, but it was planned to raise resistance troops in four other districts: *Neronian*, west of *Coupling*, where there was said to be a guerrilla potential of 4,000; *Squalid*, between Hua Hin and Chumphon (600 guerrillas); *Priest*, in the Kra Isthmus (200 guerrillas). The fourth area to be developed was west of *Neronian* but the Japanese surrender came before work could be started here. The guerrillas in these areas had fourteen radio stations; and the Siamese army had been given another six. OSS carried out comparable operations to the south of the *Candle/Coupling* activities.

The Siamese themselves had made good progress in organizing guerrilla forces in northern Siam months before British officers arrived there. On 3 December 1944 three Whites, Chew, Noon, and Noo,* parachuted to the neighbourhood of Volaithani and reached the *Coupling* sector on 3 January 1945. Pridi sent Nai Y Tieng Sirikhanta, a member of the National Assembly (code-name Pluto), to foster resistance in the north-east, with Kong as W/T operator. At the end of May Lieutenant-Colonel C. S. Hudson came to *Coupling* and Major David Smiley to *Candle*.

Smiley's reception shows that the guerrillas were completely in control of the northern part of the country. He was taken from the paddy-field where he landed to a bullock cart and escorted by fifty armed men through two villages to their camp without a single Japanese being seen. Pluto was already in touch with all the principal local officials, most of whom were helping to supply recruits. By the time Smiley arrived 3,000 had been trained in the east and 2,000 in the west. All the civil authorities played their part. The district governors collected and supplied intelligence; doctors came to the jungle to tend the sick; the Post Office allowed use of the telephone service – risky because the Japanese might hear conversations; the transport department supplied vehicles; teachers joined the resistance, bringing with them their senior pupils; railway officials supplied information about rail movements. Large numbers of the

* Respectively Major Snoh Nilkamhaeng, Captain Praphod Paurohitya, and Captain Deb Semthiti.

regular forces asked to be transferred to the resistance movement but were told to stay where they were. The Japanese would have spotted a sudden reduction in the size of the army.

Almost the only difference between the resistance organizations in the two main British sectors was the attitude to the police. In *Coupling* it was accepted from the beginning that the police – 600 of them, all armed with rifles – must make a major contribution. In *Candle*, however, because Pluto regarded the Chief of Police as a collaborator, the police were at first kept at arm's length. Eventually Pluto was persuaded that the police must be allowed to play their part when the resistance movement was called on to fight.

Apart from training, the main activities were jungle-clearing to make new dropping-zones, and building roads and airstrips. The local governors, who had powers to conscript men, ensured that there was plenty of labour. The *Candle* runway was built in six weeks by 3,000 villagers using 1,000 bullock carts to carry stone from a mountain five miles away. This splendid construction – 1,000 yards long and fifty wide – had nine inches of rock covered by three inches of gravel and earth in which grass was sown. It was christened 'Heston' after the aerodrome where Smiley had kept his private plane before the war. It was used exactly twice. The runway at *Coupling* was built by 1,400 villagers.

Provision was made for speedy communication overland. In *Candle* 200 miles of road were prepared for Jeeps that never came. There were jungle tracks throughout the whole area where a fast pony could cover thirty miles a day. Training camps were built, each with a dropping-zone cut in the jungle nearby, and each with a permanent reception committee.

The main problem was how to build up the resistance movement quickly, without forcing the Japanese to take action against it. During July the number of supply drops greatly increased – seventeen to *Coupling*, with equipment for 1,200 men, in a fortnight. Since the Liberators fixed their position on Sakon Nakon, where there was a Japanese garrison, they could hardly fail to notice what was going on, in spite of the fact that the resistance groups confined suspects to their villages and shot known informers – including one Siamese, a notorious opium smoker who was 'personally shot by Pluto'. Annamites and itinerant Chinese merchants acted as agents for the Japanese, who at first jokingly referred to 'Nai Tieng's army' as if the guerrillas posed no threat; but when they had studied aerial photographs of Heston, and realized that a British officer was leading the resistance forces they decided that they could hang back no longer.

They sent reinforcements to many towns in the north, and brought in a battalion from Indo-China. They made many arrests hoping to get information about the whereabouts of the resistance forces. A joint Japanese/Siamese commission went to investigate the underground movement on the spot but made little progress since the Siamese members kept the guerrillas posted about the commission's movements. The training camps were abandoned and the trainees dispersed to their villages. Drums were used to warn neighbours of the approach of Japanese troops. 'It was a strange sensation to hear the drums beating in one village and then the next, and right along the line taken by the Japanese.' These patrols were small and could have been wiped out, but the guerrillas were under strict orders not to show their hand as that would merely have brought stronger Japanese forces into the field.

Mountbatten told the Chiefs of Staff on 1 July 1945 that there were indications that the Japanese might take over the whole country within the next twenty-four hours. This possibility posed an awkward problem for the Allies, well aware of the unpleasant precedent in Indo-China. Should they suspend building up the resistance forces in the hope that the Japanese would call off their campaign? Or should they go all out to arm as many guerrillas as quickly as possible in an attempt to create an army that would hold its own against the enemy?

Pridi opted for the former alternative, asking that all supply drops should stop, which suggests that his earlier proposal to send the guerrillas into action was in fact an empty political gesture. Had he really believed they were a match for the Japanese he would have asked for more arms. SOE fell in with his wishes for a few days during which supply drops were replaced by bombing and leaflet-dropping sorties, in an attempt to make the Japanese think the earlier increased aerial activity had also been devoted to delivering bombs and leaflets rather than arms and equipment. Then Force 136 decided to take the bull by the horns. Emergency plans were made to rush a minimum of 450 tons of supplies to the guerrillas before the end of August, which would bring them up to operational strength.[24]

Whether they would then have been able to hold their own is open to doubt. Certainly Mountbatten's intelligence staff were satisfied that the Japanese would easily suppress a rising in July, although it might be a different story when the guerrillas were fully equipped. Hudson's verdict was: 'at the time of the surrender we were well able to defend ourselves, and could easily have produced offensive action by the beginning of September . . .'. This, however, like so much in the life of SOE in the Far East, was not put to the test.

For the whole of the war Force 136 was inhibited by the Foreign Office's insistence that the Siamese must work their passage – a process never properly defined. Pridi formed a resistance movement within days of the arrival of the Japanese. His efforts to get in touch with the Allies were ridiculed by the Foreign Office. The Free Siamese Movement was instructed by Mountbatten not to go into action before he gave the word – and therefore had no chance to prove it meant business. If words were not enough and deeds forbidden how could the unfortunate Siamese get absolution?

Italy's declaration of war was not made under duress, her campaigns cost many Allied lives, yet she was deemed in the twinkling of an eye to have worked *her* passage. There was one law for the West and another for the Far East.

# 4

# French Indo-China

IN 1940 French Indo-China was an agglomeration of peoples with little in common except geographical proximity and enforced allegiance to France.* When that country fell in June 1940 the administration in Indo-China remained loyal to Vichy, and began a close association with the Japanese to whom in September 1940 they gave facilities for operations against China. By August 1941 they had allowed 40,000 Japanese troops to enter. Meantime Japan increased her political influence both in Indo-China and Siam by mediating in the border dispute between the two. For most of the inhabitants there was little to choose between French and Japanese overlordship, and for some the goal was independence. For the time being it was business as usual with the French nominally in charge – although the Japanese could take complete control whenever it suited them. The 12,000 Europeans in the Army had served for several years without home leave and had little stomach for fighting.

The British Government in 1940 aimed to maintain friendly relations with the French administration so long as it resisted Japanese pressures. It followed that de Gaulle sympathizers within the country must not be encouraged.[1] After the outbreak of the Far Eastern war, however, it made sense to support any Free French resistance movement; but it was not until 1943 that SOE could do much about it. In that year de Gaulle appointed General Pechkoff his representative in China, with overall responsibility for resistance in Indo-China. Captain de Langlade, who had served in the Oriental Mission, was put in immediate charge. When he arrived in New Delhi in July 1943 India Command refused to recognize him because of the uncertain political position of the French, but SOE accepted him as Liaison Officer and made him head of their Indo-China Country Section. In October 1943 a small number of French officers and Annamites were brought from Algiers by Commandant de

---

* French Indo-China's population in 1936 was 24m., including 17m. Annamites, 3m. Cambodians, 1.4m. Siamese-speaking people, 1.4m. tribesmen in the mountains, 326,000 Chinese, and 43,000 Europeans (FO 371 41723, f. 60).

Crèvecoeur for guerrilla training in India, and were shared between SOE India and the Pechkoff Mission in China.

But politics immediately stopped the movement of Frenchmen to the Far East. This time the obstruction came from President Roosevelt. On 16 December 1943 he summoned to the White House the representatives of Britain, Russia, China, Turkey, Iran, and Egypt to tell them he was determined that the French, who had neglected the people of Indo-China for over a century, should not regain power there. The Secretary of State (Cordell Hull) let it be known that the State Department did not agree; but nevertheless Roosevelt's attitude delayed the arrival of a French Military Mission at Mountbatten's headquarters, thereby handicapping SOE operations in Indo-China; and it held back in Algiers a number of highly qualified French soldiers whose services would have been invaluable.[*2]

At first the British COS opposed a Military Mission on the ground that the French had neither troops nor free territory to contribute to the common cause; but later they agreed it could be useful.[3] The Foreign Office were in favour because 'the Colonial Powers had better stick together or hang together'.[4] Mountbatten was alarmed by Roosevelt's stand. He was playing into the hands of the Japanese, who were exploiting in their propaganda the Allies' continued snubbing of the French. If the French in Indo-China thought Britain shared his views it would be impossible to stimulate resistance there.[5] Further, if SOE did not have a French team based in India they would have to rely on Pechkoff's operations from China, which would complicate their overall plans. These arguments impressed COS. They may also have impressed Churchill, who according to Selborne strongly disagreed with Roosevelt's line.[6]

In spite of Selborne's assertion and in spite of continuing pressure from COS, the Prime Minister refused to approach the President. When in April 1944, urged on by Mountbatten and SOE, COS yet again asked for a French Mission, yet again Churchill said no. In May 1944 an exasperated Selborne told him he was frustrating SOE's plans for Indo-China. Why not let the Mission go, without telling the Americans? Eden repeated the argument that if the French were frozen out of SEAC they would operate from China and cut across

---

[*] On this occasion the President said the British had a good colonial record – the opposite of what he said to Stalin privately at the Yalta Conference (D. S. Clemens, *Yalta* (OUP, 1972), pp. 247–8).

SOE's activities elsewhere in the region. Still the Prime Minister would not budge.[7] Why he refused to act on the unanimous advice of Ministers and COS is not clear. It may have been partly reluctance to go against Roosevelt's wishes, and partly reluctance to help de Gaulle.

In January 1944 the Free French in Algiers gave 'Peter' Murphy* a memorandum about their participation in the Far East war intended for Churchill but withheld because of de Gaulle's bad relations with him. When Mountbatten and Pechkoff discussed this in New Delhi, the latter suggested that General Blaizot, leader designate of the proposed Mission, should break the ice by paying an informal visit to SEAC. The same idea was mooted when Gubbins met Blaizot in Algiers in June 1944 and found him 'frank, open, not politically minded, with a great sense of humour'. Murphy pointed out that a courtesy visit would not commit the British Government to anything.

JPS in London believed that Force 136's chance of success in Indo-China depended entirely on French co-operation.[8] If the Japanese took over the country (which they thought bound to happen sooner or later) a senior French officer would be invaluable to SEAC. Now, at the eleventh hour, Churchill sanctioned an approach to the American COS, who immediately agreed that the proposed Mission was a military necessity. To the astonishment of the British Joint Staff Mission in Washington, Roosevelt again shot down the proposal.[9]

The British now took the law into their own hands. They authorized Blaizot to pay a personal visit to Mountbatten; and on 21 October 1944 Churchill agreed that his visit should be extended indefnitely, and further that the French should set up a permanent Mission on the lines of the Dutch and Chinese Missions already with SEAC.[10]

The plan to bring from North Africa a force specially recruited for irregular operations also met with opposition from the Americans. SOE were doubtful about taking on what seemed to be a private army of 1,200 men – the Corps Léger d'Intervention (CLI) – but then agreed it could operate in small groups. Because of American

---

* James Victor ('Peter') Murphy had been transferred at Mountbatten's special request from the Political Warfare Executive (PWE) to advise him on Indo-China. In fact Murphy became Mountbatten's daily companion and was regularly consulted by the Supreme Commander on all his problems.

objections, however, it was not until January 1945, a year after its formation, that CLI was ordered to the Far East. Mountbatten's American deputy, General Wheeler, at first refused to issue the calling-forward order, citing a directive that no French ground forces should go to the Far East; but was persuaded that CLI was not a ground force within the meaning of the directive. At long last CLI prepared to move.[11]

There was an immediate storm in the Foreign Office, anxious to toe the American line. They said, tongue in cheek, that the order must have been issued by a junior officer unaware of the high political implications; but in fact suspected that SOE had hoodwinked Mountbatten into believing that the Foreign Office were in favour of the movement. Sterndale Bennett ruled that if Mountbatten really wanted CLI (now redesignated the 5th Colonial Infantry Regiment, partly to avoid confusion with the Ceylon Light Infantry, and partly, according to Dening, because no Briton could pronounce the original name) the matter must go to COS, and then to the Foreign Office for a policy decision. Mackenzie, on the other hand, warned London that if the French saw the British as lackeys of the Americans they would lose confidence in SOE, whose work in Indo-China would suffer. He begged London to instil a little courage and vision into the Foreign Office.

The episode ended when Sir Orme Sargent formally reprimanded Gubbins for taking the name of the Foreign Office in vain: to which Gubbins replied that the movement order came from SEAC, no doubt after consultation with the Foreign Office man on the spot. This – 'one of the lamest defences I have ever seen' – upset Sterndale Bennett, who particularly disliked the attempt to foist the blame on Dening. With the greatest reluctance he recommended that the matter should be allowed to drop. Cavendish Bentinck, Head of the Services Liaison Department, closed the Foreign Office file: 'Typical of SOE!' SOE might well have closed theirs: 'Typical of FO!' Thanks to that Department's holier-than-thou attitude SOE were once again prevented from doing their job. The 5th Colonial Regiment had been compelled to kick its heels in Algiers while the resistance movement in Indo-China was being wiped out by the Japanese. On 5 April 1945 – nearly a month after the Japanese coup which ended all hope of effective resistance in French Indo-China – the British COS told Washington that they were authorizing the immediate movement of the 5th Regiment, since to delay its dispatch 'may sacrifice the military advantages of French resistance there', a message which would have made excellent sense eighteen months earlier.*[12]

The few Frenchmen who did find their way to India were formed into the Service d'Action (SA), corresponding roughly to SOE. They provided the staff of Force 136's French Indo-China Country Section. SOE agreed to supply arms and equipment for a maximum of 3,000 guerrillas, and to put their common services at the disposal of the French.

The first task of the new Section was to assess the strength of resistance in Indo-China. Arrangements were made through the solitary radio link between the army in Hanoi and the French in Chungking to send an exploratory mission (Operation *Belief*). Three agents would parachute in – de Langlade, Major Milon (who was fully briefed about the 5th Colonial Regiment), and a radio operator. Their first attempt on 9 May 1944 ended when the Liberator's automatic pilot failed; and the second, next day, was frustrated by thick cloud. These sorties were mounted from India, which meant flying over Burma where the weather was particularly bad at this time of year. It was therefore decided to make a third attempt from Kunming, which delayed the project until the July moon.

Petrol for the sortie had to be flown from India over the Hump; and the operational aircraft had to make the same trip, through atrocious weather in which an aircraft had been lost the day before. During the onward flight from Kunming two of the Liberator's engines gave trouble, and the captain told the conducting officer, Captain R. A. Simpson, they would have to turn back. Simpson persuaded him to carry on, on the ground that the mission was important enough to risk all their lives.

They found the dropping-zone without difficulty, in bright moonlight. The pre-arranged signal – fires in the shape of a T – was clearly seen and six containers were dropped. Then the fires went out and the aircraft made two fruitless runs, wasting fifteen precious minutes, before torches were flashed to bring down the agents. They were taken to Hanoi where de Langlade handed to General Mordant, head of the resistance, a letter of introduction from de Gaulle. In spite of the letter, written in de Gaulle's own hand, Mordant 'remained reserved', which led de Langlade to conclude his mission had failed. He and Milon left for Lao-kay where Simpson was to arrange for them to

---

* The 5th Regiment finally disembarked at Saigon on 4 November 1945.

cross into China, but on the way they had a message saying that Simpson could not make the rendezvous for another two weeks. They returned to Hanoi where, after further meetings, Mordant promised whole-hearted co-operation.[13]

De Langlade's mission had been kept secret from the ever-suspicious Chinese. Simpson therefore had to invent a reason for his trip. The cover story was that 'Squadron Leader Barnes', a British Beaufighter pilot, had crash-landed in Siam, and had been looked after by a French officer in Indo-China who agreed to get him to Hokow where there was a French-speaking Chinese general, Ma Tsao Tsin, who would arrange to get 'Barnes' into China. Since there was no British French-speaking officer available in China, Simpson had been flown in from India at short notice – which was why he had no pass.

The Chinese commander in Kunming provided a pass and wrote to his brother in Meng-tze, 'a middle-aged opium smoker unavailable from mid-day to early evening', asking him to help. However, the brother refused to allow Simpson to travel by junk down the Red River because of his connection with the smuggling trade there, and he had to go overland. The trip to Hokow took nine days, one by train, one by American truck, one devoted to finding mules, and six by mule train through bandit-infested country, in almost unbearable heat. General Ma Tsao Tsin proved to be highly suspicious and kept asking awkward questions which Simpson did not attempt to answer. Eventually the General agreed to tell a contact in Lao-kay that Simpson was standing by to receive the supposed pilot, but said that an acknowledgement would take three or four days. This seemed strange as Lao-kay was just across the Red River. When Simpson discovered that no message had been sent, but instead a telegram had been dispatched to Chungking, he asked just what was the trouble. Ma Tsao Tsin had to admit that there was no trouble, but simply grumbled that this sort of mission should be handled by the Chinese equivalent of M.I.5 – and still did nothing.

Simpson now appealed to the local commander, Colonel Sung, who told his troops to look out for anyone trying to cross the river. This was fortunate, for the General had decided not to alert the military, so that they would certainly have fired first and asked questions later. On the evening of 22 July 1944 'Squadron Leader Barnes' safely crossed into China accompanied by Major Milon, whose unexpected presence undermined the cover story. After some quick thinking

Simpson explained that the French officer (i.e. Milon) had entered Hanoi from a submarine on a sabotage mission. The French resistance had teamed him up with 'the British officer' (i.e. de Langlade) who did not speak French. The French officer, who did not speak English, would get the pair across Indo-China and the British officer would take over in China.

This ingenious off-the-cuff fabrication led to complications. Ma Tsao Tsin interrogated de Langlade about his supposed crash-landing in fluent but incorrect French through Simpson. While the questions were being asked de Langlade, whose native tongue was of course French, struggled to maintain an uncomprehending silence, before replying in English to the translated questions. Milon came to the rescue by throwing in bits of local colour when de Langlade seemed to be getting out of his depth. A further problem arose when Sung explained that he had to detain for questioning any Frenchman who escaped into China; but as Milon had helped the British pilot he agreed to make an exception and waive the interrogation.

Ma Tsao Tsin had been furious when the escapers were brought in without his knowledge. However, he calmed down and indicated that he would be happy to receive a small reward for his services – a Sten gun, 200 rounds of ammunition, the instruction manual, and copies of the *Tatler* and *Illustrated London News*, which were in due course delivered to him. Simpson invited the local dignitaries to lunch, the General gave a return lunch, and on 26 July 1944 the three started on the arduous journey back to Kunming.

De Langlade reported a resistance movement within the Army which could be more important than civilian guerrillas; but there was much to be done. Arms, food, and men would have to be taken in. CLI should be infiltrated, ideally with its own motor transport. The Japanese, whose morale seemed low, were weakest in the north where parachute drops could be increased without provoking a reaction. He suggested that leaflets should be dropped on Saigon urging women and children to move north where their presence would strengthen the resistance.

That he carried a letter from de Gaulle was made known to P Division only after Operation *Belief* had been approved, which led the ever-suspicious Americans to think that Britain was surreptitiously furthering French interests in Indo-China. The American deputy head of P Division angrily referred to this 'highly dangerous and improper action on the part of Force 136'. No authority had been given to send in an emissary of de Gaulle. The failure of Force 136 to notify P Division of last-minute changes in the plan until after the emissary had departed was inexcusable. It took a flurry of telegrams to calm this storm in a teacup. Mackenzie was in London at the time and satisfied the Foreign Office that the letter was an introduction with no political content, and that it in no way changed the operation approved by SEAC. He and Taylor sent a telegram to Guinness, acting head of the India Mission, telling him to stick to this line. Gubbins told Selborne that it was beyond his comprehension how anyone could challenge de Gaulle's right to issue a letter of introduction in these circumstances; and the Minister promised every support if the fuss continued.

In spite of the manifest correctness of SOE's position the Americans persisted in seeing the episode as a deliberate attempt to undermine their policy for Indo-China. Although the letter was no more than an introduction, what really mattered was that de Langlade had been briefed by de Gaulle and they did not know what that briefing contained, although in fact it related to resistance pure and simple – to which the Americans could hardly take exception.* They were so incensed, however, that to appease them Mountbatten asked Mackenzie to replace Guinness. Mackenzie told Gubbins he did not feel justified in retaining his second in command against the Supreme Commander's wishes; and on 15 November 1944 Guinness returned to London.

When de Langlade reported to de Gaulle (now in Paris) he was asked to pay a second visit to Indo-China. On 15 November 1944 he flew to a clandestine airstrip near Dien Bien Phu in a Hudson of 357 Squadron, posing as a French Canadian member of the RAF so that if they were brought down his connection with the resistance movement would be concealed, but donning his French uniform when they had safely landed. His orders were to tell the resistance movement to lie low. It was believed that the disappearance of the

---

* The nature of the briefing is revealed in a note by de Langlade in *Espoir* (December 1981): 'Les instructions manuscrites du Général, détruites par le général Mordant, par crainte de voir ces instructions tomber en mains japonaises, étaient de me donner l'autorité pour expliquer verbalement la pensée du Général de Gaulle sur la nécessité pour la France que la Résistance civile et militaire en Indo-Chine reprenne le combat, au moment le plus propice, et sur son ordre, à lui de Gaulle, aux côtes des Alliés, de préciser à l'Amiral [Decoux] les moyens qui peuvent être apportés à la Résistance intérieure et de lui confirmer l'existence du corps expeditionnaire à Alger . . .'.

Vichy Government in August had increased the danger of a Japanese take-over and that premature guerrilla attacks might be the last straw. He spent a month in dicussions with General Sabattier (who was authorized to take over the leadership of the resistance from Mordant) and the Governor-General, Admiral Decoux, whose sympathies were turning to de Gaulle. Decoux agreed not to precipitate a crisis – not too difficult since he had been working with the Japanese for the last four years – to give SOE time to complete the buildup of the resistance forces.

The aircraft which took in de Langlade brought out Commandant Horaire Prévôt with the resistance movement's operational plan. It was totally unrealistic, being based on far greater aid from outside than could possibly be provided. On 30 November 1944 Prévôt, accompanied by Colonel Huard, who had been concerned with the formation of CLI, returned to Hanoi to try to bring some sense into the plan. They argued that instead of organizing guerrilla activities all over the country they should build up an area in Upper Laos for the reception of men and supplies from outside; and they also insisted that the resistance organizations should operate independently of the Army. When Huard and de Langlade returned to India on 13 December 1944 they were satisfied that the revised plan would make the best use of the available forces. De Crèvecoeur considered that the resistance was now under the control of the French High Command. The country had entered the war on the side of the Allies; and the Japanese would find her a hard nut to crack.


During these exchanges the buildup of arms, equipment, and men began. De Langlade brought back a request for Sten guns and ammunition, but SOE were asked not to send in men as the French did not want to have too many clandestine personnel on their hands. Bad weather in August and September limited the number of sorties, but by the end of December thirteen W/T stations had been installed and were in regular touch with Calcutta. Ten dropping-zones were in use. In the January moon period twenty-seven agents were dropped, their hosts having agreed that the risks of accommodating them must be borne. At the end of February the number of dropping-zones in use had increased to fifty, and there were twenty-one active W/T stations. Words transmitted had doubled to 3,000 daily. The resistance movement had been provided with 3,400 Sten guns with over a million rounds, 6,000 grenades, 800 pistols, ninety-four Brens with a quarter of a million shells. Large quantities of incendiaries and explosive devices had been delivered. Sixty more men had been infiltrated.

At the end of 1944 Lieutenant Lucien Doebbels visited Tonkin to inspect the material dropped and give instruction in its use. He saw to the cleaning and oiling of the weapons and ensured that they were properly stored in dry places. One hundred and fifty officers and men attended his training courses in the garrisons of Hanoi, Tong, and Langson. He also trained 150 civilians in small groups, only half of whom were competent to work on their own. The others would support the military teams.

The buildup of the resistance movement was, of course, liable to be self-defeating. The stronger the movement the more likely became Japanese intervention; and even if they did not suspect that the increasing number of flights over Indo-China were to supply the resistance, informers gave them a shrewd idea of what was happening. They believed that a large part of the French army, whose loyalty to Vichy had meant loyalty to Japan, was now transferring its allegiance to Free France. As a precautionary measure SOE decided to suspend drops to the more populous areas and concentrate on the remote mountain regions.

De Crèvecoeur looked forward to 1945 with great confidence. The achievement of the SA was modest, and could never equal that of the resistance groups in Metropolitan France, but it was getting into its stride. Political and military links had been established to assure the future of Indo-China. Through SA the French High Command could play an increasing part in support of the Allies. It had brought a new taste for adventure, with the hope of action and the equipment to carry it out. The great dividend would become evident 'au Jour-J'. De Crèvecoeur was happy to acknowledge SA was deeply indebted to Force 136.

That body's forecast was no less confident. They sought authority to stockpile stores and training material, and to provide instructors for eventual action against Japanese lines of communication. Reception committees would be established in the sparsely populated districts in the north, west, and south where guerrillas would in due course answer the call to arms. There would be thirty-three Liberator sorties every month for the whole of 1945.

The Japanese, however, had different ideas. Any chance that they would stand idly by while the resistance groups gathered enough strength to take on the occupying troops disappeared when Tokyo decided that General MacArthur planned to attack Indo-China, and that the French army must be put out of action forthwith. In the evening of 9 March 1945 Decoux was told that the Japanese Government intended to take over the French armed forces. His temporizing reply was ignored, and through innumerable acts of treachery the Japanese seized key points all over the country, dealing mercilessly with any opposition. In some garrisons more than half the French troops were decapitated. Officers were invited to social functions, taken prisoner, and killed. The official reasons for the coup, put out in a vast communiqué, were that the French troops, secretly supplied by the Americans in China, could no longer be relied on to co-operate in the defence of the country; and that the resistance movement was reaching dangerous proportions.[14]

Although there were many individual acts of heroism, for which a fearful price had to be paid, overall the resistance was a broken reed. Decoux and Mordant were imprisoned. Sabattier, who had been ordered to escape if a coup was threatened, left Hanoi on 8 March 1945 to try to rally the resistance forces. It was now obvious that SOE had been right to press for a greater French presence in the Far East. Had CLI been allowed to come as soon as it was formed, the resistance movement could have been provided with experienced leaders who understood the vital importance of strict security (which the French forces in Indo-China did not) and were equipped with highly sophisticated weapons and devices.

On 12 March 1945, three days after the coup, Churchill asked General Ismay, Military Deputy Secretary to the War Cabinet: 'How is it there are French troops and a Governor General there now? Are they survivors of the Vichy period? Have they not yet joined up with de Gaulle? I have not followed the affairs of this country for some time.' This curious minute confirms that the Prime Minister, when he steadfastly denied the Free French a chance to play a part in the Far Eastern war, cannot have applied his mind to the military problem. He asked for an account of affairs in Indo-China since 1940 to be put on a single sheet of paper, so at least he was familiar with the background when a week later the French, fighting for their lives, appealed against an American refusal to send them ammunition. He invited the President to help, not because every effort against the common enemy was necessary, but because 'it will look very bad in history if we were to let the French forces in Indo-China be cut to pieces by the Japanese through shortage of arms . . .'. The Americans gave way and allowed ammunition to be dropped to the Frenchmen fighting a desperate rearguard action as they made their way towards China.[15]

It seemed to SOE that the whole resistance movement had been wiped out overnight. Every one of their twenty-one radio stations was silent. Contact was gradually re-established, however, with those in the remoter districts, although in the main centres of population – Hanoi, Saigon, and Phnom Penh, nine had been finally silenced. It was estimated that after the coup 10,000 men were still resisting the Japanese. Four thousand were in the Black River sector of West Tonkin under General Alessandri, who were thought to have a good chance of holding on to the airfields in the area. Force 136 turned over to the General their six W/T stations in Tonkin and seven in Upper Laos. They also carried out several operations to deliver arms to those who were fighting on; and they dropped three 'action groups' made up from the best men available in India. In the region of the Red River further east in Upper Tonkin there were 4,000 more troops.

Sabattier had told Huard in November 1944 that if he had to fight it out with the Japanese he would group his forces in a rough quadrilateral between Hanoi and the Chinese border, bounded on the west by the Black River and on the east by the Red River, and that he would build up supplies there; but the Japanese kept so careful a watch on army activities in the region that this proved impossible. The troops, poorly equipped, were steadily driven towards the border, their numbers dwindling as they went. Only 5,000 reached China where they had a chilly reception from Chinese and Americans alike. In spite of their sufferings in fifty-two days of bitter fighting on the retreat, politics made them unwelcome guests.

Force 136 sent Flight Lieutenant Kino to evaluate airstrips still in the hands of the resistance. On 15 April 1945 he parachuted to Nam Tha 250 miles north of Hanoi to an excellent clandestine airfield. The runway had just been lengthened from 1,000 to 1,500 yards, and it could now take aircraft up to the size of Mitchell bombers. None the less, it seemed to him a matter of days before the French forces were completely subjugated. The greatest handicap was their poor internal communication. The clandestine radio stations could talk to each other only through Calcutta, which in practice meant that 90 per cent of their intelligence was three days old. This

played a large part in contributing to the French defeat because they
eventually arrived at the stage where they could not trust any news at all,
and rather than risk being caught they would pull out well in advance of any
danger . . . In this way a lot of the French formations never even tried to make
a stand against the Japanese columns which in a lot of cases did not exceed
one hundred men.

Apart from Sabattier and Alessandri, well-known Gaullists, all the
officers Kino met seemed to be pro-Vichy. 'Everywhere you see
photographs of Pétain, and when you question the French officer on
his sympathies he shrugs his shoulders and goes to great pains to
explain "now politics are of secondary importance . . . everybody is
against the Japanese".' He accepted that the horror of the night of 9
March 1945, when hordes of screaming Japanese charged through the
streets murdering women and children, must have affected morale at
the time; but since then whole battalions had simply retreated and
retreated, although there were many mountain passes which resolute
men could have defended against superior forces. He recommended
that Force 136 should abandon its support of the French army, which
had made poor use of the huge quantities of weapons sent in, and
concentrate on supplying their own parties in the field.

While he was at Nam Tha a handful of refugees congregated there,
desperately trying to keep ahead of the Japanese, who were reported
to be beheading women and children. Some were so terrified that
they wanted to walk to China rather than wait for an aircraft to take
them to safety. On 22 April 1945 Calcutta radioed that a Dakota
would land at Nam Tha. Four days of impossible weather followed;
and on the fifth the local commander ordered the refugees to make for
China. Before they could get very far, however, the Dakota arrived,
embarked thirty-one passengers, and after an uneventful six-hour
flight reached Jessore.[16]

Immediately after the coup there were in the field 1,210 guerrillas
proper – the direct responsibility of Force 136 and SA – located as
follows:

|  | Europeans | Natives | Total |
|---|---|---|---|
| Upper Laos | 47 | 195 | 242 |
| Central Indo-China | 213 | 742 | 955 |
| Cochin China | 13 | — | 13 |
| Total | 273 | 937 | 1210 |

These men were in difficulty right from the start. The suddenness of the Japanese attack forced most to leave home without arms or equipment, so that their survival depended on regular supply drops which proved to be impossible. SOE were committed to support the offensive in Burma. The SD squadrons (357 and 358) were seventeen Liberators short, due to operational losses and wear and tear. Bad weather increased the percentage of unsuccessful sorties. Missions to Indo-China averaged forty-four a month in January to March, but fell to seventeen in April and fourteen in May.

In spite of the arrival of new teams, including some 'Jedburghs' – two officers with their own radio operator – the resistance groups were gradually worn down. On 1 April 1945 Colin Mackenzie told London they were still causing the Japanese some trouble, adding that if only the 5th Colonial Regiment had been available the situation might have been saved. He asked what he should tell the French about London's failure to approve the dispatch from France of badly needed radio operators. The Foreign Office reaction was predictable. Sterndale Bennett accused him of 'manoeuvring to escape any blame for the inevitable collapse', and justified the delay on the ground that SOE's previous attempts to 'jump' the Foreign Office made it necessary to scrutinize all their proposals.[17]

Although the guerrillas did attempt some sabotage it was on a small scale and merely encouraged the Japanese to hunt them down more vigorously. A group under Captain Fabre at Paksane, in North Laos, for example, destroyed a number of motor launches and blew up two bridges on the main roads from the town. At the beginning of June the Japanese caught up with them and killed one officer and three other ranks, with four other ranks missing. Their equipment was seized and four of their five W/T stations destroyed. It became obvious that it was only a matter of time before all groups would be liquidated if they continued their pinprick attacks, and they were ordered to confine themselves to the supply of intelligence.

Force 136's efforts in Indo-China were totally wasted, and there is no certainty that if the Blaizot Mission and CLI had been welcomed with open arms things would have been any better. The French army, caught off guard, was no match for the Japanese. Morale was low, security poor, equipment out of date, and the loyalty of the natives suspect. Groups of CLI – experienced volunteers with sophisticated weapons and techniques – might have turned the army into a force to be reckoned with. Alternatively they might have developed their own resistance movement in the remoter parts of the country where they would have awaited the arrival of an Allied invasion force. Between them Roosevelt and Churchill ensured that neither alternative was given a chance.

# Sumatra

SUMATRA was the most difficult of SOE's territories in the Far East, for many reasons. As the last area due for liberation it came at the bottom of SEAC's priority list.* Other factors were the great distance from Ceylon; traditional hostility to outsiders, particularly among the Achinese in the north-west of the island; the Japanese anti-Dutch propaganda and their pan-Asiatic movement which led many to support the Japanese 'Co-prosperity Sphere'; disagreements between Force 136 and the Dutch in Ceylon, and between the latter and their own Government in London; and finally the preference of Admiral Helfrich, the Dutch C-in-C, for commando raids which conflicted with SOE's practice of seeking to organize dissidents into an anti-Japanese movement. On the last point Helfrich may have been right. There was in Sumatra no body of friendly natives anxious to throw out the Japanese.

Before the Japanese troops arrived the Dutch carried out demolitions with rather more resolution that did the British in Malaya. Those appointed to do the job were given miitary rank and on 11 February 1942 destroyed the oil wells and installations at Pangkalanbrandan and Pangkalansoesoe fifty miles north of Medan. According to the British Vice-Consul at Medan (Mr G. C. Whitteridge) it was thought that if this prize was denied them the Japanese might not think it worth while occupying Sumatra. Ten days later the oil wells were still burning. When Whitteridge closed his office rubber and petrol stocks in Achin had been destroyed. All cars had been put out of action except those needed by officials.

To judge from Reuter messages which emanated from Malaya, giving details of midnight conferences between military and civilian authorities to determine what should or should not be destroyed, the long-prepared scorched earth policy in the Netherlands East Indies provided a sharp contrast which the Dutch were quick to notice and comment on.[1]

The impossibility of establishing a viable resistance movement

---

* Other Dutch, and Portuguese possessions in the Far East were the responsibility of SOA, also known as SRD (Services Reconnaissance Department).

should have been accepted from the beginning. Although the warlike Achinese had been submissive for forty years there was every likelihood that they would seize any chance of freeing themselves from the Dutch. Even before the Japanese landed there was rioting in which Europeans were killed in the northern area. In southern Sumatra native police discarded their uniforms, and labourers on European estates attacked their owners, killing several. The situation became so serious that the authorities planned to disarm the police elsewhere in the Dutch East Indies lest Sumatra become a precedent. That the police, the group most likely to remain loyal to the regime, should take this line is a measure of the hopelessness of fostering organized resistance. Yet for the whole of the war Force 136 and the Dutch persisted in the belief that something might be done.

On 21 February 1942 the War Office said they hoped SOE would harass the occupying forces and recruit agents, saboteurs, and guides, some of whom would be brought out to support later military operations. Radio sets should be provided for those who would remain behind. In fact, all the available sets had already been handed over to the Dutch. Two were hidden in Java for communication with Australia. Four were intended for use within the country. Another was given to van der Post who planned to assemble groups in the jungle along the south coast of Java.[2]

In spite of the manifest difficulties, British and Dutch alike continued to be optimistic about special operations in Sumatra. When Helfrich was given command of the Dutch forces in Ceylon and India he was ordered first to use them in the defence of Ceylon, and second to train them for raids on the Dutch East Indies. On 4 March 1942 he was urged to locate in North Sumatra 'some scores of people, European or native' to act as agents in areas occupied by the Japanese. They would be sent to Ceylon where the British would advise about their training. It was believed that many native troops, renowned for their fighting qualities but poorly armed, would be willing to form guerrilla bands, if they could be given sophisticated arms to replace their rifles and swords. They would be supplied by submarines, motor torpedo boats, or landing-craft which would establish dumps on the islands lying off the west coast.[3]

The optimism continued unabated. At the beginning of April 1942 Captain H. G. C. Pel and Lieutenant Jan Scheepens were flown from Britain to Ceylon to form the nucleus of a special operations group. Both knew Sumatra intimately, having been with the Dutch army there. Major Mollinger, also of the Dutch East Indies Army, took the commando training course at Arisaig, where he impressed his instructors – 'an excellent man, who obviously means business' – before going to Ceylon to take charge of Dutch special operations. SOE London asked the India Mission to provide instructors and to supplement the stores Mollinger brought from Britain; and they endorsed the assessment of the Arisaig school: 'He is a very competent officer, and collaborating with you he should be able to do excellent work in Sumatra.' There would be plenty of opportunity to strike at the Japanese.

Mollinger found himself in command of forty men, part of the 1st Detachment of the 'Princess Irene' Brigade, which had left Britain on 7 January 1942 for the Far East, but had been diverted to Ceylon when the Japanese occupied the Dutch East Indies. These men – the 'Korps Insulinde' – were trained in India for commando work, which made difficulties for the India Mission. SOE London tried to explain to the Dutch there that special operations and commando activities were different. The latter were military, for example the destruction of a specific objective. The former aimed to develop underground organizations in enemy territory. Commando work called for officers and men with initiative, dash, and courage. Special operations needed specially qualified agents, able to organize resistance movements. This had little effect on Dutch thinking, and for several months in 1943 the *Korps Insulinde* continued to be a thorn in SOE's flesh in spite of the fact that the Dutch agreed that the India Mission should have an Anglo-Dutch Country Section with Lieutenant-Colonel Christopher Hudson in charge, and a Dutch second in command (Mollinger).

SOE hoped this would end the Dutch aspirations to carry out commando raids. Further, the Dutch Government wanted their meagre forces to be concentrated in Australia. Helfrich, however, proposed that the *Korps* should remain in Ceylon to take part in a future invasion of Sumatra. Mackenzie made it clear to London that the *Korps* was valueless from his point of view, made up as it was of Dutchmen few of whom had been in Sumatra and who did not speak Malay. The sooner it was removed to Australia the better.

In further discussions with the Dutch in London it was agreed that it was premature to talk about active resistance in Sumatra. All that could be done was to seek intelligence and make contacts – with the proviso that if there was a military case for destroying some objective

SOE were free to do so. Helfrich, on the other hand, wanted an expanded *Korps Insulinde* to carry out commando raids; and with this in mind asked that any special operations into Sumatra should be accompanied by armed guards to protect them not from the Japanese but from hostile natives. He reluctantly agreed that agents who needed this protection were not engaged on special operations; but at a meeting on 3 August 1943 he 'laboured on at some length' about the importance of the *Korps* and finally won agreement that he should retain it, but only for commando operations.

This produced a surprising reaction. Mackenzie, who had been doing his best to keep the *Korps* at arm's length, pointed out that if it severed its connection with SOE the Anglo-Dutch Country Section would lose the services of Pel and Scheepens, the only officers who knew northern Sumatra; and 'whilst we have held and still hold that armed guards are not normally required or desirable when landing agents, it is quite possible that cases might arise when such covering parties would be useful'. He asked that a formal directive to Helfrich excluding the *Korps Insulinde* from special operations should be rescinded. On 1 September 1943 he sent a message to London apologizing for this change of attitude, but pointing out that conditions had also changed.

Three weeks later he changed his attitude again. Helfrich and Pel, having been allowed to retain the *Korps*, were now planning to expand it, and Mackenzie asked London to warn the Dutch that if they tried to go it alone SOE would carry out their own independent operations in the Dutch East Indies. But London were not prepared to reopen the negotiations, and simply told Mackenzie that if he found it necessary to restrain Helfrich he must do it through the machinery of SEAC. They did at least have an informal word with the Dutch authorities suggesting that an expansion of the *Korps* should be discouraged.

The first operations into Sumatra, carried out by the *Korps*, were in fact special operations in the accepted sense. In December 1942 a party landed from the Dutch submarine O 24 (Lieutenant-Commander W. J. de Vries RNN) near Troemon on the west coast hoping to contact friendly headmen, but without success. They remained only a short time and found no headman willing to risk his life on behalf of the Dutch. In February 1943 a party of seven under Captain Scheepens were prevented by rough seas from landing on the north-east coast.[4]

The Anglo-Dutch Country Section's first operation was *Matriarch*, planned by Pel in March 1943. It was to be in two stages, again using O 24[5]: a reconnaissance near Meulaboh on the west coast, during which a headman known to Pel would be asked to find out if the leading men in his area would join a resistance group. If they were, the second stage would be set in motion. The newly formed group would sabotage oil installations, arrange the reception of supplies and agents, some of whom would be sent on to Malaya and Java, encourage rubber production (in the interests of Walter Fletcher's smuggling enterprise*), and collect intelligence to be fed into the SEAC pool.

Scheepens led the *Matriarch* shore party of five other Dutchmen and two British officers. Pel's headman put in a brief appearance, but then retired to his house, not to be seen again. The party spent five hours talking to the villagers, whom they took to be well disposed, but afraid of the Japanese. When they returned to the beach, however, they walked into an ambush which the villagers must have known about, if they did not actually tip off the Japanese. The party were fired on at close quarters by sub-machine guns, but none was hit. As they swam for the boats the firing continued. All reached the submarine safely although one boat was damaged by gunfire. They tried to make a second landing but were defeated by the strong current. Next night they managed to land, and happened on two Achinese farmers trying to catch water-buffalo for their paddy-fields, whom they took back to the submarine.[6]

They turned out to be a nuisance. After they had been interrogated no one knew what to do with them. If they were returned to Sumatra the Japanese might use the fact of their abduction in anti-Dutch propaganda. The men were unhappy and constantly talked about their families. They would never feel at home in Ceylon 'even if everything, including women, is provided for them. These men will have to fall violently in love to be able to forget their family.' It was concluded that to abduct people was playing into the hands of the Japanese – far better to carry out interrogations in Sumatra and then let the captives go free.

It was admitted that the first raids were not a success and it was doubtful whether this type of operation, 'which consists simply of

---

* See Part II, Chapter 9.

landing for a very short period from a submarine to talk to a contact, sometimes, but not always known beforehand', would ever provide conclusive information about the strength of an embryo resistance movement. The alternative was to drop in parties blind, knowing some would be lost but hoping the survivors would establish themselves permanently.

The operations next planned were to support the invasion of northern Sumatra (*First Culverin*) on which Churchill had set his heart in spite of universal opposition. When JPS and COS told him on the *Queen Mary, en route* for the Quebec Conference in August 1943, that the operation was bound to fail, he accused them in a thirteen-page minute of negative thinking. He appealed to Mountbatten and Wingate, who obligingly confirmed that *First Culverin* was feasible, if carried out during the monsoon (May to August); but when Mountbatten assumed command in South East Asia he confessed that from May to September sea conditions were impossible. Even when JPS argued that the operation would mean calling off the attack on the south of France (*Dragoon*) in support of the Allied invasion of Normandy (*Overlord*) the Prime Minister remained unconvinced. He wrote to Mountbatten on 10 January 1944 (having deleted the words in square brackets from his first draft):

After engaging the enemy by every means in your power the main thing is for you to concentrate on *First Culverin* after the monsoon. This I am determined to press to the very utmost day in day out [until I wear down all obstruction and break up all competitive schemes] . . . Here is your great chance. Do not allow anything to take your eye off it. Here alone will you have the opportunity of opening new fields in the world war, and here alone will you have my aid . . . Talk it over with Wingate and if you can prepare a good plan the rest can be made to [obey] come along.[7]

Some of Churchill's single-minded, not to say narrow-minded, enthusiasm rubbed off on the India Mission's planners who envisaged extensive operations in northern Sumatra in 1944/5 in support of an Allied invasion. They would provide guides and military intelligence for the invading forces, cut telephone lines, sabotage road and rail transport, assassinate enemy officers, attack military posts and arms dumps, organize risings in the enemy rear, spread false rumours to create confusion – a massive programme which presupposed a flourishing resistance movement ready to go into action when the signal was given, in spite of the evidence that there was little hope of establishing that movement.*

SOE's actual contribution was more modest. Their preparations for *First Culverin* (which of course never took place) were limited to the reconnaissance of possible sites for landing-strips on the west coast of Sumatra and the Island of Simalur (*Residency, Sugarloaf I*, and *Sugarloaf II*). Experts had to make feasibility studies of the chosen areas in a matter of hours, in the dark, knowing that enemy patrols might appear at any moment. They had to examine the vegetation, decide whether trees would have to be felled, whether there were dangerous hills nearby, whether there would be drainage problems, whether the runway called for much levelling. They also had to take back soil samples.

The *Residency* and *Sugarloaf I* parties left Trincomalee in HM Submarine *Templar* (Lieutenant T. G. Ridgeway) on 26 April 1944.[8] In addition to two airfield experts, Captain W. R. Annan and Captain A. F. S. Wright, there were Scheepens, Lieutenant Sisselaar, and Captain J. G. D. Lowe, with seven Dutch† and seven Indian other ranks. Altogether they made five landings. For the first they divided into three groups, one supporting the experts, the second standing by on the beach, and the third, the ferry party, remaining with the canoes some distance out. On 30 April 1944 Wright and his party went ashore in Rigaih Bay but a torrential rainstorm drove them back before they reached the site.

A second attempt next day fared better. This time Annan was in charge of the investigation, and thanks to the bright moonlight they found the chosen area without difficulty. Annan spent two and a half hours on the survey and satisfied himself that an airstrip could easily be prepared. Only one large tree would have to be felled; and the nearest hill, 150 feet high, was a safe distance away. The group got back to the boats without incident, but in the darkness the submarine rammed both boats, throwing several men into the sea.

---

* Churchill also took a side-swipe at General Auchinleck whose 'easy relinquishment of the prospect of operations in 1944 . . . need not weigh with us, as this officer will have no part in the South East Asia campaign. Commanders will be chosen of sufficient vigour of mind and compulsive improvisation to overcome the difficulties imposed by the climate and the terrain' (PREM 3 146/3, f. 125).

† Sergeants Hakkenberg, Bogers, Hanauer, van Hattem, Quinten, Serraris, and Private Moerdjono.

All were picked up, but one of the Indian troops was injured and could not take part in the later landings.

*Templar* now proceeded to Meulaboh to make another daylight reconnaissance. She sighted *en route* an unescorted 3,000 ton merchant ship presenting the ideal target. 'This "gift" was reluctantly allowed to pass unscathed owing to the restrictions imposed in the order for the special operation.' This note in the submarine's log was bitterly supplemented by the flotilla commander: 'Another case of a target lost because of a special operation!'[9]

On the night of 3 May 1944 when the experts planned to examine two sites, they were driven off course by strong currents and could investigate only one. As they moved into the jungle they met some natives who seemed friendly at first, but they ran off when one of the Indians brandished his gun. It seemed certain that the alarm would be raised, so the site was only superficially examined.

In the fourth landing there were two parties, one under Wright to examine the airfield site, the other under Scheepens to capture 'a few natives'. Wright successfully completed his survey which proved that a 1,000 yards strip could easily be built, but the plan to round up a clutch of natives failed.

One villager who appeared suitable believed the story of the landing party that they were a Japanese patrol . . . but he could not be persuaded to come out of his cottage so that he could be quietly kidnapped. His wife, also in the house, would probably have sounded the alarm if this had taken place inside, and as it was impossible to take her too (HMS *Templar* boasts no married quarters) he was left in peace[10] –

a strange excuse for failure to carry out an operation.

The final landing was at the Meulaboh site briefly examined on 3 May 1944. Scheepens opposed it, fearing that the area must now be compromised, but Lowe insisted on going, provided the others appreciated the risks. The submarine commander, who had the final decision, was unable to make his mind up whether 'one was over cautious or the other rash'.[11] Lowe and Annan swam ashore, leaving Sisselaar and four Dutch other ranks just beyond the surf line. Twenty minutes after the pair, accompanied by a Pathan, disappeared into the jungle Scheepens was proved right. There were long bursts of machine-gun fire, which ended abruptly. Although it seemed certain that the trio must have been killed or captured, the ferry party

Explosive devices: a perfect replica of a Chinese stone lantern, made of wood with a plastic veneer (*above*); faithful reproductions of Balinese carvings, cast in solid high explosive, each mounted on a wooden base and detonated by a time pencil (*below*).

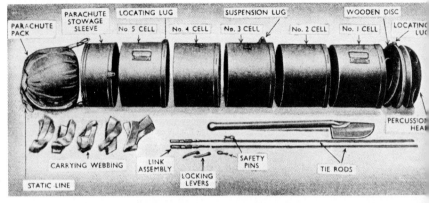

PARACHUTE PACK · PARACHUTE STOWAGE SLEEVE · LOCATING LUG · No. 5 CELL · No. 4 CELL · SUSPENSION LUG · No. 3 CELL · No. 2 CELL · No. 1 CELL · WOODEN DISC · LOCATING LUG · PERCUSSION HEAD

CARRYING WEBBING · LINK ASSEMBLY · LOCKING LEVERS · SAFETY PINS · TIE RODS · STATIC LINE

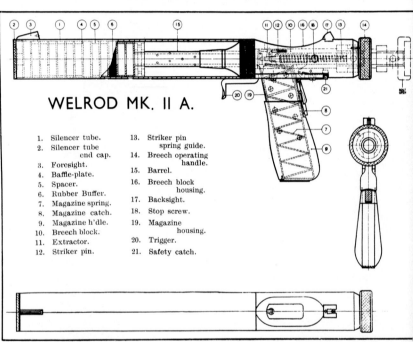

# WELROD MK. II A.

1. Silencer tube.
2. Silencer tube end cap.
3. Foresight.
4. Baffle-plate.
5. Spacer.
6. Rubber Buffer.
7. Magazine spring.
8. Magazine catch.
9. Magazine h'dle.
10. Breech block.
11. Extractor.
12. Striker pin.
13. Striker pin spring guide.
14. Breech operating handle.
15. Barrel.
16. Breech block housing.
17. Backsight.
18. Stop screw.
19. Magazine housing.
20. Trigger.
21. Safety catch.

Jungle equipment: H-type container, 5 feet 6 inches long and 15 inches in diameter, for stores dropped to agents in the jungle (*above*); the Welrod silent weapon (*below*).

Sabotage: train blown up by *Mongoose Blue* in Burma (*above*); Sleeping Beauty (SB), the one-man submarine designed to destroy enemy shipping, undergoing trials in Staines Reservoir (*middle*); Mobile Floating Unit (MFU), an innocent-looking craft intended to carry saboteurs to an enemy-occupied port (*below*).

Dropping supplies in the jungle: the agent's lifeline – a Liberator drops supplies to an SOE party (*above*); typical jungle country, showing how difficult it was for the RAF to identify a dropping-zone (*below*).

Hazardous terrain: paddy-fields (*above*); mangrove swamp (*middle*); Lysander of No. 357 (SD) Squadron landing on a Burma jungle airstrip reinforced with split bamboo (*below*).

Group 'A' Signals, Force 136, Calcutta 1945: control room and group of operators (*below*); control clerk (FANY) with wall map of operational stations (*right*).

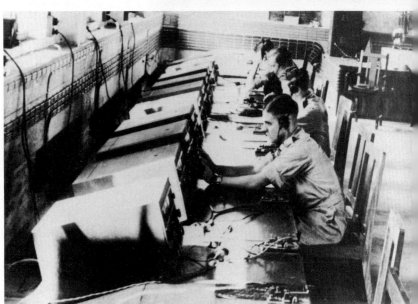

## W/T DO'S & DONT'S

**DO'S:**

1. Help your operator all the time.
2. Give him ample time to do his charging.
3. Help to die his set.
4. See that the Wireless equipment is evenly divided over your Group or Section. See that your wireless operator himself is not overloaded.
5. Give him ample time to set up his Station.
6. Remember that it is your duty to keep your wireless operator up to scratch, just as much as any other member of the Group, therefore, hold periodical inspection of his equipment, and see that he is maintaining it properly.
7. It is not your wireless operator's job to do your coding for you. He is trained and capable of doing it but he should only be asked to do so in an emergency.

**DONT'S:**

1. Do not stand over your wireless operator and pester him when he is taking a message.
2. Don't worry him when conditions are bad.
3. When helping to die the set remember, normally your wireless operator will know the best site.
4. Do not give your wireless operator a message only a few minutes before it is sked.

22

## POINTS FOR IDENTIFICATION:
### Tanks—Armoured Cars

**1. TANKETTE TYPE "92" (1932).**

This has probably been replaced by the Type "94" (1938) which is described in paragraph 2 below:—

Length—10 ft. 3 in. Width.—5 ft. 9 ins. Height.—5 ft. 4 in. Weight.—3 tons.
Speed—30 m.p.h. 12 m.p.h. cross-country.
Armament.—One L.M.G. in turret.
Armour.—Front and Turret, 14 mm. (.55 in.) sides, 8 mm. (.31 in.)
Crew—Two.
Ford—2 ft. 6 ins.
Trench crossing.—1 ft. 4 ins.
Belly clearance.—1 ft. 1 in.
Points for recognition—Engine on left-hand side in front. Turret mounted to rear of chassis, giving a boat-like appearance. Rounded turret with L.M.G. in ball-mounting. Long sloping glacis plate. Four bogies in two pairs. Front sprocket. Two return rollers.
In common with all types of Japanese Tankettes, this model is **used to tow a** light trailer.

**2. TANKETTE TYPE "94" (1938).**

Length—10 ft. 3 ins. Width—5 ft. 9 ins. Height—5 ft. 4 in. Weight—3 to 4 ton.
Speed—33 m.p.h. maximum.
Armament.—One M.G. (7.7 mm.) in turret. One L.M.G. (7.7 mm.) in hull.
Armour.—As for type "92".
Ford—2 ft. 6 ins.
Trench crossing.—1 ft. 1 in.
Belly clearance.—1 ft. 1 in.
Crew—Three. Hull gunner, turret gunner, driver.
Points for recognition—No great difference. Turret set centrally. Four bogies in two pairs. Large rear idler which also acts as a bogie. Two return rollers. Front sprocket.

23

A Dakota drops stores to guerrillas in Burma.

Record of Conference held at Camp,
30, 31, DEC. '43. between Messers CHANG HONG,
CHEN CHIN SHENG; Messers Broome, Davis,
TAN CHOON LIM; Major F.S. Chapman.

*146.A.*

## A. Terms of Coöperation.

1a. Mr Chang Hong (CH) is the elected representative of the Malayan Communist Party, the Anti-
Japanese Force and the Anti-Japanese Union,
and can put into force any decisions agreed
to in these meetings.

b. Major J.L.H. DAVIS, Captain R.N. BROOME and Mr
Tan Choon Lim are the Military Representatives
(M.R.) of the Allied C in C, South East Asia,
and are fully empowered to coöperate with
any anti-Japanese party in Malaya.

2. CH agrees that his party will fully coöperate with the Allied forces while retaking
Malaya and for this purpose will follow
the instructions of the Allied C in C in so
far as military operations in Malaya
are concerned.

## B. Details of Proposals and Decisions.

1. After giving a summary of the numbers and
resources of the various Anti-Japanese organisations in Malaya, CH asked in what way
these organisations would be expected to
coöperate.
The MR. summarised the military and Fifth
Column activity hoped for and it was agreed
that at present, beyond continuing to keep
the people anti-Japanese, the only possible
action would be to foment labour trouble
and carry out sabotage against shipping,
naval dockyards, etc. For the rest it was
agreed to be a time of preparation for future combined action. CH also undertook
to emphasize, in their present propaganda,
the need for complete coöperation with
Allied invading troops.

Jungle treaty with Malayan guerrillas, a remarkable international document written in a school exercise book. The handwriting looks very much like Spencer Chapman's (see the final plate).

2. Asked what kind of help was of expected, CH replied (a) Arms and ammunition. (b) Medical supplies including doctors. (c) Military training. (d) Financial assistance.

The MR stated with regard to (a) and (b) that the Allied C-in-C will undertake to despatch to Malaya, by all possible means, the arms and supplies needed for effective cooperation. The introduction of Doctors from outside is difficult at present but the possibility will be investigated.

(c) i The Chinese instructors who are ready in India will be introduced as soon as communication permit. ii Chinese students will be sent from Malaya for training as instructors and will be returned to Malaya. A party of 6 should be prepared to proceed to India shortly. iii The question of introducing European instructors at a later date will be investigated. (d) the MR have already asked for authority to finance. The reply is expected within a month. CH estimates that 50-70,000 $ per month will meet present requirements.

3 After the MR had stressed the urgency of setting up the wireless installation, the details of para 1 & 2 (above) were discussed and an immediate detailed plans for the first shipment of arms and medical supplies was drawn up. Investigation of further specific supply routes was ~~necessary~~ agreed upon.

_____

The above is subject to the ratification of the combined Headquarters of the M.C.P., A-J.F, and A-J.U. And is subject to agreement on the following or similar clause to be added. " That cooperation shall continue during the period in which the army is responsible for the maintenance of Peace and Order in Malaya'.

J Davis

R.N. Broome, Capt.

Lau choon lim

Gog Loon

Major

Jungle delicacy. A Sakai – Malayan aboriginal – surveys with satisfaction his evening meal of roast monkey.

"NICKELS" *from* Heaven

Liberators of 356 Squadron drop Psychological Warfare pamphlets at Pak Nam Phau, above, and at Chiengmai, below.

Liberators of No. 356 (SD) Squadron drop psychological-warfare leaflets in Siam.

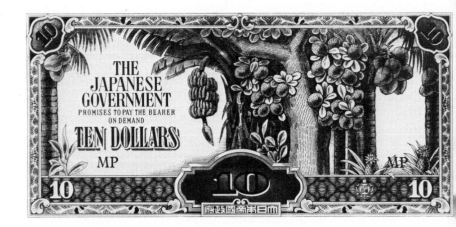

Ten-dollar note issued by the Japanese in Malaya.

Detail from obverse and the imitation issued to SOE agents, in which the forger forgot to include the smoke from the steamer's funnel. Less obvious discrepancies were the quality of the paper used and the colour of the ink.

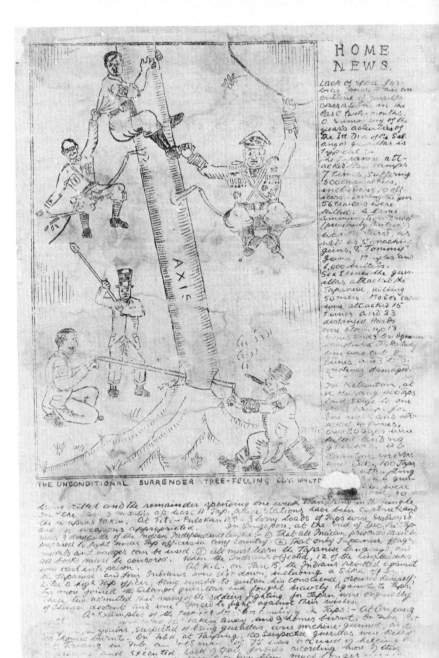

Page from Spencer Chapman's jungle newspaper circulated to guerrillas in Malaya.

paddled to the rendezvous where, after waiting in vain for half an hour, they were attacked by rifle fire and forced to withdraw to the submarine.[12]

The related operation, *Sugarloaf II*, was a reconnaissance of possible airfield sites in Simalur Island, a hundred miles west of Sumatra, by two British airfield experts, Flight Lieutenant Malcolm Bunting and Lieutenant Donald Lowe, who were escorted by an OSS party. The plan was to cross the island after the reconnaissance to the east coast where they would be picked up by the submarine from which they had landed. The supporting party, commanded by First Lieutenant R. Peterson USN, included Photographer H. Martin USNR, Sergeant M. Flaherty, radio operator, and Sergeant E. Eckhardt, Guard. They left Trincomalee on 3 May 1944 in HM Submarine *Truculent* (Lieutenant-Commander R. L. Alexander) and arrived at the disembarkation beach four days later.

The shore party – Bunting, Lowe, Peterson, Martin, Flaherty, and Eckhardt – naked to enable them to start their trek in dry clothes (which they carried in waterproof packs), were instructed to get into the water before they reached the breakers, so that they would act as sheet-anchors. A second precaution was a tow-line connecting the two boats to stop them from turning turtle. However, the men in the leading boat failed to get into the water, and when a huge breaker snapped the tow-line they and their equipment were thrown overboard. Bunting grabbed the equipment bags, which were tied together, and scrambled ashore on the next wave. Eckhardt, a poor swimmer, lost his Mae West and had to be supported by Peterson until the breakers carried them to the beach.

In the second boat Lowe and Martin got into the water as they were supposed to do, but being no longer tethered to the leading boat were at the mercy of the waves. Flaherty, who had refused to get out, was 'thrown end over end and was lost sight of . . .'. The others held on to the lifeline and were carried safely in. Flaherty turned up later, having landed some distance away unhurt but badly shaken. All were so exhausted by their experiences that they forgot to tell the submarine they had arrived safely, which caused much anxiety.[13]

They reached the proposed airfield site on 10 May 1944 and carried out their reconnaissance successfully, having to dodge several parties of villagers. Next day the difficult part of the enterprise began. They had to find a supposed trail across the island and make their way to the rendezvous within seven days. Lowe's diary gives a graphic account of their hardships:

11 May. Again rain in the morning making conditions most miserable. Going still very tough and no sign of trail . . .

12 May. Pete was definitely going slower than rest of party today but would not allow anyone to carry the heavy radio pack (40–50 pounds) which he had been carrying for the last five days . . .

13 May. Decided by now that as there were no signs of trail to make our way across Island as quickly as possible . . . Pete's feet by now an appalling sight, just like lumps of raw meat.

14 May. Set off at 0600 hours and had decided that every member should take the heavy radio pack for one hour at a time . . . Harry's shoes now unserviceable and he had to protect his feet the same way as Flaherty (i.e. wearing socks and bandages).

15 May. Flaherty, wireless operator, had left the handles of the generator behind when packing in the morning . . . Much feeling was expressed by most members of the party and the generator was thrown away.

16 May. Sibabo Bay – a truly glorious sight! About 1600 hours, however, we hit a village and were forced to skirt it. This nearly proved our undoing as we hit a mangrove swamp . . . On and on we toiled under the most stinking appalling conditions and just as light was failing I managed to take a bearing to give us at least some idea of our position. Flaherty had walked in his bare feet most of the day . . . Harry eventually arrived at the beach on his hands and knees, unable to speak . . .

17 May. We did not attempt to move until about 0800 hours and then staggered about another 200 yards along the beach to what we thought was the pick up point. At 1720 hours Mac saw the submarine emerge.

The submarine saw the party's signal, and submerged until nightfall when the six were taken on board and given badly needed first aid.

*Residency* and *Sugarloaf* were purely military, and they achieved their objectives in spite of the loss of three men. The next operations planned by the Anglo-Dutch Country Section, *Retaliate I–III*, illustrate the ease with which the planners conceived ambitious enterprises which there was not the slightest hope of carrying out.

The intention was to make contact with the Chinese in north-eastern Sumatra and to organize sabotage groups. Junks would be captured to carry agents to find places suitable for the reception of later parties. Personnel for training as saboteurs and agents would be brought out. W/T stations would be established to keep in touch with SOE, India. Preparations would be made to attack roads and railways, telecommunications, and aerodromes to assist eventual military operations. Contact would be made with the anti-Japanese movement in Malaya. Military, political, and economic intelligence would be collected. To give *Retaliate I* the best chance of success three parties would be put ashore at widely separated points, and they would be given at least six days to complete their tasks before *Retaliate II* was launched. The Anglo-Dutch Country Section was instructed to prepare detailed plans on these lines.

The final plan was more modest. It aimed to land a party on the east coast, and to capture two Sumatran Chinese. That was all.

Lieutenant W. H. van Eek, another Dutch officer, two Dutch other ranks, and three Chinese left Trincomalee on board HM Submarine *Truculent* on 12 June 1944, having made a false start the day before because of engine trouble. Ten days later they reached the point where they planned to abduct their Chinese, and disembarked three miles out. The outboard motor of their rubber dinghy – it was the first time a powered boat had been used in a clandestine operation in the Far East – stirred up a brilliant phosphorescent trail as they ran the gauntlet of innumerable fishing stakes. Five hundred yards out they met two fishing boats, the crews of which told them that the nearest Chinese were four miles inland but that there was a Malay policeman at the customs post at the mouth of the Padang River. They had no difficulty in surprising this man, who turned out to be Javanese, and having cut the telephone line, they took him back to the submarine.

After two more days on patrol the submarine came across a junk *en route* for Malaya with a crew of four Malays and a Chinese. This enabled them to complete their bag of two – although only one was Chinese – and they abandoned a plan to make a second landing. They told the Malays to take to their dinghy and sank the junk by gunfire. They arrived back at Trincomalee with their captives on 28 June 1944.[14]

Shortly after the return of *Retaliate* the Anglo-Dutch Country Section held an inquest into its performance in Sumatra and had to confess that it had accomplished virtually nothing. Its minor successes were in the field of military intelligence rather than special operations. It was the Dutch who first admitted defeat. They recorded in a lengthy memorandum that the prospects of encouraging resistance in Sumatra were bleak, thanks to highly efficient Japanese security and counter-espionage, and the support they had from Chinese and Indonesian informers in every town and village. The alternative was to mount a psychological-warfare campaign with the message that it was only a matter of time before the Japanese were defeated world-wide, and that the Dutch would deal harshly with collaborators who did not mend their ways forthwith. A stick would be held out to areas with a bad record of collaboration, in the form of aerial and naval bombardment; and a carrot in the form of food and clothing parcels to areas free of Japanese supervision. The card which the British were playing so successfully in Burma and Malaya – alliance with a communist resistance movement within the country – was not mentioned.

This realistic appraisal of the situation did not find favour with the British element in the Anglo-Dutch Country Section. Political warfare was a poor substitute for special operations. 'The possession of a crutch should not be taken as an excuse for never walking without one.' It was argued, in effect, that good money should be thrown after bad. SOE parties should be dropped blind into the interior to gather intelligence about resistance groups there – although there was no evidence that there *were* any. It was even mooted that if the Dutch would not agree to such operations they should be carried out unilaterally by the British, who could use agents from the Malaya Country Section for the purpose. The Dutch were criticized for being 'terrified of using politically-minded Chinese agents', and for having rigorously suppressed the Chinese political movement in Sumatra. In the end, however, it was agreed that the proposed psychological-warfare campaign should go ahead with the objective of turning the population against the Japanese, and thereby facilitating the gathering of intelligence needed in due course for special operations proper. It was also agreed that the India Mission's operational objectives in Sumatra should be limited to bringing out Achinese for training as guerrilla leaders. The British side made this concession grudgingly, for they clung to the belief that a resistance movement might be developed, perhaps through Dutch servicemen still harboured by the Achinese. They again claimed that the Dutch had never properly understood the role of SOE and the importance of setting up a permanent organization within Sumatra.

At the beginning of 1945 Sumatra was the only territory where SOE had no agents on the ground. The Anglo-Dutch Country Section, now headed by Lieutenant-Commander Wingender, who had replaced Pel, feared that the rapid progress of the campaign in the Far East might call for SOE support in Sumatra which they were not ready to provide. In March 1945 an attempt was made to establish the permanent organization advocated by the British. Scheepens and Major Lodge took a party of four Chinese agents to the north-west coast, where they planned to observe traffic on the main road and also to make contact with the local Achinese (Operation *Carriage*). They travelled from Trincomalee in HM Submarine *Clyde* (Lieutenant-Commander R. H. Bull), supported by a ferry party of two Dutch officers and six Dutch NCOs, landing on 1 March 1945. They were almost immediately spotted by the Japanese who opened fire, driving them back to the beach where they were picked up by the ferry party and taken to the submarine, none having been hit.

As it was obviously dangerous to remain in the area, alternative plans were discussed. One, to land at a point 140 miles further north, was ruled out as it would take *Clyde* out of her area and possibly compromise other operations there. It was agreed to try to capture some natives to get information about the coast-watching system which would be useful for future parties. The opportunity seemingly came when the submarine sighted what was taken to be a fishing boat, but turned out to be a tongkang – a small coastal vessel – carrying a cargo of petrol and nutmegs to the Japanese in Padang. Although the nine-man crew was less likely to be familiar with the local arrangements, they were nevertheless taken on board and their vessel sunk by gunfire. Scheepens still wanted to go ashore to find some local people, but the submarine commander pointed out that after the sinking of the tongkang that particular stretch of coast 'would obviously be humming' and decided to return to Trincomalee, after shelling shipping in Meulaboh Bay and government buildings in the town.[15]

It was not until the end of June 1945 that the first permanent party was introduced. Sisselaar dropped into North Central Sumatra with a W/T operator and two agents (one of whom was the Javanese customs officer brought out a year earlier by *Retaliate*) to report on communications, locate dropping-zones for future parties, and enlist the co-operation of the natives (Operation *Tether*). Lieutenant-Commander Lefrandt (Operation *Sweep*) dropped in on 1 July, followed two days later by Major Lodge and three Chinese from HM Submarine *Torbay* (Lieutenant-Commander C. P. Norman) to establish observation posts on the east coast north of Bagan Si Api Api (Operation *Steel*).[16]

It is unlikely that if these parties had been called on to support active military operations in Sumatra they would have enjoyed the success achieved by Force-136 groups in Burma. There was no powerful resistance movement looking for help against the Japanese. Instead SOE would have had to contend with militant nationalism. The war ended before they could accomplish anything; and immediately afterwards there arose 'disturbances, mass meetings, demonstrations, violent anti-Dutch and even anti-European propaganda in newspapers and by posters . . . in all the main centres'. Mountbatten banned Dutch troops from active service, so that the Dutch component in Force-136 parties in Sumatra had to be eliminated. Mackenzie wrote to Helfrich on 12 November 1945 announcing his imminent departure for Britain and expressing regret at this development; but he added that Force 136 itself was being disbanded, to be replaced in Sumatra by a small number of British intelligence parties responsible to Allied Land Forces, South East Asia (ALFSEA). Thus the Anglo-Dutch Country Section, which had had little chance of distinguishing itself in the three years of its existence, came to an unhappy end.

# 6

# China

SOE's progress in China was interrupted by Chiang Kai-Shek's expulsion of the China Commando Group early in 1942.* Killery had earlier been asked by London to step up activity in China, although it was recognized that there was little scope for special operations there because of the vast distances, the suspicious nature of the Chinese, and later, competition from OSS, which had prior rights in an American-dominated theatre. He sent Findlay Andrew, who had spent many years in the country and was a friend of most of the leading personalities, including Chiang Kai-Shek, to Chungking 'to influence Chinese politicians and keep China in the war, and at the same time do whatever was possible to restore damaged British military prestige'. He was later joined by Mr J. A. T. Galvin. For some time Findlay Andrew was under the impression 'that his was a genuine diplomatic appointment', although he was paid by MEW and ostensibly managed that Department's affairs in China.

As the creation of new secret bodies in China was banned, he hit on the idea of sharing in the work of the Institute of International Relations (IIR). This body, run by General Wang Ping-Shen, a particularly close friend, was directly responsible to Chiang Kai-Shek. It gathered intelligence in Japan and Japanese-occupied territories, and put out subversive propaganda. (It had originally engaged in sabotage but Chiang Kai-Shek had transferred this function to General Tai Li.) SOE made a financial contribution (eventually one-third of IIR's budget) and in return shared the fruits of its labours, which gave Britain access to much of the intelligence collected by the Chinese all over Asia. To give Findlay Andrew and Galvin proper standing they were appointed advisers to IIR, in which the British component was code-named the Research and Investment Institute (RII). Although the British pair had no real authority, they could influence policy through their personal contact with Wang, and through their subsidy. Findlay Andrew hoped that IIR might again carry out sabotage, but it would have meant competing with Tai Li;

* See pp. 77–9.

and in any case Chiang Kai-Shek's attitude to the China Commando Group showed that he had no wish for British-sponsored sabotage. He made other conditions. There must be no American participation, for he was anxious to play the British and Americans off against each other.

The alliance with IIR was useful. According to Keswick, who was at this time attached to the Embassy, the funds provided by SOE enabled IIR 'to spread its wings and establish itself widely throughout the East'. He believed that its development, much faster than that of other Chinese services, was due not only to British financial backing, but also to Findlay Andrew's influence. At first there were three operational districts. One included Shanghai, the coastal areas from Ningpo in Chekiang Province south to Swatow, Macao, Tientsin, and Hankow. There were two secret W/T stations in Shanghai through which IIR agents, co-operating with those of Tai Li, provided local intelligence and also acted as a clearing-house for information from Manchuria, Formosa, and Japan itself. The second district covered the five northern provinces of China, overlapping the first, as it also had agents in Manchuria, Formosa, and Japan, many of whom were planted in Japanese puppet military, economic, and political bodies. The third district organization was based in Hong Kong, and included South China, Hainan, the South Seas, with a link to Japan. Each district was managed by a business firm set up to trade in Japanese goods, which facilitated the movement of agents, and each had a director stationed in Free China in W/T contact with a 'special delegate' just inside enemy-controlled territory who was in turn in touch with agents throughout the district. Later Burma, Malaya, and French Indo-China, which were of particular importance to SOE, were brought into the scheme. IIR had an efficient printing department which produced propaganda material to Findlay Andrew's order.

The fact remained, however, that none of this was 'special operations' in the accepted sense. The beneficiaries were those who needed information about the Far East – the British Ambassador, the authorities in Whitehall, the Director of Military Intelligence in India, the Far Eastern Bureau (FEB) of the Ministry of Information (MOI). In 1945 an attempt was made to give the British effort in this field more bite when it was transferred from IIR to the International Intelligence Service (IIS) headed by General Cheng Kai-Min, the Chinese Director of Military Intelligence. This was an organization designed to undertake sabotage operations in Japanese-occupied North China, based on the town of Sian, in addition to the reconnaissance and intelligence functions of IIR. Groups of demolition experts would be supported by special assault troops, the commander under Cheng being a British officer. A formal agreement was drawn up through which SOE undertook to provide W/T sets, technical advice on communications, and British signals officers. They would also train Chinese W/T operators, and set up W/T stations to link Chungking with Sian. Had this scheme (which reflects the change of heart on the part of some leading Chinese, including Cheng Kai-Min, which encouraged them to try to reduce their dependence on the Americans and rely more on the British) gone ahead it would have enabled SOE for the first time to carry out extensive sabotage behind the Japanese lines; but the war ended before IIS could go into action.

Apart from the gathering of intelligence through IIR and the dissemination of some anti-Japanese propaganda SOE accomplished little in China before 1944. In Chungking Findlay Andrew, in addition to advising the Ambassador (first Sir Alexander Clark Kerr, and then Sir Horace Seymour), recruited Chinese agents for India Mission operations in Siam, Burma, and Malaya. Towards the end of 1943 the Chinese authorized an SOE office, ostensibly the office of the Assistant Military Attaché, in Kunming, run by Lieutenant-Colonel P. H. Munro Faure, with the title of Military Liaison Officer. It was intended to be a base for sending agents into the Lashio-Bhamo-Mandalay area of Burma, for training guerrillas for operations there, and for helping the Ruler (Myosa) of Kokang who was threatened by Chinese bandit forces (Operation *Spiers*). There was also 'the China Coast Section' based on Kweilin, whose duties were to be to recruit Chinese agents for the Malaya Country Section, and to carry out future special operations on the South China Coast in the vicinity of Hong Kong. These would include the reception of parties from SOA. The China Coast Section used as its cover BAAG, the body set up to rescue Allied prisoners of war, but it had little chance to do anything before Kweilin fell to the Japanese late in 1944, and it was reformed as 'Group C' of the India Mission with headquarters in Kunming. Group C was quite separate from Findlay Andrew's office in Chungking, and reported direct to India. It was also separate from *Remorse*, although it was recognized that the two might be able to help each other.

The India Mission's tendency to 'think big' without any real justification is nowhere better illustrated than in China. A 1943 paper claimed that it was a scandal that the Japanese were allowed to exploit Shanghai and Hong Kong unmolested, except for a few air raids. Hong Kong's well-equipped dockyards were functioning without interruption and a large volume of shipping from Japan, North China, and Formosa was passing through the port, which was an assembly point for convoys. As political considerations made it impossible to operate on the China Coast overland from Free China, an approach should be made from the sea. To avoid interference by Chungking and the provincial Governments, agents should be landed in occupied China. Possible targets were shipping, shipbuilding and repair facilities in Hong Kong; the arsenal at Canton; the naval base at Hainan; coal and shipping at Haiphong; the industrial areas of Shanghai; and coastal shipping. As the main targets would be shipping, the Chungking authorities could hardly object.

This programme would be carried out with the help of a group of Chinese communists who controlled a considerable part of the New Territories, and were said to be effectively resisting the Japanese. They managed one of the main smuggling routes to Free China but were short of weapons and would welcome outside help. They had no connection with Chungking, and 'had substantial prices on their heads'. American Chinese whose loyalty was unquestioned should be recruited in Honolulu or California and after training brought by submarine to join forces with the communists. Groups of three – one American Chinese and two locals – would carry out simultaneous attacks with limpet mines on shipping in Hong Kong. The power supply to the shipyards would be cut off, the dock labourers' tenements destroyed by fire, and the Kowloon water pipeline cut. In a second phase European leaders would go in – men drawn from oil companies and commercial firms with good local knowledge. If the plan succeeded the Chinese Government could be persuaded to take an active part in operations in the area.

That this was a pipe-dream was proved by the India Mission's two main attempts to accomplish something in South China: an operation to cripple the dockyards in Hong Kong (*Nonchalant*); and a second – *Oblivion* – to land Canadian Chinese on the South China Coast.

*Nonchalant* was mooted in October 1943 with the aim of removing Chinese dock labourers from Hong Kong in order to deny their services to the Japanese who badly needed them for shipbuilding and ship repairing, and to make them available for Allied shipyards. A formal offer of employment by the British Government was made by BAAG agents to selected labourers. They would have free travel to their place of employment, originally intended to be in Eritrea, free medical attention, free board and lodging, and the rate for the job. Their families would have a generous maintenance allowance if they accompanied them, and at the end of the war all would be repatriated at the British Government's expense. The men had to make their way to Waichow in Free China – sixty miles from Hong Kong – where SOE would arrange their onward transport.

The scheme ran into trouble before it was launched. In February 1944 it was decided that extra labour was no longer needed at Massawa. SOE feared that this would be seen as yet another let down by the British; but as yet no one had been approached. The BAAG agent in Macao who had been assigned the job of recruitment had great difficulty in getting to Hong Kong – because of the vigilance of the Japanese the round trip could take as long as six weeks. Nevertheless, in spite of the fact that there was no work for the men the scheme was allowed to go ahead, and by October 1944 fifty-two had reached Waichow. BAAG were reluctant to arrange their onward movement as there were already 1,000 Hong Kong dockyard workers in the town agitating for work, and it seemed wrong to give priority to late-comers. Meantime, desperate efforts were being made to find alternative employment – perhaps the official recruits could now be sent to Manila, or parachuted into Siam to sabotage the wooden ships now being built in Bangkok. (It was later pointed out that the place where they would be most useful immediately after the defeat of the Japanese would be Hong Kong.)

All these efforts were wasted. At first the ever-suspicious Chinese refused to allow the recruits to leave Waichow without specific authority from Chungking – although SOE had earlier asked that *Nonchalant* parties should be allowed to travel to Ceylon 'on important war work'. Twelve of them found employment locally, but the balance of forty continued to rely on BAAG who thought they had a moral obligation to support them. Before their onward travel was approved the Japanese advance isolated Waichow and there was no possibility of bringing them out even with the blessing of the Chinese. At last, in March 1945, SOE decided to cut their losses and end a scheme that had cost several million dollars. The men were given three months' wages and told that their agreement with the British Government was ended. They could have argued reasonably that the changed military situation was no fault of theirs, but however just that claim there was no hope it would be entertained.

Even if *Nonchalant* had gone ahead it would have accomplished nothing. One thousand dock workers had found their way to Free China without any help from SOE; and the removal of a further fifty-two out of the total dockyard labour force of 11,000 was unlikely to damage the Japanese war effort seriously.

*Oblivion*, like *Nonchalant*, had its seeds in the ambitious plan of 1943. It was one of four separate schemes for the South China Coast put forward in 1944, of which three would have involved a total of twelve British officers, twenty-one British other ranks, and sixty-nine Chinese agents and W/T operators. One was to arm and train two battalions of what was described as 'the Hong Kong anti-Japanese force', for attacks on Japanese lines of communication; the second to use the same force for sabotage in Hong Kong and the New Territories; and the third to arm and man six Chinese junks to direct aerial attacks on ocean-going vessels, and to capture or sink Japanese shipping.

The fourth scheme – to infiltrate a group of Canadian Chinese into mainland China, where they would join forces with the communists to start special operations in the neighbourhood of Hong Kong – was proceeded with. (It was rightly surmised that the Americans would not allow their nationals to join forces with the communists, especially in what might become an enterprise to recover a British colony.) Major F. W. Kendall, the Canadian who had formed Z Force in Hong Kong in 1939, was put in charge. When he discussed the plan in Washington the Americans opposed it on political grounds; but the Canadian military authorities, the Royal Canadian Mounted Police, and the British Columbia police gave him enthusiastic support. A training camp was found for the Canadian Chinese in a secluded part of the Okanagan Valley, and given special protection. Kendall undertook not to remove any grizzly bears they might encounter; and a marginal note added to the file in London asks, 'Have the grizzlies made a similar undertaking?'

It was at first difficult to find the ideal recruits – patriotic Canadians who still had some interest in their country of origin. In British Columbia, where Kendall had hoped to assemble his team, second-generation Chinese were still discriminated against in certain ways.

Many were therefore embittered about their Canadian citizenship and disinclined to volunteer for dangerous activities on behalf of Canada or the British Empire. 'Another factor which we were dismayed to come across was a very distinct apathy towards the whole war in the west of Canada.' These difficulties were overcome by drawing on Chinese already in the Canadian Army, who proved very satisfactory. Their training went so well that in August 1944 it was proposed to expand the scheme and set up a number of permanent India Mission posts along the South China Coast.

It was recognized, however, that there might be problems. BAAG had given the Chinese an undertaking that they would not become involved with communists; but *Oblivion*'s objective was to raise communist guerrillas and the Chinese would not believe that BAAG was not also involved. (Some argued that if a choice had to be made between the two organizations SOE would now give better value.) Furthermore, the *Oblivion* Chinese were Cantonese who could operate only within a narrow radius of Hong Kong. It was finally agreed that as a first step one or two British officers would establish themselves on the China Coast with the fourteen members of the *Oblivion* party, to make contact with the local anti-Japanese element, and report on the prospects of organizing resistance when the Allies eventually attacked Hong Kong. With this in mind, the four W/T operators in the group went to Meerut for final training, and the rest went to Australia.

The plan envisaged a landing at Mirs Bay or Bias Bay. Major R. (later Sir Ronald) Holmes (also formerly of Z Force) and Sergeant Vincent Young would lead all fourteen Chinese; and they would be followed by two further landings at intervals of three months. They would carry out industrial and shipping sabotage in the Hong Kong and Canton area; provide photographs of landing places and suggest possible Fifth Column activities; carry out coast watching; and help the communists to develop anti-Japanese propaganda. Their stores, including a great deal of specialized equipment, were packed and ready by the middle of December 1944. All that was needed was a submarine and the order to start.

The American opposition, however, which had been feared all along now became a decisive factor. General Wedemeyer, the recently appointed China-theatre commander, made it clear that all clandestine operations in China were subject to his approval. So far as *Oblivion* was concerned he said it would be an appalling waste to land a party on the China Coast from a submarine based in Australia. SOE had no doubt that his decision was influenced by political considerations, which was confirmed when a number of variations on *Oblivion* were rejected by Wedemeyer on the ground that they involved contact with the communist party. In fact, that objection did not apply to one of them: Operation *Resurrection* was a plan to reassemble as many as possible of the original Z Force and smuggle them back to Hong Kong to the cave they had occupied in 1941. Immediately before the Allies invaded Hong Kong the *Resurrection* party would attack the defences which the Japanese had built on and around Taimoshan Mountain, especially the guns which commanded Hong Kong and the surrounding area in a 360-degree traverse – a sensible scheme which had nothing to do with politics, and which might have had great importance.

The Canadian Chinese recruited for *Oblivion* proved so successful in training that 150 more were chosen and sent to SEAC to act as interpreters for the Malaya Country Section. They arrived in India in April and May 1945, and some of them were dropped into Malaya where they gave a good account of themselves.

SOE's only active operation in China (with the exception of *Nonchalant*) came through their association with BAAG. They paved the way for it when they seconded some officers to BAAG to help them in their escape work in 1942, and provided them with a W/T network. A proposal in 1943 that BAAG should be disbanded on the ground that the number of escaped prisoners was drying up was defeated partly because of the value of the intelligence it was supplying to the 14th USAAF, and partly because SOE would lose cover for their operations. There was no hope that the Chinese would allow Force 136 to start from scratch. As SOE activities would be carried out in the name of BAAG it was left to their commandant, Lieutenant-Colonel L. (later Sir Lindsay) Ride, to veto any which looked like cutting across his own plans or jeopardizing his organization.

Although offensive operations had been contemplated when this arrangement had been made, the rapid advance of the Japanese at the end of 1944 forced SOE on to the defensive. In September 1944 when Ride and General Sir Adrian Carton de Wiart, Churchill's special envoy to Chiang Kai-Shek, visited the Kweilin front, they suggested that British and American groups should be asked to put obstacles in the path of the advancing Japanese. The Americans were unenthusiastic, in spite of the fact that the 14th USAAF wanted to delay the capture of Kweilin airfield; but a British party including SOE officers on loan to BAAG went to help the Chinese army. They found that the Chinese were systematically destroying all railway bridges, but were leaving the highway intact. Therefore the British party, including Majors E. B. Teesdale, Cowie, and Salinger concentrated on road bridges. They also destroyed a large water-tower which the Chinese had failed to deal with, stocks of timber, and five roadside villages which would have provided cover for Japanese vehicles. They mined a 200-foot reinforced-concrete bridge and instructed Chinese engineers how to fire the charges, which they did successfully two weeks later. Teesdale admitted that none of the demolitions would present a serious obstacle to determined troops, but he nevertheless believed they helped the 93rd Chinese Army to make a stand twenty-five miles from Kweilin, compelling the Japanese to abandon their planned frontal attack on the town along the main road, and to make slower progress in an outflanking movement through the hills.

The success of the SOE party (to which an OSS officer had been attached) encouraged the Americans to co-operate. At the request of the Chinese, SOE and OSS prepared to carry out further demolitions on the roads approaching Kweilin. Teesdale and his colleagues mined three large timber- and stone-pier bridges using 100-pound bombs from the airfield at Kweilin, and employing coolies from nearby villages for the excavation work. The OSS team, operating on the Lipuhsien road, the destruction of which would finally cut communication with the unoccupied provinces of Eastern China, were given a last-minute order by the Chinese military commander to hold their hands. Unfortunately they ignored it, with disastrous consequences. The Chinese were regrouping their forces and this road was essential for the movement of troops, and ammunition which was being flown in to the only remaining airstrip at Kweilin. Marshal Chang Fa-Kwei ordered that all the explosives already laid should be removed, to avoid further interference with his plans, but Teesdale prevailed on him to leave the charges in position, so long as there were guards to ensure that they were not prematurely detonated. According to him Chang was very friendly and 'went out of his way to express gratitude for our assistance, even to the extent of making embarrassingly pointed distinctions between ourselves and the Americans'.

At the end of October the situation deteriorated at an alarming rate, and although the SOE team stressed the importance of further demolitions outside Kweilin the Chinese refused to allow them until it was too late. Teesdale's party withdrew to Kunming having made a smaller contribution than they would have liked.

Scorched earth was no more popular in China than it had been in Malaya in 1941. When Captain P. Dendy came specially from India to carry out demolitions at the Ping Kwei mining complex in Kwangsi Province, where there were tin- and coal-mines in the path of the advancing Japanese forces, a telegram from the Provincial Government forbade demolition. They instructed that the lighter equipment should be removed to a place of safety and the heavier put out of action by removing key parts. When Dendy said he did not take orders from the Provincial Government, but proposed to carry out a thorough demolition job, he was told that there were 100 Chinese soldiers at the mines and that any attempt to approach the plant would be resisted by as much force as was necessary.

In spite of earlier rebuffs SOE continued to hope that they might achieve a major success in China; and towards the end of 1944 a new attempt was made to get approval for Force-136 operations. Lieutenant-Colonel D. G. Gill Davies, in charge of the China Coast Section, and later of Group C, was convinced that SOE could repeat in the Far East the success they had enjoyed in Europe. He envisaged a Sino-British Resistance Group – 30,000 guerrillas to be raised in Kwangsi and Kwangtung Provinces who would be commanded by British officers, and eventually play a major part in the recapture of Hong Kong.

There was much to be said for the plan. It was desirable that Hong Kong, being a British possession, should be liberated by the British, albeit using Chinese guerrillas in the first assault. There would have to be an all-British follow-up, however, either airborne, sea-borne, or both – otherwise Chiang Kai-Shek might claim that the Colony, wrested by the Japanese from the British Empire, had been reconquered by the Chinese. But there was a great deal to be said against. Although when Carton de Wiart had informally mentioned to Chiang Kai-Shek the plan to raise guerrillas, the latter had seemed favourably disposed, it was unlikely that his support would be forthcoming when he realized what the ultimate objective was. Moreover, it was no part of United States policy to help to restore the British position in the Far East. Whatever the military advantages, Wedemeyer, who also had been told about the scheme in very general terms, would either obstruct it, or order the guerrillas to operate away from the Hong Kong area. Alternatively he might approve the plan and implement it through OSS.

When these considerations were put to Mountbatten by his Chief of Staff (Lieutenant-General F. A. M. Browning) with his own opinion that the scheme was impracticable, he decided to ask COS in London whether they intended that a British force should recapture Hong Kong. If they did, a full-scale operation should be planned, possibly employing troops based in Australia, and making use of Force 136 for clandestine operations before and during the assault.

In spite of the powerful objections to the Sino-British Resistance Group SOE persisted in backing it; but suggested that before the plan went ahead the British clandestine services in China should be amalgamated. This was debated at six meetings of the Joint Intelligence Committee in London where the SOE representative argued the Force-136 case in vain. The Group, like the China Commando Group and the IIS demolition squads in North-West China, was fated never to get beyond the planning stage.[1]

Even if it had had the whole-hearted approval of COS it seems certain that Wedemeyer would have vetoed it. He made it abundantly clear soon after his appointment that he was appalled by the lack of co-ordination between the Chinese, American, and British clandestine organizations; and he made no secret of the fact that he would remove any body which in his opinion was not essential to the Allied war effort in China. At a meeting of the American and British clandestine chiefs, when he behaved like an ill-mannered head-master addressing a group of wayward schoolboys, he said that all clandestine operations would be co-ordinated through General Cheng Kai-Min and himself. 'I ask you not to let any of your subordinates pull fast ones. I hold you responsible ... If your activities or any personnel in your activities are being used for unauthorized purposes they will be expelled from the theatre.' He sensed that the meeting (which George Taylor reported as being quite cordial) was disconcerted by his attack, for he found it necessary to assure the company that he was not an ogre.

It is clear he was giving notice that the elements in his theatre whom he saw as interlopers from Mountbatten's Command, working for British interests rather than those of the China theatre, had had their day. Further, a dispute between him and Mountbatten about their respective rights to carry out clandestine operations in Indo-China, in the course of which he implied that Mountbatten was a liar and both went out of their way to be difficult in a remarkable exchange of telegrams worthy of Fourth Form schoolboys, did not help SOE's cause. Even if there had been no American political objection to Force-136 operations in China, SOE had now no hope of accomplishing anything there.[2] Wedemeyer agreed that their existing activities, which amounted to virtually nothing, should continue. Anything new must be submitted to him and Cheng Kai-Min, and would be approved if the resources of China Command allowed, and there was no internal political complication. That was quite enough to keep Force 136 inactive for the rest of the war in China.

# 7

# Burma

THERE are two Burmas: 'Burma proper', the vast central area of paddy-lands and evergreen forest drained by the Irrawaddy and Sittang Rivers, people in 1941 by thirteen million Burmese, a million Indians, and a handful of Chinese; and the surrounding mountain ranges forming a giant horseshoe – the Arakan Yomas, the Chin and Naga Hills on the Indian border, inhabited by 50,000 Chins, the Kachin range on the Chinese border with 150,000 tribesmen, the Shan Plateau, with a million of Siamese origin, and finally the Karen Hills on the border of Siam with half a million of Siamese/Chinese descent.*

Geographical separation was mirrored by political division. Many Burmese looked forward to the end of British rule dating from the arrival of the East India Company in 1824; but the hill tribesmen, who enjoyed British protection against the dominant Burmese, feared they would suffer under independence. It was the hill communities that were most likely to co-operate with the British in resisting the Japanese.

At the time of World War II, communications were limited. The Irrawaddy, flowing into the Bay of Bengal near Rangoon, was navigable to Bhamo, 900 miles north. A metre-gauge railway with feeder lines ran from Rangoon to Mandalay and on to Myitkyina. The main all-weather road connected Rangoon and Mandalay through the valley of the Sittang River; and there was a good road system in the Shan Plateau. Movement on foot was easy during the dry season, but in the monsoon – May to October – travel off the all-weather roads was difficult and unpleasant.

The survivors of OM and others who had helped to raise the Burma levies arrived in India throughout 1942, worn out by the extreme hardships of the journey.† It was not until early 1943 that they were fit enough to start training for their eventual return. In July 1942

---

* There were another half million Karens scattered over the Irrawaddy Delta area.
† Lieutenant-Colonel Peter Lindsay never fully recovered from the strain of the journey and was invalided out of the India Mission.

Major R. E. Forrester became head of the India Mission Burma
Country Section.* He planned an operation in which eight parties
would carry out sabotage in support of an Allied offensive; but when
it became obvious that there was no hope of an early offensive the
plan was abandoned. The Burma Country Section could do no more
than explore areas where SOE might operate when the Allies *did*
return; and they launched a series of operations for the purpose.

One was aimed at the Indian community in Rangoon. Sunil Datta
Gupta, a member of the Indian Communist Party, parachuted into
the Tharrawaddy district in June 1943 (*Mahout*) to create unrest
among Indian dockers and railway workers, but was not heard of
again until Rangoon fell in 1945. He got a job in the railway sheds
where he carried out minor sabotage before being arrested in
September 1944. Over a period of many months he was subjected to
every known torture, which he claimed was a rare distinction,
reserved only for the most stubborn interrogatees. The one torture
omitted from his catalogue – cigarette burns – was added by a friend
who corroborated his statement. In October 1943 two more Indians
failed to link up with Gupta. One, who got in touch with British troops
near Mandalay in March 1945, said that he himself had been
arrested and that his companion had died. There were no more
attempts to approach the Indian community, partly because of lack
of suitable agents and partly because strikes and sabotage would
have little effect until they were combined with a major offensive.

SOE planned to cultivate the Kachins north and south of the Upper
Irrawaddy Valley, whose morale was low after the British withdrawal. A Kachin officer (Captain Kumje Taung) and four Kachin
other ranks were dropped in March 1943 to establish an 'underground railway' on the European pattern so that stores and agents
could be sent in (*Dilwyn I*). But it took another Kachin (Major Shan
Lone) four months to cover the 180 miles between Allied territory
and *Dilwyn's* terminus in the jungle, and the underground railway
idea was abandoned. Nevertheless, *Dilwyn* sent out useful information about Japanese movements, and raised the morale of the
neighbouring tribesmen. It also helped wounded and stragglers from
the first Wingate expedition to make their way to Assam and China.[1]

When the India Mission accidentally discovered in March 1943
that Wingate proposed to send a glider-borne expedition to the

---

* He was succeeded by Lieutenant-Colonel Ritchie Gardiner in July 1943.

Kachin Hills (*Dahforce*) to create a diversion in support of his second expedition, Mackenzie was understandably annoyed. It would be better to use the India Mission party already on the ground, whose security might be jeopardized if an independent force operated in their area. Brigadier Guinness who had stumbled on the *Dahforce* plan had 'a stormy $1\frac{1}{2}$ hours' with Wingate, who 'disliked and suspected' SOE. As a compromise it was agreed that *Dilwyn* should receive *Dahforce*. They would send the crack signal 'Plain sailing' if it was safe for the glider-borne troops to lands. If not, the signal would be 'Stormy weather'.

A few hours before *Dahforce* was due to leave Major L. V. Lovett-Campbell of SOE, who had joined *Dilwyn* on 5 March 1944, signalled 'Plain sailing' and proceeded to the reception point. Wingate, however, had assumed that the crack signal would be confirmed immediately before his troops emplaned, and when no further message came assumed that SOE had let him down. Lieutenant-Colonel D. C. Herring, in command of *Dahforce*, wanted to send in one glider to find out what the situation was, but the flight commander would allow only a mass landing. Herring discussed the problem with Wingate by telephone.

The conversation will long live in my memory. The line was bad and we were only able to talk to each other with difficulty. Finally, my new orders, which were given to me couched in Biblical terms,* were received and understood. *Dahforce* deplaned from the gliders, hastily threw aside several thousand pounds of arms, ammunition, and explosives, disposed of 5 or 6 wireless sets, and emplaned into 3 DC aircraft.

Wingate insisted that *Dahforce* should land 100 miles south of *Dilwyn* who waited three days for their arrival 'in a somewhat understandable bad humour'. Eventually the SOE party united with *Dahforce* and greatly helped in the recruitment of levies.

There was little hope of stimulating resistance among the Shan tribes in the north-east whose easygoing nature encouraged them to accept the Japanese. In any case, the comparatively open Shan country did not lend itself to guerrilla operations. Nevertheless, a base was established on the Burma/China border to renew contact with some Shan leaders more warlike than their fellows.

The Burma Country Section tried to get in touch with the Chinese

---

* We can only speculate as to chapter and verse.

community through agents from China. Eighteen – the Pandas, who were supposed to know Burma and Burmese, although several did not – took the usual training courses, which only seven passed. One was dropped without W/T to collect intelligence in Mandalay and return overland through China; but no more was heard of him until 1945 when what little information he had gathered was hopelessly out of date. The Pandas proved so unsatisfactory that all were sent back to China, except one or two who were trained as W/T operators.

The warlike Karens were well placed to attack the road and railway from Rangoon to Mandalay, and the main road north from Toungoo, the importance of which had been demonstrated during the British retreat. They had hidden the arms then issued and could muster 2,000 rifles. The steep, broken nature of their country and heavy jungle made it an ideal centre for guerrilla operations. Moreover, it was possible that Lieutenant-Colonel Seagrim, who had remained behind after helping to organize the Burma levies, had developed a resistance movement in the Karen Hills.

In February 1943 Operation *Harlington* was planned to make contact with the Karens. A Karen officer, Lieutenant Ba Gyaw and three other ranks landed in a small area of paddy-fields east of Shwegyin. Their W/T set was supposed to follow immediately, but between March and September no fewer than nine attempts to drop it failed – seven due to bad weather, one through engine trouble, and one when the dropping-zone was not identified. It was finally decided to send it in with Major J. R. Nimmo on 12 October 1943. Within two days he was in touch with Ba Gyaw who had joined up with Seagrim, and confirmed that the Karens were eagerly awaiting the return of the British.

On 9 December 1943 Captain F. C. McCrindle parachuted in to join *Harlington*. Ten days later they reported that the enemy had sent a force of 300 to track them down. In January the Japanese were still hard on their heels, and Nimmo was caught. McCrindle suffered the same fate. The Japanese Military Police (Kempei Tai) now arrested and tortured hundreds of Karens because of their support for the British agents; and in an effort to help them Seagrim gave himself up in March 1944. Ba Gyaw was captured. They and several members of their party were imprisoned in Rangoon and in September Seagrim, Ba Gyaw, and five others were executed. The rest of the group were sentenced to eight years' imprisonment.[2]

The last of these exploratory operations was *Flimwell*, to encourage the Karens in the Irrawaddy Delta 'to dislocate the social and economic order established by the Japanese' – a tall order. *Flimwell* got nowhere. The Karen officer and W/T operator who went in first were picked up when they landed – the former on the roof of a house. There was no follow-up as it was decided that the Delta Karens were too widely scattered. Plans to contact them were not revived until early 1945.

While these attempts to get in touch with a resistance movement were in progress, one of the 'Burma for the Burmese' groups within the country was trying to enlist Allied support. This was the communist 'Thakin' ('Master') Party led by Thakin Soe. For some years before the war they had fought colonial rule and continued to work against the Allies until the Russians entered the war, when they decided that to co-operate with the Allies against the Japanese might smooth the path to post-war independence. A second group planned to achieve independence by a different route – co-operation with the occupying power. Thakin Aung San, General Secretary of 'Our Burma League' (*Dobama Asi Ayon*), had fled the country in 1940 to avoid arrest on a charge of sedition, and in 1941 he took twenty-nine fellow nationalists to Japan to receive military training. These men returned to Burma after occupation to join the Burma Independence Army (BIA) founded by the Japanese and commanded by Aung San.* Although he believed that co-operation with the Japanese gave the best hope of ending the colonial rule, he accepted from the beginning that if the Japanese proved unreliable he should look to the Allies as Thakin Soe was doing. In June 1942, the Japanese, rightly suspecting that BIA was too interested in politics, ordered it to cease all political activity, and to re-form as the Burma Defence Army (BDA), which was renamed the Burma National Army (BNA) on 1 August 1943 when the country was formally given independence by Japan. A group of young officers had to be dissuaded from organizing armed resistance to the Japanese in the middle of 1944; and shortly afterwards the various anti-Japanese movements came together to found the Anti-Fascist Organization (AFO), with BNA – which did not openly oppose the Japanese until 1945.

* He was rewarded with the Order of the Rising Sun, Third Class, with Middle Cords (WO 203 4464, no. 69A).

The India Mission was, of course, badly informed about the complex political situation in Burma and its implications for resistance; and when in July 1942 two young members of the Thakin Soe group, Thein Pe (*Merlin*, to use his SOE code-name) and Tin Shwei (*Lancelot*), came to India professing hostility to the Japanese they were greeted with suspicion. It was eventually accepted, however, that they were genuinely anti-Japanese, if not pro-British. In December 1943 Tin Shwei returned by motor launch with an official message to the anti-Japanese elements. He was brought out in February 1944, accompanied by Nyo Tun, head of the Thakin Party in Arakan (*Galahad*) and a wife acquired during his tour as SOE agent (*Guinevere*).* They carried papers of great value which made it clear that a genuine resistance movement did exist. The part that Aung San might play was not considered at this stage – as C-in-C of BDA established by the Japanese he seemed an improbable ally, although a message from Seagrim had suggested that the time might come when Aung San would be fighting on the Allied side. This idea was confirmed by captured members of BDA who said their officers had told them the time was coming when they would have to turn against the Japanese.

Nyo Tun volunteered to return to Arakan to pretend collaboration with the Japanese; and was escorted through the British lines in April 1944 accompanied by a W/T operator and two specially released Burmese political prisoners. Nothing was heard of his mission (code-name *Billet*) until he returned by the same route in June. His companions had been captured and he had been on the run for two months. He had managed, however, to arrange for five members of the resistance to come to India for training, and he had asked Thakin Soe to send another thirty. (Eventually over seventy men were sent to India for training.) As the Japanese now knew that Nyo Tun was working for the Allies a rumour was spread that he had been drowned, which was believed by the enemy.

The five men found by Nyo Tun reached the British lines at the end of July. One, Tun Kyaw, held a key post under the Japanese Chief of Intelligence in Arakan. As he was supposed to be on leave for only a few weeks, he was given a quick course in India and sent back overland with instructions to locate dropping-zones, arrange further receptions, and send out military intelligence. An aircraft sent to drop

---

* It is not clear if the choice of name was an attempt to deceive the Japanese, or due to imperfect knowledge of the Arthurian legend.

a W/T set to him failed to spot his ground signal, which consisted of candles in cigarette tins totally invisible from the air. Yet another attempt to establish W/T contact with Burma had failed.

Overland contacts were building up evidence of a resistance movement and it even seemed possible that it might turn on the occupying forces without help from outside. The India Mission redoubled its efforts to get in touch so that it might direct the movement into the most profitable channels. Aung Myint, one of the five who had come to India, carried a microfilmed message to Thakin Soe asking how strong the movement was and what arms it needed. Another agent, Ba Thein, parachuted to Rangoon with a copy of the message, hoping to pass information from the resistance to two agents who followed him with a W/T set; but their parachutes failed to open and both were killed. In a second attempt to give him a W/T set *Donkey*, a Burmese, dropped in during the November moon period. Since Ba Thein had no experience of reception the pilot was briefed to drop *Donkey* on any likely formation of lights, which he did, but unhappily they had not been lit by Ba Thein. However, *Donkey* persuaded the villagers among whom he landed to give him sanctuary, and within two days was in touch with the India Mission. At last, after many vicissitudes, there was a W/T link with Burma.

In June 1944 Lieutenant-General W. J. (later Sir William) Slim, GOC-in-C, Fourteenth Army, complained that he was not getting enough intelligence. The armed patrols of 'Z' Force, which gathered intelligence up to sixty miles into enemy territory,* had done a good job but must be expanded. Force 136 had furnished useful information, but nothing about Japanese lines of communication. The enemy had moved large formations over great distances in total secrecy. For example, 151 Regiment had moved from Central Burma to the Bishenpur front without being identified until it joined battle with his forward troops.[3] His criticism may seem harsh, since intelligence was not an SOE function, but it led SEAC's P Division to examine the secret organizations in July 1944.† It was found that

---

* Z Force (GSI(z)) also had certain security functions within India.

† The organizations, apart from Force 136 and Z Force, were: ISLD, the SEAC name for the Secret Intelligence Service (SIS); the Combined Operations Pilotage Parties (COPP), commandos engaged in marine sabotage; Air Sea Rescue; Psychological Warfare Division (PWD); Deception Division (D. Div.); E Group (the prisoner-of-war escape organization); the Burma Intelligence Corps (BIC), which provided guides and

there was overlapping of function, and confusion – but not enough to be dangerous. Although amalgamation would increase efficiency the consequential political and organizational difficulties would far outweigh the military advantages. (This sounds like the administrator's case for doing nothing.)[4]

Slim remained critical. In September 1944 he sent Mountbatten a signal inveighing against the deplorable state of the clandestine forces, and claiming there was no intelligence coverage in Burma at all. One remedy was to put SOE parties in the field under formation commanders, which Force 136 had strenuously resisted on the ground that they must be controlled by SEAC headquarters. Although they agreed to this in principle in May 1944, it was not until November that Colin Mackenzie recorded that for the first time units of Force 136 were 'properly co-ordinated with military operations'. SOE had liaison officers with the Fourteenth Army, XV Corps, and Northern Combat Area Command (NCAC).[5] Slim continued to maintain that SOE showed an inadequate return for its manpower, whereas OSS was giving excellent service in NCAC. He recommended that Force 136 should cease to operate in Burma and be replaced by OSS. He summoned Lieutenant-Colonel Cumming, the Group A Operations Officer, to defend SOE.[6] Cumming ventured to observe that the General was not in full possession of the facts. Much of the intelligence supplied to NCAC came in the first place from Force-136 patrols. Further, it was easier to come by reliable information among the friendly Kachins where OSS operated than among the Burmese in the areas in which the Fourteenth Army was interested. Slim grudgingly accepted this but continued to press for centralized control by the army of all special forces on his front.[7]

On 4 January 1945 Browning and Major-General G. P. Walsh (Chief of General Staff, ALFSEA) met to resolve the problem. Browning admitted that unified control would be ideal, but given the multiplicity of organizations, co-ordination by P Division was good enough. Walsh repeated Slim's proposal that OSS should take over, and suggested alternatively that Force 136 and Z Force should

---

interpreters for forward patrols; V Force, which operated fighting patrols and collected intelligence deep in enemy territory; and finally the American OSS with SOE and SIS functions, and Office of War Information (OWI) corresponding to the British Political Warfare Executive (PWE). There were thus twelve secret organizations in all.

amalgamate. On behalf of P Division, Garnons-Williams agreed to the amalgamation, subject to a questionnaire to the Fourteenth Army and XV Corps.[8]

This asked if Force 136 had any value as a sabotage organization, and in raising guerrillas. Should it be used to collect intelligence, amalgamated with Z Force, or disbanded? Slim replied that it might play a minor part in sabotage under Fourteenth Army direction, although major targets were best destroyed by air. There *might* be scope for raising guerrillas, especially in the Karen Hills; but unless Force 136 accepted a primary intelligence function it should be disbanded. The XV Corps reply was much the same. Force 136 had provided intelligence leading to successful air strikes; and it had had some success in raising guerrillas in Arakan. However, there were strong arguments against keeping it in West Burma where the lines of communication were so poor that there was little scope for sabotage. Force 136 should be combined with Z Force with intelligence as their primary function; and the new formation must come under military command.[9]

In the light of these replies it was decided to combine the forces and use them on long-range intelligence, with sabotage and guerrilla work as secondary roles; but for reasons which are far from clear in the papers the decision was not implemented. Z Force was military, Force 136 quasi-military. Their administration and method of accounting were different. These impediments, which seem hardly insurmountable, were enough to continue Force 136 as a separate organization. No doubt Slim would have preferred the merger to go ahead, and that the new formation should be under his command for all purposes; but his wishes were met to the extent that it was firmly established that SOE's primary function was intelligence; and that in the battle area, at least, it would come under the direct control of the Fourteenth Army and XV Corps rather than SEAC.[10]

Some SOE parties deprecated the priority thus given to intelligence gathering which ruled out action against the enemy until the army gave the word. *Bison*, operating between Mandalay and Kyaukme, early in 1945 were given five tasks: to establish communication with base; report traffic on roads and railways; report possible bombing targets; harass enemy convoys, and save key installations from destruction by the Japanese – the two last only on orders from the army, which were never given. The leader accepted that the intelligence function was important, although it meant that their training for special operations was wasted. He was convinced that without prejudice to the supply of intelligence they could have done a great deal of damage with grenade necklaces, which a single man could have detonated, with 'beehive' explosives buried in the bank at a bend in the road, and by simply tossing grenades into personnel lorries, which never had hoods and travelled slowly going up the hills. He appreciated that intelligence parties should not do this sort of thing, but thought it would do no harm if carried out 'well away from our front door step'.

The defeat of the Japanese at Kohima and Imphal in Assam in May and June 1944, when they made their last desperate attempt to break through to India, was the beginning of the end of their occupation of Burma. It was now planned that the British forces in Arakan should capture Akyab; that those on the central front should fight their way back cross the Chindwin River; and that the American/Chinese forces in NCAC should recover the Northern Shan States and regain command of the Burma Road. By the end of March 1945 all these objectives had been attained. The Fourteenth Army crossed the Chindwin River, at the cost of 50,000 casualties, in the middle of December 1944. XV Corps occupied Akyab at the beginning of January 1945. The American/Chinese forces reached Kyaukme at the end of March to bring the Burma Road once again under Allied control, and provide overland communication between Mandalay and China.

The last operations were helped by Force 136 in the old *Dilwyn* area where they had retained a W/T station after the withdrawal of *Dahforce*. They raised levies through six additional parties (*Badger*, *Cheetah*, *Monkey*, *Gazelle*, *Squirrel*, and *Bear*) which operated with success against both the Japanese and so-called Chinese guerrillas who were no more than robber bands engaged in systematic looting. They supplied useful intelligence to the 10th USAAF, the only air force operating in the area; and they also carried out specific tasks for the American forces. Thus, when the latter asked for details of the Lashio defences a group from *Badger* (Kachins who had dropped blind in November 1944 between the Burma Road and the Salween River) entered this closely guarded strong point and gathered information about the whole defensive layout. *Monkey* rescued forty-two prisoners of war. A member of *Gazelle* penetrated the Japanese 56th Division headquarters to find information wanted by the Americans.

In spite of their contribution and the fact that Force 136 had been in unbroken contact with the Kachins for a long time, Lieutenant-General J. W. Stilwell, Commanding General in the China–Burma–India theatre, used all his influence to have them removed from the Kachin Hills. He argued that the United States would not interfere in operations in a predominantly British area simply because they happened to have some units there; and in any case he believed that OSS would do better if they were allowed to work on their own. Nevertheless, he said he would bow to SAC's decision 'if he insists that the British party should remain and continue to operate in the Bhamo area'. On 21 September 1944 Mountbatten sent him a personal telegram reminding him that SOE had at their disposal a body of Kachin officers and men whom he wanted to operate under Stilwell's command along with OSS; but after further friction Force 136 withdrew – an unfortunate move in the eyes of one Kachin officer (Captain Zau June). He concluded a report on his own operations in the area by saying that although Force 136 had recruited 3,000 Kachins who 'were just on tip toe to take up arms on signal word "Go", then, however, the Americans came in and stepped into our shoes'. This was unfortunate because they did not have the interests of the Kachins at heart, they indulged in 'forceful conscriptions', which was a crime, and all the chiefs and elders 'prayed and cried' that Force 136 should remain as the true representative of the British Government. Whatever the merits of the case, the field was left to OSS.

After the Allied successes in December 1944–March 1945 the way was clear for the Fourteenth Army, which reached Meiktila, ninety miles south of Mandalay, in early March, to drive down the Sittang and Irrawaddy Valleys to Rangoon and capture the capital before the monsoon broke. The distance to be covered was 350 miles, which, since the rains usually came between 10 and 20 May, implied a much faster rate of advance than anything achieved so far. The monsoon would halt forward movement and give the enemy time to re-form, so that a delay of even a few days could be fatal. The Fourteenth Army would be left with a line of communication vulnerable in the dry season, and impossible to maintain during the monsoon.

Toungoo, on the Sittang River roughly half-way between Meiktila and Rangoon, was of crucial importance since the only road by which the Japanese could reinforce from the north passed through it. The value of this road had been established in 1942 when the enemy used it as a base to strike into the Shan States, which hastened the success of their campaign. The danger now was that they would reverse that operation and build up a substantial force at Toungoo to slow the progress of the Fourteenth Army. It was equally possible that the Japanese forces west of the town would attack from the Pegu Yomas.

The Fourteenth Army specified exactly what they wanted from Force 136. They must be ready in January 1945 to supply intelligence about enemy road and rail movements in the Sittang Valley between Mandalay and Toungoo. Next month they must establish teams in the Pegu Yomas Range to watch the Sittang Valley between Rangoon and Prome, and the two main roads leading east across the Karen Hills to Loilem and Bawlake. In March they must cover the road from Taunggyi in the Southern Shan States to Bawlake, which might become an important enemy escape route – or the route through which they would bring reinforcements. Force 136 was to confine itself to the provision of intelligence and avoid clashes with the enemy; and it was also to explore the possibility of raising Karens.[11]

To understand the importance of Force 136's role it is necessary to visualize the geography of Lower Burma, where the final route of the Japanese was planned. The Irrawaddy and Sittang Rivers run parallel in the centre of the country, north to south, separated by the Pegu Yomas mountain range, and entering the Indian Ocean on either side of Rangoon. The Irrawaddy is flanked to the west by the Arakan Yomas Range, and the Sittang to the east by the Karen Hills. It was down these valleys that the Fourteenth Army proposed to drive the Japanese forces; but since the mountains precluded outflanking movements on any great scale, the enemy would have every opportunity of making an orderly withdrawal, and re-forming troops which still had a lot of fight in them at a point of his own choosing. Force 136 was to make that orderly withdrawal impossible. They would, as it were, be stationed in secret butts in the hills, waiting for the beaters to drive the game into their line of fire. Indeed, this seems to have been the India Mission's own conception, for the formal record of Japanese casualties inflicted by Force 136 is entitled the 'Game Book'.

The operations mounted by Force 136 to help the Fourteenth Army to achieve its objectives, as it fought its way from Shwebo to Rangoon, were *Elephant*, *Nation*, and *Character*; but before these had got properly under way the Force had played a significant part in XV

Corps' advance in Arakan to Akyab, through Operation *Manual*.

The main objective of *Manual* was to provide intelligence for XV Corps, which authorized the India Mission to drop two two-man Burmese parties in Arakan. *Hound* dropped blind and provided a reception committee for *Lion*. They quickly established W/T communication with headquarters, although their signals required judicious interpretation. *Hound*'s first read: 'Dropping obvious money provided to keep their tongues'; while *Lion*'s Chinese operator reported: 'We and stuffs arrived here safe. All we drop on trees. Now hide jungle ready move at night.' In passing on the latter message an India Mission wit endorsed it: 'Your pidgin!' *Hound*'s W/T operator, a six-foot stalwart from the distant Chin Hills, was also endowed with a sense of humour. When told by headquarters how to deal with hostile villagers he signalled briefly: 'Natives friendly'.

Both *Hound* and *Lion* reported Japanese positions which enabled the RAF to carry out successful bombing raids, but it was felt that a more professional intelligence service was needed. On 27 December 1944 a Jedburgh team* (*Camel*) dropped to *Hound* with two W/T sets. The British members – Major T. A. Carew, Captain J. H. Cox, and Sergeant Sharpe – had been a mere three weeks in India, with only ten days' jungle training. The Burmese Nyo Tun attached to them took umbrage when he was not put in command; but was consoled with the honorary title of Head of the Military Mission to the Anti-Fascist Organization, Arakan. A team of eight Arakanese dropped along with *Camel* to spread rumours and divert attention from the area where Carew would operate. In the first week he moved forty miles south without finding the support Nyo Tun had promised, and on 1 January 1945 signalled the India Mission that it was pointless to carry on. Next day, however, he reported a concentration of 800 Japanese troops which the RAF attacked with devastating results. This advertisement of British power brought in scores of recruits.

At this time the political implications of seeking help from AFO and BNA had not been formally considered by the British authorities. SEAC were aware that the immediate military benefit might be outweighed by long-term problems created for the Civil Affairs Service (Burma) (CAS(B)) when it took over the administration of the country, and for the Government of Burma when it returned from exile; but it believed that to accept their offers of help was the lesser of two evils. The alternative might be to fight large numbers of Burmese in addition to the Japanese. SOE, aware that they were in the wrong

---

* Usually two officers with a W/T operator.

by so doing, deliberately kept CAS(B) in the dark about their plans for closer association with the resistance.

In January 1945 CAS(B) officers advancing in Arakan with the British troops began to arrest *Camel*'s guerrillas. Carew made his way to the front line to protest, to find that CAS(B) suspected that he was somehow improperly in league with Nyo Tun, who was high on their black list. After lengthy discussion in which the Commander of XV Corps, Lieutenant-General A. F. P. (later Sir Philip) Christison, took part, Carew was authorized to tell his Arakanese that so long as they behaved themselves and handed back their arms at the end of hostilities they would not be charged with crimes against the state. *Camel* was overrun by the advancing troops on 22 January 1945, having carried out admirable intelligence work and killed nearly 100 of the enemy. The group's 200 guerrillas from the AFO, the first to work under British direction, were paid off in cash or with the gift of a longyi (sarong).

XV Corps also asked SOE to mount an intelligence operation south-east of *Camel*'s area, covering a road running east into Central Burma which wound through hilly country and was difficult to reconnoitre from the air. *Mouse* (Major Kemball, Major Blaythewayte, and three Arakanese) failed to spot a reception prepared by *Camel* and had to drop blind. They were pursued by the Japanese for the whole of the three months they were in the field, but managed to keep XV Corps fully briefed about traffic on the road, which led to twenty air strikes, some highly successful. Although intelligence was their main task, *Mouse* also recruited 120 guerrillas who accounted for more than fifty Japanese killed.

*Camel* brought into the open the question SOE had deliberately ignored – whether or not to welcome the co-operation of AFO and BNA and to arm their members? In spite of the support XV Corps had had in Arakan it now criticized the India Mission for recruiting these men. Some were wanted on serious charges, including murder. The killing of Japanese stragglers was not a sufficient reason for their employment, which would store up trouble for the future when 'dacoits armed with modern weapons and plenty of ammunition would conceivably tie down a considerable military force, and if Burma is used as a line of communication, future operations against the Japanese might be seriously impeded'. Although this verdict came from XV Corps it probably originated in complaints from CAS(B) after their brush with *Camel*.[12]

Mackenzie had foreseen this problem in November 1944 when he replied to a request from Thein Pe for the wholesale issue of arms to the resistance movement. He promised, without consulting London, that SOE would provide enough arms, ammunition, and financial aid to guarantee success; and in reporting this to London he said he hoped they would back him up. He also said he was seeking the support of the military and the Government of Burma so that if the CAS(B) attempted to interfere with his plans they would be overruled. He claimed that experience in Arakan showed that weapons would be returned at the end of hostilities. If arms were denied to the Burmese of the plains (i.e. AFO and BNA) when they had been freely issued to the hill tribes, it would sow the seeds of post-war grievance.* Further, if AFO and BNA were snubbed, the Anti-Japanese Union and Forces (AJUF), the corresponding organizations in Malaya, would lose faith in Force 136.[13] Dening sent a copy of Mackenzie's paper to the Foreign Office with the comment that Force 136 might be making a case 'because they are afraid HMG will interfere with their operations'. A minute on the Foreign Office file agrees, but adds 'it seems to be a case which is not lacking in merit'.[14] Mackenzie's was a bold decision. 'It is indeed remarkable that official assurances which contained such far-reaching implications for the future should have been made without consulting the Chief Civil Affairs Officer, and apparently without the approval of the Supreme Allied Commander.'[15] Mackenzie had no doubt that it was right to arm the Burmese resistance, and he was equally certain that if the matter were discussed CAS(B) would fight tooth and nail against the proposal.

He was quite right, for when CAS(B) were consulted (in February 1945) they said AFO and BNA were communist terrorists and that the price of their co-operation would be the right to take part in the government of Burma after the war. Lieutenant-General Sir Oliver Leese, C-in-C, ALFSEA, accepted CAS(B)'s advice and on 15 February banned the issue of arms to AFO. Mackenzie's second in command, Brigadier J. (later Sir John) Anstey, pointed out that rejection of AFO offers of help might induce them to make last-minute bargains with the Japanese, and indulge in a period of lawlessness and looting,

* This argument suggests that Mackenzie was well aware of the importance for post-war Burma of holding the balance between the Burmese and the hill tribes, and weakens the claim made by some that Force 136 inspired the hill people's post-war demands for autonomy.

thereby jeopardizing the safety of Force-136 parties already in the field. He submitted that the India Mission should seriously consider suspending the dispatch of further parties. 'This, however, is a defeatist policy, and I recommend that we continue to press for powers to enlist the aid of the AFO on the score alone of providing protection for our parties which are sent into the field to obtain intelligence for the army.' Mackenzie agreed and appealed to the Supreme Commander, who instructed Leese to countermand his order. Nevertheless the embargo continued, which put Force 136 in an impossible position. Men in the field could not tell if a guerrilla was a member of AFO and therefore not entitled to arms. Mackenzie told Mountbatten that he must cancel all future missions – which meant that Force 136 would no longer be able to satisfy the army's intelligence requirements, now SOE's primary function.[16]

Mountbatten could not ignore this powerful card. Although Leese had not carried out a direct order, he took a gentle line with him. Arming AFO was a political decision reserved to himself. 'I should be obliged therefore if you would issue immediate instruction to Force 136 to proceed with their planned operations . . .'.[17]

This took care of the question of arming the Burmese resistance, and represented a victory by Force 136 over CAS(B); but a new conflict arose when the latter learned that the Burma Country Section proposed to get in direct touch with Aung San. This truth was strenuously denied by SOE and Mackenzie ordered the Burma Country Section to tighten their security 'to prevent any leakage in future' to CAS(B), 'which must be considered hostile'. SEAC's hand was forced towards the end of March, when it seemed possible that BNA would move against the Japanese with or without Allied help. Aung San had just been given a rousing send-off in Rangoon as he left to fight 'the enemy' – unspecified, but presumed by all except the Japanese to be the Japanese. Slim welcomed the prospective rising, and Mountbatten told COS on 27 March that it would be a bonus, although not an essential part of his plan. He was sending SOE Liaison Officers to tell the BNA leaders that their help would be appreciated, and that good service would count in their favour if they had to stand trial for past offences. He added defensively that in supporting any rising Britain would be doing no more than she had done in Italy, where a former enemy had become a co-belligerent.*[18]

_____

* A curious note on the SACSEA file says, 'If he felt all this he should have signalled home a month ago.'

Eden did not like this. He minuted the Prime Minister: 'The tone of this telegram is reminiscent of too much we have had from SOE in the past. Surely we should not boost these people so much. They will give great trouble hereafter.' Churchill replied: 'I cordially agree with you. General Ismay should convey these opinions to the Chiefs of Staff Committee.' However, the War Cabinet's India Committee had already given their qualified approval to Mountbatten's proposals. AFO and BNA must be told that Britain attached no great importance to their contribution; and they must be forcibly reminded – more forcibly than the Supreme Commander seemed to contemplate – that they had a lot of leeway to make up as ex-collaborators. 'In fact they have to work their passage home.' PWD must advertise that Burma was being liberated by the Allies, *not* BNA. COS for their part approved Mountbatten's proposals so long as they did not call for additional air support.[19] However, the rising had begun even before Mountbatten referred the matter to COS – a fact which considerably irritated him when he became aware of it. From 24 March onwards members of BNA were defecting in increasing numbers, and by the end of the month virtually the whole force had abandoned the Japanese cause. It was not until 30 March that Mountbatten received the War Cabinet instructions about the line he was to take.

At least the War Cabinet decision made it easier to approve a request by Slim that Aung San should be brought to his headquarters for discussions about the co-ordination of their operations, although at first Mountbatten would not agree to the meeting. He told Slim to reflect on the implications – there was a danger that the Burmese would regard such a meeting as evidence of Britain's wish to forgive and forget. Eventually, on 20 April 1945, Mountbatten gave the go-ahead, provided it was made crystal clear to Aung San that only military matters were to be discussed, and that he might still have to answer for his crimes;[20] but before the meeting could take place British forces had made such progress that the operational contribution which BNA could make had greatly diminished.

This fact was seized on by CAS(B) whose defeat by Force 136 still rankled. Major-General C. F. B. Pearce, Chief Civil Affairs Officer (Burma) (CCAO(B)), who had earlier complained that his advice to the Supreme Commander about politics in Burma was impaired because Force 136 refused to reveal their plans to him, now took the initiative. He demanded that since it was admitted that Aung San had outlived his usefulness he should be treated as a war criminal.

Leese was in a quandary because Aung San was *en route* for Slim's headquarters. He asked for urgent guidance, and was told by Mountbatten that on no account was the Burmese to be arrested. He must be treated as a friendly guerrilla commander, thanked for his help, warned that he might have to stand trial in due course, and promised that future co-operation would count in his favour. He should be asked to place himself unreservedly under the orders of the Allied Command and to issue orders in writing to his subordinates to do likewise.[21]

Air Marshal Sir Philip Joubert, Deputy Chief of Staff, Information and Civil Affairs (DICA), complained to Mountbatten about his decision not to arrest Aung San, on the ground that if the Supreme Commander showed excessive clemency towards BNA those elements hostile to the British would cause even more trouble. He added, in rather lordly fashion, that he proposed to consult the Governor of Burma with a view to reopening the whole matter.[22] Mountbatten reacted swiftly. No useful purpose would be served by Joubert's approaching the Governor of Burma. 'Moreover, since you apparently do not support my oft-declared policy, I do not wish you to discuss the matter with him.'[23]

It is difficult to imagine the consequences if Civil Affairs had had their way. A key reason for working with BNA was that it reduced the incentive on their part to end colonial rule by stabbing the British in the back, as they had just stabbed the Japanese. If Aung San, protected by a safe conduct, had been arrested, his troops must have turned against the British, with disastrous results. At the beginning of June Lieutenant-General Sir Montagu Stopford, in command of XXXIII Corps, estimated that had this happened the Allies would have had to find two additional divisions, at the expense of the force earmarked for the invasion of Malaya; and the clearance of Burma would have been delayed for months.[24]

Although the Fourteenth Army now had little to gain, Slim's meeting with Aung San went ahead. '. . . On 15th May the British forces in Allanmyo observed a boat crossing the Irrawaddy towards them. It flew a red flag with white stars and contained Aung San and some of his staff.'[25] The party was flown to Fourteenth Army headquarters at Meiktila, and at their meeting next day Aung San gave Slim details of BNA's dispositions. Slim accepted his offer of help, undertook to employ the organized units of BNA operating against the Japanese, and to provide them with rations, on the understanding that they would take their orders from the local British commander. Most of the discussion, however, was devoted to the future organization of the Burmese forces, and to disabusing Aung San of his belief that he was an Allied commander representing the Provisional Government of Burma headed by Thakin Soe. Slim made it clear that he and his army had no legal status; and sent him back to Rangoon to pass this on the AFO Supreme Council and prepare the way for further meetings with the Allied High Command.[26]

Of the Force-136 operations mounted to help the advance of the Fourteenth Army – *Elephant*, *Nation*, and *Character* – the first was the least important. In the middle of December 1944 when the Fourteenth Army was closing in on Shwebo they badly needed intelligence from the neighbourhood of the town. *Elephant* was intended to meet this need, to make contact with the AFO leaders in Upper Burma, and to organize guerrilla bands. It was led by Tin Shwei (*Lancelot*) with another Burmese and two Chinese W/T operators. The last, survivors of the group from China (the Pandas) who failed to qualify as agents, refused to leave until they had talked with one of the Chinese representatives in India, it was presumed to receive secret instructions from Chungking. The party was dropped successfully but instead of getting on with the job Tin Shwei made the long trip to Rangoon to agree a line of action with the AFO leaders. Thus both Chinese and Burmese members of *Elephant* were seeking guidance from their own people as much as from SOE.

The Burma Country Section was naturally displeased with *Elephant*'s failure to carry out instructions, and when Tin Shwei was chased by the Japanese all the way from Rangoon to Mandalay they observed with satisfaction, 'if he was half the headache to the Japs that he was to us, then he achieved something!'. Although they were not supposed to go into action, on 8 March 1945 *Elephant* organized a group to take on the Japanese in the suburbs of Mandalay, killing a few soldiers and BNA's Japanese advisers; but they were forced to disperse immediately. For the next ten days they had minor encounters with the enemy, killing some and suffering casualties themselves. Although *Elephant* made no attempt to provide intelligence, their brush with the Japanese – the first open revolt of BNA – persuaded Fourteenth Army commanders that the Burmese resistance could make a useful contribution by operating on their flanks and carrying out specific acts of sabotage behind enemy lines.

*Nation* and *Character* were on a vastly greater scale – by far the most important of Force 136's operations in Burma. *Nation*, organized by Jedburghs, was intended to work with AFO and BNA in the Pegu Yomas Range between the Irrawaddy and Sittang Valleys. It was founded on *Donkey*'s drop in the neighbourhood of Pegu at the end of 1944.* Three weeks after he landed *Donkey* began to send useful reports about Japanese dispositions; and on Christmas Day a member of AFO, Ba Han, who had been brought to India for training, was sent in to put him in touch with reliable AFO supporters who would hide him. Ba Han also arranged a courier service between *Donkey* and AFO headquarters in Rangoon, and distributed midget radios and duplicators to resistance leaders for propaganda purposes.

On 19 January 1945 Force 136 received through *Donkey* their first message from Thakin Than Tun, Minister of Agriculture in the Ba Maw puppet Government, and acting head of AFO in the absence of Thakin Soe, who had been driven underground. His request for a large quantity of weapons was refused on the ground that there was as yet no one to control their issue, supposed to be limited to one hundred per British officer in the field; and he was asked where SOE parties could best be received. The answer was throughout Lower Burma, where he promised to provide reception committees. The Burma Country Section, recollecting Nyo Tun's resentment at having to play second fiddle to a British officer in Arakan, feared that Than Tun and other AFO leaders might be equally difficult. They therefore sent Tun Kyaw (who had taken part in Operation *Manual* in Arakan) to explain how that very successful campaign had been organized, that its success was due to collaboration between the guerrillas and the regular forces, and that a small well-controlled operation was much to be preferred to an uncontrollable rising of the masses. Tun Kyaw was also to persuade Than Tun to sever his connection with the puppet Government and move to a secret hide-out near Toungoo. In spite of this public-relations exercise the Minister did prove difficult, perhaps because he was aware that BNA was about to defect and wanted to give them as much time as possible before Force 136 arrived in great numbers to steal their thunder.

On 18 March 1945 Than Tun moved to the chosen hide-out in the

* See p. 169.

Pegu Yomas west of Pyu (having begged that the RAF should refrain from bombing the route he was to take. The first British party to reach him, the Jedburgh *Weasel* (Major Carew, Captain Brown, and Sergeant Sharpe, who had taken part in *Manual*), arrived at his headquarters on 21 March – from a dropping-zone twenty miles away – and were coldly received. The Burmese said he had the situation well in hand, and implied that British help was unnecessary. 'He had read the 10-odd pages of the guerrilla warfare propaganda pamphlet and imagined he knew the subject from A to Z . . . His plans seemed very phoney and consisted mainly in attacking police stations.' When he was told that the guerrillas would be armed only if they took their orders from Carew 'he became huffy' and it took four days to get him to see reason. He refused to allow *Weasel* freedom of movement, which made their task of receiving further parties and stores much more difficult. 'Many was the abortive sortie which left Jessore only to return later with its full load on board, having found no reception.'

Meantime Force-136 W/T teams were arriving in the *Nation* area. *Terrier* was dropped near Toungoo on 27 January 1945, and made contact with the India Mission next day. Another team, *Elk* (which later became *Yak*), dropped blind into the Tharrawaddy district. They landed ten miles off target, in bright moonlight in the middle of a village festival, and had to abandon their W/T equipment and make a run for it. They reached Rangoon safely, however, where they received new W/T sets in the next moon period. Later they moved to Pyapon. Other W/T stations were established at Allanmyo, at Thaton near Moulmein, and at Tavoy in the Tenasserim peninsula.

It had been intended that the Jedburgh operations should be controlled by *Weasel* from Than Tun's headquarters, but Carew was too fully occupied coping with the Burmese leader to have time to direct the others – and in any case it was probably better to leave them with complete freedom of action. The most successful was *Reindeer*, led by Major D. J. C. Britton, in the area due west of Toungoo. Britton got on with the job of raising and training AFO guerrillas, who proved to be so enthusiastic that he had to restrain them from going into action prematurely. By 12 April he had 300 men under arms and an intelligence network covering a radius of twenty miles.

At this time the Japanese were moving troops by rail north through the Sittang Valley to Toungoo, and they had to detrain during the day through lack of air support. This gave Britton the chance to call in highly successful air strikes. As the Fourteenth Army advanced he was asked to intensify his efforts, and between 19 and 27 April – when they were overrun by the army – *Reindeer* made a remarkable contribution, directing the RAF to ammunition dumps and motor-transport concentrations, cutting the railway in several places, sinking river boats, and capturing or destroying stores – all in addition to carrying out innumerable attacks on enemy troops. Britton, whose brilliant leadership was largely responsible for the success of his guerrillas, was asked by the army to co-operate with them in mopping up Japanese troops who had escaped to the hills.

*Pig* (leader Major Cox) dropped on 30 March and reached *Weasel* two days later, where they remained a fortnight arguing with Than Tun about their next move. Eventually they left for Pyu by bullock cart overnight and ran into a platoon of the rebel Indian National Army, four of whom they killed before making their get-away. Captain Brown was captured, but later managed to escape. *Pig* had only a few days in the field before being overrun.

*Chimp*, led by Major R. A. Rubinstein, who like several of the other Jedburgh leaders had earlier served with SOE in Europe, was dropped on 10 April near Pyinmana where the army badly wanted intelligence about Japanese dispositions. He had no difficulty in raising 200 guerrillas through the local AFO leader. They operated successfully until they were overrun on 19 April, when they moved south of Toungoo to link up with *Reindeer* – whose leader was killed in action the day they arrived. Here the combined teams provided a first-class intelligence screen until the Japanese surrender.

*Zebra* (Major Hood) and *Jackal* (Major Harrington) dropped on 1 April, but like *Pig* they were frustrated by Than Tun 'at this juncture at his most difficult'. After ten days it was agreed that they should move west to Tharrawaddy away from the *Nation* area, which entailed a journey of ninety-five miles across the Pegu Yomas, completed in seven days – a remarkable feat. *Zebra* took over an area near Tanbingon, while *Jackal* moved thirty miles south of Tharrawaddy town. They started operations at the end of April and by the end of May had killed 800 of the enemy.

The other *Nation* Jedburghs were *Giraffe* (Major McAdam) and *Cow* (Major McCoull), which were dropped in the Thaton area north of Moulmein – one of the main escape routes for the Japanese forces – at the request of the Fourteenth Army. They were received by the

Burmese W/T station *Rabbit*, which had done an excellent intelligence job. By the end of April the enemy were in full retreat through Thaton, bound for Moulmein. *Giraffe* and *Cow* established observation posts on all their escape routes to the south and carried out many successful ambushes; but by the middle of May when it became clear that the Fourteenth Army were not going to follow the Japanese across the Salween River, the enemy re-formed in the *Giraffe/Cow* area and made determined attempts to liquidate them. They were cut off in relatively open country between the Salween River and the Coast, and eventually had to make their escape to *Mongoose* (Major A. A. E. Trofimov), the most southerly of the *Character* operations.

When plans were made to support Fourteenth Army operations Force 136 ignored the Irrawaddy Delta areas, as it was assumed that their help would not be required there; but when it looked as if the Army might not get to Rangoon in time, Operation *Dracula*, the secondary airborne and sea-borne assault on Rangoon, suddenly became more important. The Jedburgh *Panda* was therefore dropped to a reception by the Burmese W/T station *Yak*, 'whose ideas of reception lights were possibly over-secure, in that they consisted of six candles in holes in the ground put out at 2 yard intervals'. By a miracle *Panda* saw them and were in touch with the India Mission on 4 April, the day after they landed. There was no jungle in which to hide and *Panda*, primarily concerned with intelligence for *Dracula*, had to keep on the move. The Japanese heard of their arrival and succeeded in capturing their AFO W/T operator, but he managed to escape thanks to an RAF air strike on the Japanese holding him. To increase the volume of intelligence a second Jedburgh, *Dog* (leader Major Clowes), was dropped on 24 April. *Panda* and *Dog* reported that there were very few Japanese in the neighbourhood, with the implication that *Dracula* was hardly necessary. Nevertheless both sea-borne and airborne operations went ahead, although they proved to be little more than training exercises.

According to the Game Book* *Nation* accounted for 3,381 Japanese killed, 201 wounded, and 156 prisoners. Allied losses were thirteen killed and fifty-two wounded.†

*Nation*'s contacts were mainly with AFO, whose rank and file came in for universal praise, unlike members of BNA in the same areas.

* See p. 174.
† The records vary. Another gives 4,250 Japanese killed, 440 wounded, and 250 prisoners, with Allied losses as thirty-six killed and fifty-two wounded.

*Reindeer's* AFO guerrillas were 'simple village folk with no particular knowledge of politics' whose loyalty to their immediate leaders was unquestioned. Harrington, leader of *Jackal*, said AFO were prepared to listen to advice and obey orders. 'The BNA imagined they were soldiers and as such waffled about "positional warfare" and yearned for pitched battles and glory . . . they always thought they knew better and could not be relied on to do what they said they would.' Rubinstein of *Chimp* found the 'vigour and enthusiasm' of his AFO levies totally lacking in the members of BNA whom he met, who would do nothing unless they knew it had been approved by Aung San or his staff. Another verdict was that AFO 'were responsible people who wished to get their country going again, and were willing to cooperate with the British, provided they got their independence in a few years'.

Operation *Character* was *Nation's* counterpart in Karenni. It had the same objectives: to keep the Fourteenth Army informed about Japanese dispositions and, when called on, to harass the retreating enemy. From the Karen Hills the road and railway running south from Pyinmana to Pegu could be kept under surveillance. Another line of communication, for both Japanese reinforcement and retreat, was the road from Toungoo in the Sittang Valley through the Karen Hills to Bawlake and Loikaw, and on to the border with Siam. In a meeting at his headquarters on 5 March 1945 Slim said that Force 136's main contribution, apart from the provision of intelligence, would be to prevent the Japanese from moving forces south from North and Central Burma, and to oppose reinforcements coming up from Moulmein into the Sittang Valley, or the Rangoon area. For the purposes of *Character* the region was divided into three zones: north, central, and south. In these zones guerrillas were to be raised by Special Groups* reinforced by Jedburghs.

At first three Special Groups were assigned to Karenni: *Walrus*, led by Lieutenant-Colonel Tulloch, in the north; *Otter* (Lieutenant-Colonel Peacock) in the centre; and *Hyena* (Major Turrall) in the south. Later the southern zone was divided into two, the more southerly half being allocated to *Mongoose* (Lieutenant-Colonel

---

* There was misgiving in the SOE Council in London about using these Special Groups on the ground that their task was not genuine special operations; but Gubbins argued that they were the best means of capitalizing on the contacts which Force 136 had made earlier in the Karen Hills.

Critchley). The original plan was that the Special Groups should operate under a single command in the field (as had been intended for the *Nation* Jedburghs), but this was abandoned when it became obvious that difficulty of communication made centralized control virtually impossible. Indeed, the Special Group commanders found it a problem to keep in touch with their subordinate parties. Between them they had twenty-six W/T stations but it was often necessary to use runners to keep in contact. There was so much dissatisfaction with the signalling arrangements that some units were forced to improvise in the matter of codes – a serious breach of security.

The India Mission believed that the Karens would welcome the return of the British, although there was some fear that the reprisals when the Japanese were hunting for Seagrim might still affect morale.* At first the hillmen showed reluctance to co-operate, but as more British parties arrived, followed by large quantities of arms, the mood changed, and there were more volunteers than could be armed. The enemy failed to realize the magnitude of the operation or its tactical significance. Although there were minor skirmishes near the dropping-zones the fact that the Special Groups lay low while they recruited guerrillas meant that, unknown to the Japanese, a force of nearly 7,000 levies had been armed by the middle of April.

It is impossible to follow all the operations of the four Special Groups and their numerous sub-parties; but the performance of *Walrus*, the most northerly Group, is typical of the rest. Their first wave – two majors, a second lieutenant, three sergeants, and fourteen Burma Sappers and Miners – under Tulloch, took off from Jessore on 24 March 1945. They found their chosen dropping-zone easily, but saw that it had been cleared by burning and was covered with dangerous stumps. Tulloch selected an alternative eight miles south of Loikaw which also proved dangerous because the party dropped from only 400 feet. As a result one Burmese was killed on landing, Major Lewes of the Burma Rifles broke a foot, and most of the others suffered minor injuries, which affected morale. They hastily hid parachutes and stores in the nearby jungle and set off for the foothills, taking with them only a week's rations.

Next day a small patrol captured a villager to get information about Japanese forces in the neighbourhood. He led them to a cave deeper in the hills and told them where they could find guides. Several

* See p. 166.

minor headmen came forward with offers of help, and on 26 March a local chief promised to raise 1,000 men. Tulloch signalled to headquarters for arms, which were brought in two days later by *Walrus*'s second wave – three majors, three captains, and two sergeants. He now had 100 armed men for immediate protection, and quickly formed an intelligence ring. On 2 April, when 400 had been armed, they had their first encounter with the Japanese, killing thirty out of a party of forty and driving the survivors into the garrison at Loikaw. By 13 April the Group had 2,000 under arms and was ready to start operations on a large scale.

This was good timing, for on 13 April *Walrus* (and *Otter*) were warned that the Japanese were trying to send their 15th Division south to reinforce Toungoo before the Fourteenth Army could get there – the move which Slim had anticipated. The British forces were nearing Pyinmana, and the race for Toungoo looked like being a dead heat. Five days later Tulloch was ordered to concentrate all his forces on the Loikaw–Bawlake road to harass the enemy as they moved through the Karen Hills. He moved all his parties down to the road and for the next two months they attacked it unceasingly. There were regular demolitions, hardly a day passed without an ambush, and Japanese casualties mounted steadily. *Otter*, *Walrus*'s neighbour to the south, was equally active, carrying out ambushes and blowing up bridges in the path of the 15th Division. Their combined efforts held up the Japanese for a week, allowing the Fourteenth Army to establish itself in Toungoo and block the exit from the hills. But for the contribution of the guerrillas a considerable part of the Japanese forces would have confronted the advance guard of the Fourteenth Army, and possibly held it up long enough to put at risk the whole operation to recover Rangoon.

The Japanese now abandoned the attempt to break out at Toungoo and cut the Fourteenth Army line of communication, and concentrated on building up their forces in the hills in the Mawchi/Kemapyu area. This meant that the Special Groups were victims of their own success in bottling up the enemy, especially after the capture of Rangoon on 3 May 1945 'when the Army appeared to rest on its laurels and the Japs were quick to seize on this respite and reorganize and re-equip their battered forces'. This had an effect all over the *Character* area. The Japanese still had 50,000 troops in the Karen Hills and now took counter-measures, moving in well-organized convoys protected by tanks and armoured vehicles which it was virtually impossible to ambush successfully. For the whole of the time until the Japanese surrender the guerrillas had to withstand regular attacks timed to coincide with major enemy troop movements. *Walrus* was forced to surrender control of the important Bawlake–Mawchi road. *Otter* was limited to minor hit-and-run attacks. 'All parties were on the defensive against a hungry enemy adopting a policy of looting and burning villages and killing the inhabitants.' *Mongoose* in the south was driven into the hills after a series of attacks on its headquarters near the Karen village of Papun. *Hyena* maintained thirty-three ambush parties on the main track from Kemapyu to Papun for a time but after a series of bitter engagements were forced to go to ground.

To make matters worse *Character*'s survival was threatened through shortage of aircraft. It was estimated on 13 May that another four weeks were needed to clear the whole area, but the Fourteenth Army could not release aircraft to support the many thousands of levies now in the field. SEAC pointed out, however, that *Character* had been mounted at Slim's request, and the Fourteenth Army agreed that the levies were doing a good job. The supplies they needed would be sent in until the monsoon broke, at the expense of the Army's general programme. In the event *Character* had to be maintained for another three months, during which the shortage of British officers and other ranks became more of a threat than the shortage of supplies.[27]

The Special Groups now began to suffer from exhaustion and sickness due to the appalling climatic conditions. On 21 July Stopford, in command of XXXIII Corps, told SEAC that he feared that *Character* would die out through inability to make good losses due to casualties and over-strain. The operation was still paying off, having in the preceding month inflicted more casualties on the enemy than did the regular forces.[28]

*Character*'s last important action came at the end of July in the *Mongoose* area when the remnants of the 28th Japanese Army re-formed and made a determined attempt to cross the Sittang River from the west and break through to Moulmein. *Mongoose* had a party of 750 guerrillas waiting for them south-east of Shwegyin. Three thousand Japanese reached the west bank of the Shwegyin Chaung, where they built rafts, but the *Mongoose* forces on the other bank pinned them down and left them a sitting target for the RAF. The Japanese lost 1,240 men in ground actions and many more in bombing and strafing. This one-sided battle went on until 8 September, in spite of leaflets dropped to the enemy to tell them that their Government had surrendered.

At first the RAF was critical of the intelligence supplied by *Character*, but it quickly improved. A report from 224 Group recorded that in the weeks before the fall of Rangoon almost all their long-range fighter-bombers were employed on Force-136 targets, and that so many high-grade reports came in that it was impossible to act on them all. There were many notable successes, the principal being an attack on the railway station at Pyu which coincided with the arrival of a troop train and caused over 1,000 casualties. The Group was so impressed with Force 136's later intelligence that they proposed that when operations began in Malaya at least one squadron should stand by to carry out immediate strikes when a mobile target was reported – something that had not been done in Burma.[29] Force 136 for its part said that the RAF could not be praised too highly for its skill in dropping the Special Groups and Jedburghs, in keeping them supplied, and providing arms for the guerrillas.

*Character* was by far the biggest operation mounted by the Burma Country Section. According to the Game Book the levies killed 10,964 enemy troops, wounded 644, and took eighteen prisoners; and they were indirectly responsible for many thousand more enemy casualties through the air strikes they called up.*

* A report by MacKenzie summarizes casualties inflicted in the whole of Burma by Force 136 as follows: 16,879 killed; 995 wounded; and 285 prisoners. In addition 4,000 Japanese were killed by the Burma National Army. Mountbatten's final report gives a total of 22,307 enemy killed by all the clandestine forces in SEAC for the loss of sixty-eight white officers.

# Malaya

MOUNTBATTEN'S directive 'to liberate Burma at the earliest date', which he received on 3 February 1945, said that his next task would be the liberation of Malaya. Detailed planning for that operation (code-name *Zipper*), originally timed for November 1945 but brought forward to August, began in May. Force 136, fortified by their experience in Burma and the knowledge of a substantial resistance movement in Malaya, made their own preparations. Guerrillas would be armed and trained throughout the country, ready to support *Zipper* when the signal came.

The Malay peninsula, running south from Burma and Siam, is 700 miles long and 250 wide. The fertile coastal belt is bounded by mountains almost entirely covered with primary jungle well suited to guerrilla activity. The population during World War II was about five and a half million – 2.3 million Malays, 2.4 million Chinese, three-quarters of a million Indians, and 100,000 British and other races. At the time of the Japanese invasion the Straits Settlements of Singapore, Penang, and Malacca were a British Colony; Perak, Selangor, Negri Sembilan, and Pahang a Federation; and Johore, Kedah, Trengganu, Kelantan, and Perlis were unfederated states with British advisers. Most of the population in the Straits Settlements and Federated Malay States were Chinese concentrated in the towns. In the unfederated Malay States the majority were Malays engaged in agriculture.

At the time of the Sino-Japanese war the illegal Malayan Communist Party (MCP) welded smaller left-wing parties into a country-wide organization, the Anti-Enemy Backing-up Society (AEBUS). It tried to weaken the British war effort by fomenting strikes; but when Russia joined the Allies in June 1941 threw all its weight behind the British through 'centrally directed State Committees, Town Committees, Village Committees, and finally small cells. The organization was financially sound . . . Its propaganda by means of underground newspapers and pamphlets was exceedingly good'. It provided eleventh-hour trainees for 101 STS and offered to raise a fighting force. Just before the fall of Singapore its members were advised to move into the jungle, take every opportunity to harass the Japanese, and await the return of the British.

The Malays, strict Muslims with no strong political convictions, accepted things as they found them and could not be expected to support a resistance movement with enthusiasm. Most of the Indians were Tamils working on the rubber estates for a few years before returning to India, with no long-term interest in the future of Malaya. It was therefore to the communist Chinese that the India Mission had to look for its main support.

For a long time nothing was known of the fate of the European left-behind parties and the Chinese graduates of 101 STS,* apart from the news picked up by Davis and Broome when they visited Selangor in February 1942; but it was hoped that some would be able to help in directing resistance forces. In fact few of the forty-odd Europeans were able to accomplish much. Six were killed in action or executed. Most of the others were captured and taken to prisoner-of-war camps in Malaya, Sumatra, and Siam, where seven died. Five members of party No. 4 in Negri Sembilan were captured in July 1942 and imprisoned in Changi Gaol in Singapore. Only four avoided capture and survived: Spencer Chapman himself, and Frank Quayle, Robert Chrystal, and William Robinson, from Party No. 3 in Selangor. (The last died in a guerrilla camp in Perak.) A few other Europeans remained at liberty, including Mr J. K. Creer, a District Officer in Trengganu, and Mr Pat Noone, an authority on the Sakai, the aboriginals of Malaya. Creer survived the war but Noone disappeared in his beloved jungle and was not heard of again. Of the European party in Pahang led by John Cotterill, Tyson died in January 1943 and the others joined forces with the guerrillas in July 1943. They finally linked up with Major A. C. Campbell-Miles's *Tideway* group in September 1945. Cotterill had fallen in with Spencer Chapman in 1943 when they discussed plans for escaping from Malaya but decided it was hopeless.

Garden's experience shows how the left-behind parties were hopelessly handicapped by being put into the field too late. His party left Kuala Lumpur on 8 January 1942 for the Bentong–Kuala Pilah Road to carry out demolitions on the eastern railway and roads in the area, believing that the army would hold out long enough to allow them to establish a base. The 9th Indian Division retreated past their chosen hide-out much sooner than expected and they had to

* See pp. 62 ff.

abandon their explosives and food. They decided there was nothing for it but to try to escape to India by boat; but after being joined for a time by some members of the other groups, they were captured by the Japanese on 19 March while pushing heavily laden bicycles, no longer fit to ride, through Kuala Kutsu on their way to the west coast.*

It is difficult to write without passion about the fate of the left-behind parties, condemned to failure by complacent civil and military authorities even before they had taken up their stations in the jungle. What might they not have accomplished given the time enjoyed by their brothers in Burma! It is wrong to single out any for special mention but an exception may be made for the engineer John Reid. When the other members of his party failed to appear he went alone to their hide-out. Those who knew him thought his jungle experience and resourcefulness gave him a sporting chance of survival; but like so many of his fellows he was captured and died in Changi Gaol on 12 May 1944.

The India Mission was already planning activities in Malaya in 1943 – guerrilla warfare in remote areas, small-scale sabotage, industrial go-slow, *coup de main* parties to attack oil installations and shipping (given the highest priority by COS). All this was academic until contact was made with a resistance group, which was not easy. Malaya was beyond the reach of the available aircraft, and the sea approaches too dangerous for surface craft. This left submarines, badly needed for other purposes.

Nevertheless, a series of submarine sorties to the west coast of Malaya was authorized in May 1943 (Operation *Gustavus*). There were four objectives: to establish a submarine link between Ceylon and Malaya; to create an intelligence system; to contact the guerrilla forces; and find survivors of the left-behind parties. John Davis, who had escaped from Sumatra in 1942, landed on 24 May 1943 from O 24 in the Pangkor-Lumut area in the Malacca Straits, taking with him five Chinese agents.[1] They had been recruited in Chungking by Lim Bo Seng, a very able man with important manufacturing interests in Singapore who had done much to rally the Chinese before the city fell. The plan was to take over a junk, but after boarding one Davis decided it was too small to act as a staging

---

* Major Cauvin's ISLD party survived in the jungle, although he committed suicide and one other member died. There is an account of the adventures of this party in *Red Jungle* by John Cross, who took over the leadership (Robert Hale, 1957).

post, and that his party should land by folboat. The shallow water
kept the submarine far from the beach and they had to paddle more
than five miles against strong tidal currents. After several hours'
exhausting effort they reached an unguarded area where they buried
their W/T and stores. Their first contacts were friendly and helpful
Chinese market gardeners.

The five agents were safely planted; but since the guerrillas were on
the far side of the closely patrolled coastal belt Davis could not get in
touch with them immediately. He managed to acquire a junk to
make contact with *Gustavus II* (the second of the monthly series,
using O 23 – Lieutenant-Commander A. M. Valkenburg RNN), which
was successfully accomplished on 25 June 1943.[2] The agreed
recognition signal – a red blanket over the port quarter and three
men standing in the bows – was easily spotted, and Broome and Mr C.
(later Sir Claude) Fenner, who had intended to join Davis, identified
him on the junk; but as Davis considered that more time was needed
to prepare for the infiltration of agents, all three, and one of the
Chinese, returned to Ceylon with O 23, leaving a Chinese in charge of
the junk.

Davis returned on 4 August 1943, accompanied by Fenner, in
O 23 (*Gustavus III*) making a successful rendezvous with the junk,
which used the same recognition signal.[3] This eliminated the
dangerous folboat trip and simplified the ferrying of stores and
equipment. Fenner went back to Ceylon to report that Davis's agents
had been in touch with a group claiming they were preparing
rebellion against the Japanese. After Fenner had left, Davis met Wong
Man Wa, one of the guerrilla leaders in Perak (code-name Chen Ping,
or CTP), and became aware for the first time of the real strength of the
resistance movement. AEBUS had been replaced by the Anti-
Japanese Army (AJA) which operated from camps in the jungle; and
the Anti-Japanese Union (AJU) which provided the guerrillas with
money and food. Together they were known as the Anti-Japanese
Union and Forces (AJUF). The movement was country-wide, and
although it was certainly communist, for the time being, at least, its
sole objective was the destruction of the Japanese.

Davis was joined in September by Broome (*Gustavus IV*) again
using O 24.[4] The British party now moved to the Perak Hills, partly
because the Japanese knew they were in the coastal jungle, but more
important to keep in closer touch with the guerrillas. Unfortunately it
was considered too dangerous to carry unusual equipment, in

particular the bulky W/T sets. Chen Ping promised to take them by junk up the Perak River to avoid the swamps between Lumut and the hills; but the junk failed to appear and they spent a miserable night in pouring rain with no food, fearing they would become fugitives in the not very extensive Sigari jungle. However, the junk did turn up next day – 9 October 1943 – and instead of keeping Pangkor Island between them and the mainland they sailed boldly through the crowded Dindings Channel 'on the principle of doing the unexpected'.

Chen Ping went down with malaria and they spent an unpleasant five days in a vegetable-garden house near Jenderata, at the mercy of the mosquitoes. For the next week they walked through rubber plantations, being well received by the Chinese and taking a chance with the Malays, who were more likely to inform on them. At one point they passed noisily under a Malay house – supported on stilts – but happily the owner identified them as a wild pig. On another occasion 'our guides lost their way and their heads, and we spent 3 hours puddling about in the swamp, waking up scores of Malays and leaving tracks like a herd of elephant'. They finally found sanctuary in a tiny tract of jungle where they lay all day within twenty yards of some Tamil cultivators. On the fourth day they were entertained to coffee and cakes in a coffee shop which was the guerrillas' regular meeting place; and two days later reached the camp.

On Christmas Day 1943 they were joined by Spencer Chapman, who for the last two years had been visiting AJUF camps, trying single-handed to give the guerrillas some idea of training and discipline. He had heard four months earlier in Negri Sembilan that someone in Perak with a new kind of tommy-gun (it was the Sten) wanted to meet him; and he guessed that an agent must have come in. He was just in time to join the first formal conference with AJUF on 31 December.

Chang Hung, representing MCP and AJUF, was empowered to negotiate an agreement, subject to ratification by these bodies. He gave details of the Chinese resistance throughout the country and confirmed that when the invasion came the guerrillas would take their orders from the Allied C-in-C. Davis, authorized by Mountbatten on 29 November 1943 to 'aid and strengthen' the resistance movement, outlined the military and sabotage activities expected from the guerrillas; but asked that for the moment they should do no more than sabotage shipping and foment labour trouble. He promised the Allies would send in everything needed – arms, ammunition, medical supplies, and money. It was doubtful if their request for doctors could be met, but if possible they too would be provided. Chinese instructors standing by in India would come as soon as aircraft were available; and guerrillas would be taken to India for training. At no point did the guerrilla leaders suggest they expected political concessions in return for their co-operation.*

Although it was not known at the time, Chang Hung (who went under ten other names, including Lai Tek, and Mr Wright) was hedging his bets by acting for the Japanese. A Chinese with Annamite blood, he came to Singapore in 1933 from French Indo-China where he had been acting as an informer, to work in the same capacity for the Malayan authorities. He joined the communist Seamen's Association and, helped by a claim of Ho Chi Minh's friendship and support, became Secretary General of MCP. He was arrested by the Japanese soon after they arrived in Singapore and released on condition that he worked for them. As earnest of his good faith he told them about a secret meeting of resistance leaders at the Batu Caves in Selangor (for which he happened to arrive too late), which enabled him to eliminate an important section of the guerrilla movement. He also divulged information about Force 136 activities – enough to keep him on good terms with the Japanese, but not enough to arouse suspicion among the guerrillas. It may be presumed that had the Allies invaded Malaya he would have continued to serve both sides, giving preference to whichever seemed more likely to win.†

In November 1943 0 24 brought in Lim Bo Seng (*Gustavus V*).[5] Broome tried to make the rendezvous but could not get through the road-blocks between the camp and the coast. Chen Ping, however, who could travel more freely, met Lim Bo Seng and escorted him to the camp. The December sortie (*Gustavus VI*) was abortive. HM Submarine *Tally Ho!* (Lieutenant-Commander L. W. A. Bennington) failed to make contact on 9, 10, and 11 December; and nothing was found in the 'post box' arranged on one of the Sembilan Islands.[6] However, a Chinese agent made a successful rendezvous with an

---

* The English version of the treaty is neatly written in ink on two sides of a leaf torn from an exercise book, one of the more informal records of an international agreement.

† After the war he resumed working for the Malayan authorities, who knew about his dealings with the Japanese, although the communists at first did not. They denounced him, however, in September 1945, whereupon he disappeared from Singapore taking with him a large part of the funds of MCP.

extra sortie (*Emergency Gustavus VI*);[7] but since he left the camp before the conference with AJUF he did not take with him information about the guerrillas' strength and dispositions – essential for planning the invasion of Malaya. *Emergency Gustavus VI* was the last contact with Davis and Broome for over a year.

Meanwhile the *Gustavus* party built up an intelligence organization through Wu Chye Sin (code-name Ah Ng) one of the agents originally brought in, who 'consistently displayed not only courage but daring, initiative, intelligence and sound commonsense' which made him 'the key man from the beginning'. His cover was a business in Ipoh dealing in black-market food, lubricating oil, and gold. He also ran a junk service which helped *Gustavus*'s monthly submarine rendezvous; and he cashed the gold sent in by the India Mission (pretending it came from Siam) by arrangement with a Japanese official. He soon owned a lorry, a private car, and a motor boat plying between Singapore and North Malaya. He was on good terms with Chinese detectives 'some of whom were satisfactorily compromised' and who, it was hoped, would keep him posted about enemy moves. Once, when he heard that the Japanese were sending out Malay search parties to find *Gustavus*, he contrived to lead on a wild-goose chase the party assigned to the *Gustavus* area.

The other members of the ring were 'Bill' (not one of the India Mission) who acted as Ah Ng's manager in Ipoh; Lee Han Kwong (Ah Tsing) who ran a fish business at Pangkor, and managed the early submarine rendezvous; Lung Chiu Ying (Ah Ying) installed in a coffee shop in Sigari, who took over the nerve-racking junk rendezvous work; Yee Tien Song (Sek Fu) for whom a shop was bought in Tapah; Tan Sieng Yang (Ah Lim); and the ablest of them all, Lim Bo Seng.

On 1 March 1944 Lim Bo Seng left camp to develop the intelligence system and try to raise money. He gave Ah Ng the names of three friends in Singapore who might help with cash; but one was too frightened to help, and the other two gave only vague promises. On 20 March *Gustavus* received a letter from Lim Bo Seng at Silibin, reporting that Ah Ng had returned to Singapore to continue fund-raising. He also referred to a mysterious visit which Bill had had from two men claiming to be AJUF representatives, whom he suspected of working for the enemy. Bill told them nothing about his relationship with the guerrillas.

The next news was brought by Ah Tsing, in a state of great

excitement. He reported that three days after the visit of the 'AJUF representatives' Bill had been arrested by the Japanese and had revealed what he knew – a good deal more than it should have been – about the *Gustavus* intelligence network. Ah Tsing himself had been arrested the following day, and had confirmed what Bill had said, since there was no point in denying it. He was taken to Ipoh where he was well treated, in the hope that he would work for his captors. A chance to escape came when the women guarding him were frightened from the room by a number of Japanese wandering around naked – as was their habit. Pretending he was going to have a bath he escaped through the second-storey bathroom window. He hailed a taxi, telling the driver he was a guerrilla who had just escaped from the Japanese. The driver 'responded magnificently, and shouting "We're all of one blood" ' drove at full speed to Bidor, where Ah Tsing disappeared into the jungle *en route* for *Gustavus*, having first borrowed money from the local AJUF to pay the fare.

Ah Tsing knew nothing of the fate of the other members of the ring. In captivity he heard the police say they had to go to Tapah where Sek Fu was established, and guessed they might be going to arrest him, and in fact he was arrested. After interrogation by the Kempei Tai in Ipoh he was imprisoned at Batu Gajah, along with Lim Bo Seng, who also had been picked up, as had been Ah Ng. Ah Ng, Ah Lim, and Sek Fu survived but Lim Bo Seng died in prison towards the end of 1944. Two of the crew of Ah Ng's junk were compelled to reveal the *Gustavus* rendezvous points, and one of them committed suicide after his release. The W/T and arms dump at Lumut was found. Bill was allowed by the Japanese to return to his business in Pankor, where he was kept under surveillance.

On 13 April 1944 Spencer Chapman, accompanied by 'Black' Lim, a camp guard, left in search of Noone, who had been working with AJUF, but had left because they would not allow him to deal with the Sakai. He was said to be at Grik, 100 miles to the north. They fell in with a band whom they took to be members of AJUF, but who stole their weapons and refused to let them leave. Eventually they released Lim, and Spencer Chapman escaped, only to be captured by a Japanese patrol. He again escaped, and for the next month endured all the hardships of the jungle – leech bites, malaria, hunger, headaches, and giddiness – knowing he was being hunted. He found sanctuary in an AJUF 'traitor-killing' camp 'among tin tailings and tapioca fields, skilfully concealed in a minute patch of secondary jungle . . . the food was excellent, rice and sweet potatoes, a leaf vegetable, and salt fish twice a day, and coffee once a week'. On 16 July he was strong enough to return to *Gustavus*, which he reached on 25 July, after 103 days.

He found that W/T communication with the India Mission had not yet been established, in spite of another series of submarine sorties. *Remarkable I* (*Tally Ho!*) which hoped to land a Chinese agent, a W/T set, and 1,000 pounds of stores, and to bring out one or more of the *Gustavus* party, looked in vain for the small junk they were supposed to contact – the recognition signals were a red blanket hung over the port side, lowering of the sail, and assembling the crew aft for fifteen minutes in every two hours. *Tally Ho!* returned with stores and agent to Trincomalee.[8] Next month HMS *Trespasser* (Lieutenant-Commander R. M. Favell) fared no better. *Remarkable II* planned to land a British and a Chinese W/T operator, but after patrolling for three days in the agreed area south of Pulo Jarak without seeing any signal, returned to base.[9] The April sortie (*Remarkable III* – HMS *Tantalus*, Lieutenant-Commander H. S. Mackenzie) of Captain F. P. W. Harrison, a Chinese W/T operator, and three Chinese agents was instructed to put two agents ashore in a blind landing if there was no sign of a reception committee. The crew of a sampan rowed towards the rendezvous, but without displaying the recognition signal, which included a shirt tied by its arms to the rigging. 'As a last hope a visual reconnaissance of its crew was carried out through the periscope by a member of the *Remarkable* party who would have recognized them. The result was a complete blank, as regards both the recognition of the sampan's crew and likewise the stare with which the latter viewed the periscope.'[10]

The blind-landing plan was now put into operation. Just after midnight on 25 April 1944 the two Chinese agents left in their folboat. They went off 'full of confidence and disappeared from sight going strongly straight for the objective' – the western tip of Long Island. 'The night was dark but clear and the sea could not have been calmer, so the folboat should have had no difficulty.'

On 11 and 12 June 1944 *Remarkable IV* (*Tantalus* – Major Tremlett, Captain Hislop, a Chinese W/T operator, and a Chinese agent) attempted to rendezvous with the two agents landed blind in April; but yet again the recognition signal was not seen. Earlier on the submarine's patrol – on 1 June – a junk was seen near the rendezvous in which a Chinese was ostentatiously waving a red flag – near enough the pre-arranged signal of a red blanket to be suggestive. No other craft was around at the time, yet the man continued to wave until the junk was out of sight. The submarine commander guessed that it was a decoy and that some previous agent had 'blown the gaff' – not one of the two agents landed blind by *Remarkable III*, since their rendezvous dates were 11 and 12 June.[11]

SOE Colombo had been warned by 'a secret source' that the Japanese might be lying in wait for *Remarkable III*, and they may also have been on the look-out for *Remarkable IV*. The 'secret source' may have been the ISLD *May* and *Moon* parties established at Ipoh and Kuala Lumpur in April and May 1943; but there is a mystery which neither the papers nor the surviving witnesses can solve. A memorandum on ISLD's Operation *Mud* dated 31 January 1944 records that on 14 September 1943 the leader of *Gustavus* (John Davis) had asked that in order to avoid compromising SOE parties ISLD should attempt no more blind landings. In the same report Davis passed on information from an AJUF official about the *May* and *Moon* parties. 'The first party had landed at Kuala Bernam, but on wading ashore ran into a Chinese who tried to arrest them. They got away after a mixture of threats and pleadings . . . The second party landed further south, nearer to Selangor.' Both continued to operate for the rest of the war. They had W/T, ineffective at first because of damp, but which may have been made serviceable. In any case, at least one member of the parties managed to return to Colombo in May 1944.

Why then, if Davis was aware of these parties, did *Gustavus* make no attempt to communicate through them with SOE Colombo? Although his report of 14 September 1943 is quite specific, Davis now has no recollection of *May* and *Moon*. A report on the latter which is recorded in the index to the SEAC War Diary, which may throw light on the mystery, cannot be found by the Ministry of Defence. The position is hardly clarified by the record of a meeting between Mackenzie and Major Boris Hembry of ISLD on 6 May 1945 when the latter said it was believed that although *May* and *Moon* were operating in AJUF territory their presence was not known to AJUF – although it *was* known two years earlier. Mackenzie acceded to his request that *May* and *Moon* should continue to work independently of Force 136 in Malaya, although Force 136 had by now become the senior partner by virtue of its much greater numerical strength. Hembry, like Davis, has no recollection of *May* and *Moon*, nor has Mackenzie, so that three of the leading actors are unable to explain the mystery of the papers.

It was now decided to suspend the *Remarkable* series and to try instead to infiltrate agents overland. (The aircraft available at this time could not make the round trip to Malaya.) This idea was not followed up, however.

*Gustavus*'s attempts to bring to the hills the W/T equipment hidden at the coast had been frustrated by increased Japanese activity in Perak. it was not until May 1944 that the W/T-set batteries and hand generator were manhandled through the swamps from Telok Anson to a guerrilla camp. The heavier equipment, including pedal and motor generators, could be taken only as far as the foothills. When Davis and Broome went to collect the W/T they found that the Japanese had removed it along with reserve food, medicine, and miscellaneous stores hidden in a nearby cave. Worst of all, *Gustavus*'s 'security bag' containing money, signals plan, and records of their dealings with the guerrillas was found, in spite of the fact that it had been carefully buried. Spencer Chapman's diaries had also gone.

After 'a miserable month' in which they had only tapioca and a small quantity of salt fish to eat *Gustavus* set up a new camp at Gurun, to which the supplies brought in by Lim Bo Seng in November 1943 were taken – small radio receivers, two B2 W/T sets, medicine, and tinned food. The W/T sets were in perfect condition, but the pedal generator and batteries had been ruined by damp – there were two gallons of water in one of the cases. The motor generator had been abandoned, being too heavy.

*Gustavus* now had W/T sets in good working order, but no batteries, or generators to charge batteries. They sent the unserviceable dynamo for repairs but it came back still useless. The guerrillas, ever anxious to help, acquired a number of car batteries, and on 5 November 1944 *Gustavus* managed to pick up All India Radio on one of the small radios. But this was less than half the battle. They could not yet tell the India Mission about the guerrilla dispositions and their wish to co-operate. But they contrived to rehabilitate the pedal generator, and coupled it to a car battery. They also got news of their survival to *Carpenter*, which had infiltrated South Johore in October 1944 by submarine from Australia (HMS *Telemachus*, Commander W. D. A. King).[12] ON 16 December *Carpenter* told the Malaya Country Section that Davis, Broome, and Chapman were safe in Perak. A further report from *Carpenter* on 19 January 1945 said that

*Gustavus* were now ready to transmit; and on 1 February Colombo picked up their signal. After more than a year of silence there was two-way communication between *Gustavus* and the India Mission.

As a result Operation *Funnel*, led by Major J. P. Hannah, dropped to *Gustavus* on 26 February 1945.* Davis, confident that he could now implement the undertaking given a year ago, summoned the guerrilla leaders to a second conference. The meeting

was a great affair. A special camp was built near the edge of the jungle. AJA managed to buy up all the pigs and poultry in the countryside. *Funnel* gold must have helped. A guard of honour 100 strong was provided and two days were given up to conferencing, feasting and cordiality. Broome passed out on the way down and was given a spoonful of rum to revive him, and promptly became hopelessly drunk. However, he managed to take the salute of the guard of honour in royal style, firmly supported by two *aides de camp*. I ate myself silly. The whole atmosphere was one of the greatest confidence and optimism. The break-up too was ceremonial. Wong Man Wa wore the only tin helmet known to exist in Perak ... It was next seen being used as a cooking pot ...

The conference, in which the guerrillas were again represented by Chang Hung, agreed that AJUF would appoint a commander to keep in touch with Davis. The AJUF 'regiments' in the States would receive a British Group Liaison Officer, and each patrol within the regiment would be joined by a Patrol Liaison Team. In the buildup period before the guerrillas were ordered into action these forces would be independent but subject to general direction from AJUF headquarters. They would still act independently after D-Day, but on orders from the Allied C-in-C through the Group Liaison Officers. Each group would have a medical officer who would move from patrol to patrol. Arrangements for financing the guerrillas were agreed. A system of code-names was evolved, Wong Man Wa, who became head of the guerrilla forces, taking *Kaput*, and Davis's organization *Malt*.

*Carpenter*, which had passed on the news of *Gustavus*'s survival to the India Mission, was operating in Johore, at the other end of

---

* *Funnel* would have gone in earlier but ISLD had priority for the next mission to Malaya. A joint SOE/ISLD mission was not proceeded with because of a personality clash; and when W/T communication was established with *Gustavus* SOE decided to go it alone. The ISLD mission (*Evidence*) operated near the *Gustavus* area and claimed that the poor co-operation they received from the guerrillas was due to *Gustavus*'s influence – which was strenuously denied. This episode is not untypical of the relationship between the two organizations.

Malaya. As the commander of HMS *Trespasser* had pointed out, it was much easier for a submarine to land a party on the east coast of Malaya where there were no mangrove swamps, the coastal belt was less populous, and deeper water allowed the submarine to get closer in. The Navy, however, was reluctant to send submarines from Ceylon into the Malacca Straits further south than the Pangkor-Lumut area where *Gustavus* landed. The alternative for Ceylon-based submarines was to go round the west coast of Sumatra and through the Sunda or Lombok Straits; but one based on Australia could approach the east coast of Malaya without too much difficulty. It was therefore decided to land a party in South Johore with six months' stores – which called for the biggest available submarine. HM Submarine *Clyde* was earmarked, but because of engine trouble was replaced by *Telemachus* which arrived at Exmouth Gulf in Western Australia in September 1944; and on 5 October landed five British officers and seven Force 136 agents led by Major W. B. Martin on the coast of South Johore. The disembarkation had been carefully rehearsed because of the size of the party and was carried out so efficiently that the submarine's forehatch was open for less than an hour, in spite of the fact that only one of the Landing Craft, Rubber (LCR) outboard motors would start. There was a minor hitch when it was found that local Japanese stations were using the same frequency as *Carpenter*'s 'walkie-talkie'. Another problem was the fogging of the submarine's periscope when looking across wind in high humidity. The commander noted that in the last five years he had often drawn attention to this fault and expressed the hope that it would be remedied before the next war.[13]

The ferry party was supposed to return with the submarine, but it failed to contact them on 6 and 7 October and the commander decided that it was too dangerous to remain any longer, particularly as further communication with the shore might reveal their presence to the enemy. The ferry party were therefore left to become part of *Carpenter* for the time being. W/T communication with Colombo was established on 15 October – the longest range so far achieved – nearly four months before *Gustavus* made contact with headquarters.

*Carpenter* was soon transmitting useful information about the movement of Japanese warships in and out of Singapore – although the navy felt that the absence of a trained naval-intelligence officer was a handicap. This service was continued to the end of the war. Martin got in touch with the Johore AJUF (No. 4 Regiment) and confirmed to the India Mission that the resistance would be a force to be reckoned with. *Carpenter*, however, being a long way from the main guerrilla forces, was less well-informed than *Gustavus*. Martin was killed when the Japanese attacked a group collecting stores dropped from a Liberator on 25 January 1945.

At the beginning of February *Carpenter II* led by Major Hart and comprising another British officer, an NCO, and five Chinese agents landed from HM Submarine *Thule* (Lieutenant-Commander A. C. G. Mars), which had sailed direct from Trincomalee, with 4,000 pounds of stores and equipment.[14] *Thule* took off three members of the original party. *Carpenter III*, again using *Thule*, arrived at the end of May with 8,000 pounds stores, three officers, and sixteen Royal Marines – a large party made possible by the removal of the reload torpedoes. Fourteen LCRs with eleven outboard motors were used. When disembarkation was complete the motors were recovered and the landing-craft sunk.[15] From this time *Carpenter* was regularly reinforced and continued its twin tasks of organizing local levies and coast-watching.

Although there was no doubt that the Chinese were by far the biggest element in the resistance movement, SOE realized that in the interests of harmony in post-war Malaya the Malays must be seen to play a part. The first operation with this objective was *Likewise*, in which Captain P. G. Dobree, formerly of the Straits Settlements Agriculture Department, Captain (later General Tan Sri) Ibrahim bin Ismail, and four Malays tried to land from a submarine (HMS *Severn*, Lieutenant-Commander R. H. Bull) in August 1944 west of Kedah Peak. None of the outboard motors of their LCRs would start – except one which then fell overboard. The operation was abandoned.[16]

*Likewise II* (Dobree) and *Oatmeal* (Ibrahim) followed; but when the latter was captured, the former was called off (when six days out from Trincomalee) since *Oatmeal* knew its plans and might have revealed them to the enemy. Ibrahim and three Malay other ranks had intended to land from two Catalinas off Kelantan on 31 October 1944; but rough seas and a large number of fishing boats prevented them from going ashore. They went instead to the Island of Perhentian Kechil, ten miles out, where they were informed on and arrested. The Japanese treated them comparatively well, administering only 'slaps and knocks on the head', and promised to spare their lives if they acted as double agents. Then began a game of cat and mouse in which neither side knew which was cat and which mouse.

His captors, who had found Ibrahim's signals plan complete with security checks, ordered him to get in touch with Colombo, which he did on 13 November 1944. When headquarters asked for a security check he was faced with an impossible problem. If *Violin* (their W/T code-name) gave the 'We're caught' response the Japanese were bound to spot it, and *Oatmeal*'s fate would be sealed; but if he signalled 'All's well' he could be leading future operations into a trap. Ibrahim persuaded the Japanese that the 'All's well' response in the signals plan in fact meant the opposite, and 'I succeeded somehow in making them believe that the right answer to the check had been taught to me verbally.'* It is astonishing that this bland statement that black was white should have been accepted, but it was and the agents were safe – for the time being. Although Ibrahim did not know it, headquarters had no doubt that *Oatmeal* was operating under duress since the news of their arrest had reached the India Mission through *Appreciation*, the SOE W/T station in Bangkok, and through *Carpenter* in South Johore.

The deception game now began in earnest. The Japanese problem was how to use *Violin* to mislead SEAC. Ibrahim's problem was how to go along with them but make certain their plans failed. The problem facing Lieutenant-Colonel Peter Fleming, who was in charge of SEAC's Deception Division to which SOE had transferred the operation, and whose stock-in-trade was the manipulation of double agents, was how to keep the charade alive without doing what the Japanese wanted, yet without endangering *Oatmeal*.

Ibrahim and his colleagues were taken to the area where they were supposed to be established to enable them to include authoritative local colour in their reports. In December D Division instructed them to cross to the west coast to join forces with another agent, a sensible delaying tactic since the move would take several weeks. They replied, of course with the approval of the Japanese, giving the route they would take. In fact they were flown across country as it was feared that if they went by rail under escort they might be spotted by another Allied agent; and at the end of January 1945 – dressed as 1st Class Privates in the local volunteer force – they were installed in a house north of Taiping.

* The actual question was: 'Have you met Miriam?' The 'All's well' response was: 'Two Scotsmen left here two days ago.' The 'We're caught' response was: 'Yes, I've met Miriam.'

For the next six months *Oatmeal* discussed with headquarters the reception of a further party – which would of course have walked into the arms of the enemy. From time to time their Japanese controllers became impatient, but Ibrahim managed to convince them that this was the pace at which special operations moved and that his headquarters would smell a rat if they were asked to speed things up. In July 1945, however, D Division sensed that something more than an exchange of signals was becoming necessary and they promised a drop of arms and equipment on 27 July. The Japanese were delighted and 'went around quietly congratulating each other'. Their euphoria was premature as the next signal said the aircraft had engine trouble. The drop would now be on the thirtieth. On that day Ibrahim was escorted to the chosen dropping-zone where a sudden rainstorm made a drop impossible, and the only notable event was that one of the reception party fell into a pig trap. 'Luckily for him there were no bamboo spikes.'

Finally, stores including a W/T were successfully dropped on 7 August, but due to a packing error the signals plan and crystals were not included in the container. The missing items were promised for 19 August; but on the eighteenth *Oatmeal* received a signal announcing the unconditional surrender of the Japanese. The game was over – just in time.

Neither side profited from *Oatmeal*. Had Malaya been invaded while *Violin* was still operating the Japanese might have tried to deceive the Allies about their defensive strategy; and since D Division knew that *Violin* was under duress they would have tried to guess the enemy's true intentions. They would no doubt have used *Violin* to give the Japanese High Command a false impression of the Allied invasion plans. The only tangible result of *Oatmeal* was that Ibrahim was given a decoration by the Japanese for his supposed services.

The initial link with the Malay resistance came through Operation *Hebrides*, dropped east of Grik in North Perak, and led by Dobree – the first blind drop in Malaya. The aim was to open up communication with the hill area of Northern Kedah, and if possible to find Noone.* The drop, from a Liberator, took place at dusk during the new-moon period in December 1944, and was completely successful. W/T communication with Colombo was quickly established and much valuable intelligence transmitted, not only about Japanese dispos-

* See p. 192.

itions in the immediate neighbourhood. Dobree had thirty main agents and many more sub-agents, some operating as far afield as Singapore.

Conditions in the area were very bad. Food was scarce in spite of attempts to grow crops in jungle clearings, using Sakai labour. There was much sickness, no medicine, even in the hospitals, and prices were astronomic. There was no shortage of arms – British, Japanese, and police rifles, tommy-guns, and pistols – but what little ammunition they had was unreliable. The few cars and buses in the region were falling to pieces and at one stage provisions could be moved only by bicycle or elephant.

Dobree had no doubt that a separate Malay resistance movement could be organized. His appeal for volunteers in the Grik area met with a great response – every bachelor wanted to join, and there were not enough arms for all. He chose 100 whom he christened the Loyal Malay Army (Ashkar Melayu Setia), hoping to expand it after *Zipper* (the invasion of Malaya) had been launched. When another British officer was dropped to support him, he sent him to Kedah with a few members of the Loyal Malay Army to recruit a similar organization there. It was found, however, that in spite of their enthusiasm the Malays had a poor sense of security, and it was decided not to arm large numbers but to employ a small number of the more discreet on intelligence work, which they carried out with great success.

Although Dobree was mainly concerned with developing a Malay resistance movement he inevitably came into contact with the local AJUF. He found that in some areas they were hand in glove with the police, who allowed them to come freely into the towns to collect weapons to be hidden until D-Day, when the police planned to join the guerrillas. The Japanese were using large numbers of informers of all races in the region, a serious threat. They were also offering huge rewards for the capture of Europeans dropped by parachute – none of which was ever earned. *Hebrides* also had to deal at times with Kuomintang (KMT) bands in North Perak and Kelantan who occasionally clashed with AJUF. Three other groups went in to recruit Malay guerrillas: *Fighter*, in Kedah under Major G. A. Hasler; *Beacon*, near Kuala Lipis in Pahang (Major J. A. Richardson); and *Multiple*, under Major Derek Headly, formerly a member of the Malayan Civil Service, east of Raub in Pahang. It was expected that the number of Malay guerrillas – far fewer than the Chinese – would increase when the Allied landings began. Richardson was assured by Che Yeop Mahideen, Assistant District Officer at Raub, that 500 Malays could be raised with the backing of the Sultan of Pahang (who in 1942 had ordered village headmen to help Miss Nona Baker and her brother when they took to the jungle).[17]

In Malaya the India Mission faced the problem it faced in Burma – to arm or not to arm the left-wing resistance movement? Mackenzie told Mountbatten in February 1945 that if arming the guerrillas was ruled out in Malaya – where Davis had already signed his treaty promising to help them – he must stop sending in further parties, the line he had taken in Burma. Mountbatten referred the problem to the Chiefs of Staff on 19 April 1945, explaining that AJUF was by far the most important resistance group in Malaya. Malay resistance was of political rather than military importance; and KMT were no more than robber bands. He accepted that AJUF were politically dangerous and might try to seize power post-war 'on democratic pretences', as had happened in Greece. To arm them might seem to help them towards that goal.[18]

Nevertheless, the risk must be taken. He had no doubt that AJUF, helped by British officers, would hasten the eviction of the Japanese and save many British lives. In any case AJUF already had large quantities of arms acquired when the British withdrew in 1942; and in the coming campaign they would no doubt acquire many more abandoned by the retreating Japanese. If through the India Mission the British Government co-operated with AJUF, who had made no political demands, it would stand them in good stead in the post-war period; and it would also enable the British authorities to keep in touch with the policies and plans of the Communist Party. He therefore proposed to instruct SOE to carry on organizing, training, and arming AJUF; and at the same time to support the purely Malay resistance to act as a counterbalance. He suggested that any dangers would be minimized if Britain's post-war constitutional proposals for Malaya were published.

COS, taking their time from the War Cabinet, shied away from pronouncements about the post-war period. Relations with the guerrillas must be purely military – again the line taken in Burma. The Malay resistance must be given the maximum encouragement. SEAC were authorized to give 'such support as will assist in controlling them' to AJUF, one of those nebulous directives which left the Supreme Commander free to do as much as he dared or as little as he wanted. KMT were to be further investigated before COS would give instructions about them.[19]

The effort required from Force 136 in Malaya was suddenly intensified when it was decided to bring *Zipper*, planned for November, forward to August. A superhuman effort was needed from all Force-136 headquarters staff, in particular those concerned with training, operational planning, and the provision and dispatch of stores and equipment. The SD Squadrons were also called on to go flat out, being helped by the weakness of the Japanese air force in Malaya which made virtually no attempt to interfere with the aircraft carrying men and stores. They were attacked only twice, and none was shot down. Japanese tactics on the ground also helped. As a rule they waited an hour or two before attacking a party that had received a drop, which gave the Force-136 teams time to get the stores safely away and prepare an ambush. The rate of the buildup differed in the various parts of the country, depending on the distance the supply planes had to travel, the availability of suitable dropping-zones, and the degree of co-operation offered by AJUF.

The forces which the India Mission would have deployed in Malaya had Operation *Zipper* gone ahead were certainly as well prepared as those of *Nation* and *Character* in Burma; and there is little doubt they would have made an equal contribution to the Allied victory. The Group Liaison Officers all had experience of Malayan jungle conditions and were well qualified to get the best out of the guerrillas. Of those working with AJUF three had been in the Malayan Police Service: Lieutenant-Colonel D. K. Broadhurst in Selangor, who had been in the campaign of 1941–2 and had escaped via Sumatra after being behind the enemy lines for six weeks; Fenner in Negri Sembilan, who had spent six months in submarines acting as conducting officer; and Lieutenant-Colonel I. S. Wyllie in South Johore. Two – Campbell-Miles in North Johore and Hislop in Kedah – had been planters: Hannah in Perak had spent three years in Malaya and the Dutch East Indies as a prospector; and Major J. R. Leonard in West Pahang had been a game-warden in the Federated Malay States. They would have been in control of more than 4,000 armed members of AJUF and some thousands of auxiliaries.* At the time of

---

* It is impossible to be more precise. A paper by Lieutenant-Colonel Innes Tremlett dated 15 August 1945 shows 3,000 AJUF, 500 KMT, and 'small groups of Malay levies'. In an appendix he lists 2,021 AJUF, 272 KMT and bandits, and 187 Malays with British Group Liaison Officers – total 2,480. But whereas he attributes 139 AJUF

the Japanese surrender Force 136 had introduced over ninety British officers; and they had forty-eight W/T stations in the field. They had introduced six Gurkha Special Groups comprising two British officers and sixteen Gurkha other ranks.

Japanese maps found after the surrender revealed that most of the guerrilla positions were accurately pin-pointed, but it is unlikely that this would have militated against their success had they been ordered into action. Guerrilla groups in Burma survived on the run and still did great damage to the enemy; and there is no reason to think it would have been any different in Malaya.

---

to *Galvanic* in Selangor, the true figure was 700. *Multiple* in Pahang is given fifteen Malays compared with the actual figure of 244. (Information supplied by Lieutenant-Colonel Broadhurst and Lieutenant-Colonel Headly.) Tremlett puts arms supplied to the field at about 2,000 whereas the records show nearly 5,000.

# 9

# *Mickleham, Remorse,* and *Grenville*

THE Japanese occupation of Malaya and the Dutch East Indies drastically reduced the amount of rubber available to the Allies. Mr A. C. Baker, formerly Adviser to the States of Kedah and Kelantan, pointed out that since there was far more rubber in the occupied countries than Japan needed the producers must be embarrassed by large surplus stocks. Why not open purchasing centres, say in the islands close to Sumatra, and let the producers know they would be paid a good price in silver for any rubber smuggled past the Japanese? Baker provided the name of a Chinese admirably qualified to run this trade: 'a man of great ability, entirely unscrupulous, and devoted to making his own fortune. He should be very useful so long as no patriotism, no acceptance of personal risk, is expected of him, and he is not paid until he delivers the goods.'

The Combined Raw Materials Board approved the scheme; and Mr Oliver Lyttelton, Minister of Production, agreed that Britain should join. SOE would handle the transaction as 'a covert project of the buccaneering type'. Although it had little chance of success it should go ahead not only because of the shortage of rubber, but also in the interest of British prestige, sadly damaged by events in the Far East. Walter (later Sir Walter) Fletcher, a London rubber-broker, was appointed to manage the British organization. He had served in the first war and for months had been badgering the authorities for a job. To Hugh Dalton he was a 'thug with good commercial contacts' who would do well in SOE; and an official recorded that 'though not exactly the person to be trusted with the private means of a widow or orphan' he was tailor-made for rubber smuggling. Hambro described him as 'an international authority on rubber, with SOE temperament, drive and initiative. I can think of no-one with a better chance of making this odds-against proposition a success.'*

---

* Fletcher was the son of an Austrian Paul Fleischl who became naturalized. He was a large man who was counted as two passengers in an aircraft in the interests of safety.

Fletcher went to Washington in July 1942 to discuss plans with Major L. W. Elliott, the American who had been evaluating the scheme, and who proposed to concentrate on Borneo where Japanese patrols were relatively inactive. A generous price would be offered for crude rubber delivered to the Tanimber Islands, 300 miles north of Darwin, agents being sent in to make advance payments. The first British plan was to bring the rubber from Sumatra to Ceylon, a distance of over 1,000 miles; but Fletcher decided this was too far. Instead he would put agents into Burma, Siam, Malaya, and Sumatra to send rubber into Elliott's area. The Dutch authorities were sceptical but eventually agreed to help. Fletcher asked the Treasury for £500,000 but had to be content with £100,000. The US Board of Economic Warfare put up only $100,000.

As soon as Fletcher reached India in October 1942 he changed his plan again. Now he would move rubber from French Indo-China using agents recruited in China. When London warned him that this would be difficult because of Chungking's 'present resentment of foreigners' and suggested he should rely on rubber merchants and Chinese secret societies, he decided to hijack a ship carrying rubber from Indo-China to metropolitan France. An agent equipped with a suitcase radio would board the ship in Saigon, keeping in touch with a partner in the city through whom news of the ship's movements would be passed to SOE in Kunming, and then on to the Royal Navy, who would intercept the vessel. Alternatively the shipmaster could be bribed to hand over the rubber at an agreed rendezvous.

London pointed out that an agent could not transmit without alerting the ship's own radio operator, and favoured the alternative of bribery. The agent must persuade the master to surrender the cargo, for which he would be well paid on his return to Saigon. This took no account of the fate of the agent if his proposition was rejected,

---

The India Mission's principal jester, he wrote of himself:

> Garrulous, old, impulsive, vague, obese,
>   Only by luck not 'known to the Police',
> Wedded to Wine and Food, and oft-told tales,
>   Stuffed over-full, as *foie gras* is in Quails,
> A mind once keen, now almost in eclipse,
>   A figure, too, that looks like an ellipse;
> This, and no more, be Walter's epitaph:
>   'In War's worst hour he sometimes made us laugh'.

After the war he became MP for Bury.

nor of the shipmaster's fate when he got back to Saigon. However, it proved impossible to find an agent and yet another of Fletcher's schemes came to nothing. He consoled himself with the thought that the recent Allied victories in North Africa would prevent the Axis from sending rubber cargoes through the Mediterranean – although a ship leaving Saigon would be fair game whichever route it followed.

The more Fletcher grappled with his problem the more insoluble it became. He could find no suitable agents. In any case, there was no way to put them in the field. Every inch of submarine space was booked. The RAF was prepared to help – but there was no rubber for them to carry. Fletcher recorded: 'The main conclusion I arrive at is that any large immediate results are not to be looked for, but that good results can be obtained within reasonable time, say twelve months' – after the Allies had recaptured Rangoon. Meantime there was nothing for it but to find, train, and infiltrate agents, spread the news that rubber would fetch high prices, establish collecting points, build a fleet to pick up the rubber, and encourage the producers to keep on tapping. Eventually there would be a steady stream of smuggled rubber.

Before long Fletcher had to admit that this was pie in the sky, but he ingeniously substituted another pie. It was uneconomic just to smuggle rubber. Other commodities must be added. 'There is at the moment quite a big traffic in tungsten, largely under the wing of the Yunnan Government, going from Siam right through to Japanese receivers in Southern China.' If the price was right this traffic could be diverted to the Allies. They could set up an organization in Sumatra to handle quinine *and* rubber. 'It is to throw away the services of valuable agents to work *Mickleham* [the code-name for the rubber-smuggling project] in a rigid rubber waistcoat, although rubber must obviously be the main objective.' At this point Fletcher had no agents whose services might be wasted.

The Americans were no more successful. Elliott reported that there was no hope of getting any rubber from the Dutch East Indies since all the suitable collecting points were in enemy hands. He could do no more than try to infiltrate agents to encourage growers to continue tapping and stockpile their production against the day when the Allies could take it out.

Fletcher, well aware that he had accomplished nothing, and that the Ministry of Production who wanted the rubber would soon react to this fact, decided to attack. At the beginning of 1943 he set up an economic intelligence unit under Major J. A. Newhouse, which confirmed that several strategic materials – agar-agar, cutch, benzoin, silk, and mercury in addition to quinine – could be smuggled from Japanese-occupied areas. Fortified by this advice he proposed that his establishment should be increased from four to fifty. He would proceed to China to get the personal blessing of Generalissimo Chiang Kai-Shek, which would ensure Chinese co-operation generally. He even claimed that it was just as well he had not found rubber so far in Indo-China since his over-eagerness to buy might have pushed prices up. Nevertheless, 'I hope to be organized in that area fairly soon.'

The case for continuing *Mickleham* was put to the Minister of Production in February 1943. After discussion with the Americans, who would have to fly out any supplies smuggled into China, it was agreed, perhaps astonishingly, to carry on with the scheme. The suggestion that it might be possible to get materials other than rubber tipped the balance. Fletcher, accompanied by Colonel L. O. Davis, who knew China well, visited Chungking to put his proposals to the Chinese authorities, who were invariably suspicious of British activities in their midst. But they seem to have been bowled over by the huge extrovert civilian, for they agreed without demur to his plan to smuggle strategic materials from enemy-held territory to China. They even allowed him to form a small company, admittedly with Chinese participation, to handle the commodities in question. He now sent home enthusiastic reports couched in language which must have raised the chaste eyebrows of Whitehall: 'there are plenty of fish ready to play, but I shall have to follow a narrow way between having too many at it, and not being in the hands of one man . . . After many talks and meals with the big boys in the racket [i.e. the smugglers] I am sure they will produce results.'

So far as rubber was concerned they did not. In June 1943 Fletcher and Mackenzie accepted that there was no hope of bringing any rubber from the occupied territories until they had put in agents with good W/T communication, and could guarantee sea transport. That would take another six months. Fletcher's stay in China, however, had convinced him that there were good opportunities for acquiring other materials; but this called for an operation wider in scope and different in character – so complex that he must return to London to explain it. Mackenzie told SOE headquarters that there would be some advantage from the special-operations point of view if

*Mickleham* continued to function in China. It would help him to make contacts, to gather intelligence, and to provide new channels into occupied territories – quite apart from any acquisition of raw materials.

After prolonged discussion and much special pleading by Fletcher, the Minister of Production ruled that *Mickleham*, which had failed to produce one pound of rubber, must be wound up. Undaunted, Fletcher now developed the argument Mackenzie had put forward. The real value of his organization was to provide cover for agents. He added a new argument. *Mickleham* could be used to exploit the currency black market and circumvent China's galloping inflation. While he was trying to buy rubber he had seen how the Americans bribed the Chinese, often with war materials, which the British could not do, partly because they must not pass on Lend-Lease equipment. He had also noted that the Chinese war-lords were interested in acquiring goods that would maintain their value.

He told London that his purchasing power would be much increased if he were allowed to use diamonds as currency. No doubt the South African Government had large stocks. 'Smuts is just the sort of man whose imagination would be fired by the plan to mobilize usefully for the war effort packets of stones lying hidden in safes and vaults . . . It would be nice if Smuts would follow the precedent set in other directions by letting us have the stones free . . .'. He admitted that at first blush it might seem to make more sense to use sapphires, emeralds, and rubies which were available in the Far East, but the advantage of diamonds was that they were produced within the Empire. Further, he had no wish to compete with the Rajahs who had vast quantities of the other stones. An incredulous marginal note added to his letter in London asks: 'Do you understand that Fletcher hopes to pay for rubber with *rubies?*'

In spite of their incredulity London agreed to look at his proposal. They asked for more details. Presumably he wanted finished gems and not industrial diamonds? Did he intend to use the stones 'to influence personally' [bribe does not appear in the Treasury vocabulary] senior men in the Chinese Government? If so, hard currency would do just as well. On the other hand, diamonds would be very attractive to rubber growers. What unit of value did Fletcher contemplate? What would a one-carat diamond buy?*

* In March 1943 a one-carat diamond was valued at 15,000 Chinese National Dollars.

Fletcher's first black-market transaction was in rupees. In May 1943 he negotiated a sale at the rate of fourteen Chinese National Dollars (CND) to the rupee, compared with the official rate of six, thus showing a 'profit' of more than 130 per cent. The rupees were delivered to a Chinese intermediary in Calcutta, with the approval of the Indian Exchange Control, against CND handed over in China. Fletcher was satisfied that inflation, fuelled by printing money and crowding huge number of soldiers and unproductive government servants into underdeveloped Free China, would cripple foreign interests there. If *Mickleham* went, ideal cover for black-market deals would go with it. British Government costs would soar.

There were three official rates: eighty CND to the pound for military missions and business firms; 120 for diplomatic missions; and 160 for European salaries. Since the open-market rate was 400, the purchasing power of monies remitted to the British Military Mission in Chungking was cut by four-fifths; that of the Embassy by about one third; and that of British business men by more than half. The Treasury readily accepted Fletcher's argument and agreed that *Mickleham* should be turned upside-down. The profitable sideline – dealing in the black market – now became the main objective. The acquisition of raw materials was to be no more than cover for the new institution, code-named *Remorse*, whose services had to be used by all British bodies in China. As Fletcher pointed out: 'If three or four organizations are all punting around they will not only spoil the rate for each other, but be exploited by by no means ignorant banks and exchange dealers.'

*Remorse* was authorized in January 1944 to acquire CND 'through discreet banking and exchange transactions', by buying goods and reselling them for CND, and by smuggling into China diamonds and other costly goods for sale on the black market. The banking procedures were formally approved by the Treasury and Bank of England. British organizations must tell *Remorse*, say in January, how much they would need in March. In February *Remorse* would base the March rate on recent transactions and announce how much their account should be credited; and at the beginning of March the equivalent in black-market CND would be paid into the organizations' individual accounts with the Chartered, or Hong Kong and Shanghai Bank in Chungking. *Remorse* was instructed to buy CND from people known to be favourable to the Allies with sterling accounts in London, which could be drawn on only for approved purposes.[1]

Fletcher, who in the view of a senior colleague had so far been more trouble than he was worth, now had the full authority of the British Government to run the biggest currency black market in history. He made the most of his chances, setting up headquarters in Kunming under Colonel L. O. Davis, with branch offices in Kweilin, Meng-tze, and Chungking. He also had an office in Calcutta to keep in touch with the Indian Exchange Control. His staff were known as representatives of the Ministry of Production and to enhance their cover carried on some trading for that Department.[2]

The British Ambassador to China, Sir Horace Seymour, was convinced that *Remorse*'s activities could not be hidden from the Chinese authorities. Some of SOE's operatives would land in a Chinese gaol – an unpleasant experience – and he would of course have to disown them. Fletcher guessed that although the Minister of Finance (Dr Kung) must have a shrewd idea what was going on, since the British organizations suddenly reduced their transactions through the Central Bank of China, he would turn a blind eye. In the end it was deemed prudent to tell Kung in June 1944 that some sales of sterling in the open market (not, of course, the *black* market) were contemplated, the proceeds to be used only for the expenses of missionary societies, the Red Cross, relief funds, and the expenses of British nationals. For the sake of appearances the British organizations continued to buy some CND at the punitive official rates, but they looked more and more to *Remorse*; and in October 1944 London agreed that transactions through the Central Bank should be phased out.[3]

To ensure success *Remorse* required the backing of Chinese with political and commercial influence. Fletcher's earlier company was too small to handle the ventures of the new enterprise, and was replaced by a department of the China Syndicate (comprising banks, transport companies, and representatives of the Provincial Governments) known as Syndicate B, on which *Remorse* had a seat. A fifteenth of the profits went to the Chinese Secret Service run by General Tai Li, 'a necessary insurance against guerrillas and obstruction by Customs' – proof that the Chinese knew perfectly well that the British were operating on the black market.

The commodities *Remorse* smuggled into China had a high resale value. In March 1945, for example, diamonds fetched the equivalent of 1,340 CND to the pound, more than twenty times the official exchange rate. Occasionally an eager customer ordered an item in advance – a necklace of eighty-one pearls valued in Britain at over £2,000, or a ring with an eight-carat diamond which cost £2,305. In July 1944 *Remorse* smuggled in a consignment of 200 high-quality ladies' and gentlemen's Swiss watches, many of them gold, worth £4,000. The organization had particular success with Welbikes, the miniature motor cycle designed for the forces. Two presented to the Governor of Yunnan so impressed him that he ordered forty. The value of goods sold on the black market – including four million CND worth of watches, ten million of diamonds and pearls, twenty-four million of drugs, especially the new sulpha drugs, and sixty million of cigarette-paper exceeded 200 million CND.

This, however, was dwarfed by the straight exchange transactions which brought in nearly 14,000 million CND. The number of *Remorse's* customers grew from a mere handful to thirty-three, including seven military organizations, eleven diplomatic missions, the Red Cross, the Friends' Ambulance Unit and other relief bodies, ICI Ltd., Reuters, and seven other commercial firms. it was estimated that during its lifetime *Remorse* gave the Allies additional spending power of over £77 million.

In addition to acting as clandestine banker to the Allies in China (except for the Americans, who made their own arrangements with the Chinese Government) *Remorse* helped in a number of military operations. In April 1945 they financed the French troops who fought their way out of Indo-China into Yunnan (Operation *Waldorf*), and whom at first neither the Chinese nor American army were prepared to help. For six weeks they provided food, clothing, medicines, blankets, and camps until eventually the Americans came to their rescue. *Remorse* also financed Operation *Nonchalant*, the scheme to entice dock labour from Hong Kong. When the Government of India restricted exports of textiles to China, the Chinese retaliated by banning the export of silkworms to India, which meant that the Kashmir silk industry could not produce the silk needed for SEAC's parachutes. *Remorse* came to the rescue by buying eggs on the black market in China and smuggling them to India.

When General Wedemeyer assumed command of the American forces in China at the end of 1944 he insisted that the activities of all clandestine organizations in China should be disclosed to him. This led to a curious three-way diplomatic fencing bout. SOE wanted to keep *Remorse* secret from the Americans, but fearing that they must find out about it, evolved an insurance ploy. The Ambassador would remind the Chinese that officers of the Ministry of Production were buying raw materials, using the open finance market. If the Chinese were thus put in the picture *Remorse* would no longer be a clandestine body and need not be disclosed to Wedemeyer.

Seymour said this exercise in semantics was unnecessary. He had already given the Americans a hint about *Remorse*; and to mention it again to the Chinese would embarrass them. Wedemeyer must be made aware of *Remorse*'s activities. SOE London disagreed. Both Americans and Chinese had been told about *Remorse* 'in a sufficiently proper fashion'. To mention it again to the Americans would be seen as the awakening of a guilty conscience. Wedemeyer would say: 'Just as I thought! You British are coming clean bit by bit, as and when you think we have found something out, and I will have no more of it!' Nevertheless, it was left to Seymour to follow his own judgement, provided he made it plain to the Americans that *Remorse* was not a military body but simply an agency of the British Treasury.

The Ambassador sent his Financial Counsellor, Mr Geoffrey (later Sir Geoffrey) Wallinger and Colonel Davis – the latter in civilian clothes to avoid any suggestion that *Remorse was* a military body – to call on General Ormsted, Wedemeyer's Chief of Staff. Ormsted was forced to listen to a long exposition of the innocent history of *Remorse*; and was told that the British wanted to remove suspicion that one of their organizations was operating behind the back of the Americans. He had probably no idea why he was thus being taken into the Embassy's confidence, and thanked the British representatives, saying 'It was not his task to tell us how we were to run our affairs.' A satisfactory ending, SOE decided, to an episode which illustrates the lack of trust between the Allies in the field of special operations in the Far East.

Although it was understood that all Allied agencies in China, except the American, would draw their black-market currency from *Remorse*, some tried to work independently. In April 1945 the Indian Exchange Control complained that cheques drawn by the French Military Mission in Chungking were being presented to banks in Calcutta. This confirmed the suspicion that the French, who had asked for nothing from *Remorse*, and could hardly be living on thin air, must be competing in the black market. It was believed they were using the French Consulate and the French Missionary Fathers as their agents. In June 1945 they made the mistake of buying 50,000 rupees' worth of CND from one of *Remorse*'s own contacts; and then used *Remorse*'s W/T channel to arrange reimbursement in Calcutta.

In spite of representations to the French Embassy these private dealings continued; and when the Embassy asked for information about the alleged deals, *Remorse* thought they wanted it simply to be better able to cover their tracks in future. When the French Military Mission ran out of funds, however, and asked for an immediate 150 million CND in July 1945, and 324 million in August, *Remorse* had only seventeen million available for them. Further, they would receive Chinese dollars at the rate of only 250 to the pound compared with the 575 which their other clients would enjoy.[20]

*Remorse* was as great a success as *Mickleham* was a dismal failure. Fletcher's desperate fight to keep the rubber-smuggling scheme in being long after any reasonable person would have abandoned it – surely he cannot have imagined that any of his hare-brained plans would bear fruit? – meant that he was still established in China at the moment when his peculiar talents could make a significant contribution to the Allied war effort in the Far East. He eagerly seized the opportunity, and when the Japanese surrendered could claim that virtually single-handed he had credited the Allies with the sinews of war to the tune of £77 million.*

The other currency enterprise undertaken by SOE in the Far East was the counterfeiting of Burmese military rupees and Malayan military dollars printed by the Japanese. This was first mooted in March 1942 by Galvin in Chungking. He proposed that counterfeit notes should be provided for agents, and possibly even for the purpose of weakening the Japanese economy by flooding South East Asia with yen. The Reserve Bank of India objected, fearing reprisals in kind. Most Japanese agents captured after September 1942 carried counterfeit India ten-rupee notes, which suggested that the enemy was equipped to embark on a massive circulation of forgeries – although their product was not very good. The notes were slightly smaller than the genuine, the colouring was not quite right, and the paper was limp and without 'crackle'. In spite of this the Indian authorities continued to make difficulties, although the Chancellor of the

---

* Equivalent to about £900 million at present-day prices.

Exchequer (Sir Kingsley Wood), the Secretary of State for India, and the Foreign Secretary had approved the project. They thereby delayed a complicated and costly process – mint specimens had to be found, plates made, the notes printed on identical paper, and then aged by soaking in weak tea, folding and crinkling, and finally rubbing in a judicious amount of dirt.

It was eventually agreed to provide counterfeit currency for agents, and by July 1944 SOE London had printed and dispatched to India a million Japanese/Burmese ten-rupee notes and 200,000 one-rupee notes; and roughly the same quantities of Japanese/Malayan ten-dollar and one-dollar notes. These were issued to agents along with a supply of genuine currencies in use at the time, and a small quantity of gold sovereigns – the last to be used only in an emergency. One party going into Burma took 10,000 genuine Burmese and India rupee notes, twenty sovereigns, and 15,000 *Grenville*, as the counterfeit military notes were code-named. Curiously, the Burma hill tribes, who in any case preferred coins, distrusted the artificially soiled notes, although they were prepared to accept any in mint condition, 'which they keep flat in a book or carefully rolled' – showing how difficult it is for the planners to get everything right first time.

The Japanese spotted the Malayan forgeries – SOE's note was one-tenth of an inch too long, the smoke from the steamer on the back of the ten-rupee note was omitted, and an expert could feel that the paper was not quite right. Still Force 136 continued to issue the notes, claiming that most of the people who would handle them were not experts. At the end of hostilities the remaining stocks of *Grenville* were destroyed in the presence of at least two officers of field rank.

# 10

# Psychological Warfare

THE Far Eastern Bureau of MOI was formed in Hong Kong in September 1939 to disseminate news and information about Britain throughout the Far East. It later moved to Singapore, and with the fall of Singapore to New Delhi.[1] When OM 'secretly' entered the propaganda field in Singapore, FEB resented the unknown competitor. In London MOI hastened to defend its outpost. There had appeared in Singapore 'a body of men under a Mr Killery' engaged in propaganda which was its responsibility. What was the explanation? The row was settled when the Resident Minister in Singapore (Mr Duff Cooper), the former Minister of Information, set up a committee on which both bodies were represented, so that the right hand might know what the left was doing.

This unhealthy rivalry was perpetuated when psychological warfare was included in the India Mission's charter, in spite of misgivings by SOE headquarters who noted: 'In general we would rather avoid getting involved in propaganda work at all as it invariably leads to departmental brawls, particularly with the Ministry of Information.' Policy direction was now provided by the Political Warfare (Japan) Committee (PWJC) on which were represented all interested Whitehall Departments.[2]

When SEAC was established in November 1943 SOE, FEB, and India Command were still all operating propaganda services.[3] After much debate it was agreed that SEAC's new PWD should deal with 'combat propaganda', aimed at enemy forces in forward areas, 'strategic propaganda', to further strategic plans, and 'consolidation propaganda', to win civilian co-operation when the Japanese had been thrown out. FEB would be responsible for long-term political propaganda. GHQ India would carry out propaganda in the Indian languages to Indian civilians and prisoners of war. SOE would produce leaflets inside enemy territory for immediate operational use. Finally, in August 1944 PWD took over from India Command broadcasts to the Japanese forces. A Political Warfare Liaison Committee was set up to keep these organizations in touch with each other.[4]

This tidied up, or made less untidy, the British component in the propaganda sphere. The integration of the American component, OWI, was more difficult. Mountbatten insisted that PWD, like other Divisions in his headquarters, should be staffed by Britons and Americans; but because of divergent British and United States policies in the Far East, OWI would not co-operate, even when assured that PWD would avoid propaganda with post-war or political implications. The Americans' 'courteous refusal' to accept his directive upset Mountbatten, as it denied the principle of Allied command. The impasse was removed when it was agreed that OWI should work independently, without cutting across British policies. PWD would not issue propaganda objectionable to the United States; and a Combined Liaison Committee ensured fair play.[5]

This was by no means a formality. For example, a seemingly innocuous British leaflet announcing that Burma Government servants who had not collaborated would continue their duties under the British military administration, which concluded, 'The era of face slapping is over,' was objected to by the Americans on the ground that it was not concerned with military operations and had implications for post-war policy. They asked Mountbatten to withdraw it; but he saw nothing wrong. The leaflet dealt with the establishment of British military administration in Burma, which was no business of the United States. Unless the Americans could be more specific about their objections the RAF would continue to drop the leaflet.[6]

There remained one anomaly. Now that Mountbatten had his own PWD there was no need for an SOE propaganda section. When the Supreme Allied Commander suggested that SEAC should take over the SOE propagandists, Gubbins's first reaction was to object. But he changed his mind and yet another curious compromise was reached. The India Mission's Political Warfare Section retained its identity, but was attached to and functioned as part of PWD, which satisfied honour on all sides. At last the Allies had a psychological-warfare machine capable of functioning efficiently and without friction.[7]

Hardly had this happy state of affairs been reached when FEB claimed propaganda rights in Malaya, Siam, and Sumatra on the ground that military operations had not started there. Joubert reminded Mountbatten that FEB had agreed to keep off 'combat areas'; and he pointed out that they could be defeated were Mountbatten to declare the whole of SEAC a combat area. It was decided, however, that this would be cheating, and only Burma was thus designated. As it happened, FEB's ambitions in the other countries were largely frustrated by refusing them the aircraft needed to drop their leaflets.[8]

The final organizational change came in 1945 when PWE, hitherto responsible for propaganda in enemy and enemy-occupied countries in the West, took over propaganda policy in the Far East. A proposal that PWE should absorb SEAC's psychological-warfare activities prompted Mackenzie to point out that SOE were making a substantial contribution in this field, and that he reserved his position; but before another round could be fought in this never-ending contest the end of the war stopped the bout.[9]

Two months before Killery arrived in Singapore in May 1941, the Governors of Burma, the Straits Settlements, and Hong Kong were told about his secret activities and promised that they would be put in the picture before any subversive propaganda campaign was launched in their territory.[10] Killery, who knew the Far East well, believed his best chance of success lay in a 'whispering campaign' – the spreading of rumours to further the Allied cause – based on Shanghai. He ruled out one alternative 'black' propaganda activity, the creation of a 'Research Unit' (RU) on the European pattern – a clandestine radio station pretending to operate within Japan on behalf of supposed Japanese dissidents – partly because the ban on short-wave receivers reduced the potential audience in Japan, and partly because of the difficulty of finding a speaker whose Japanese would be acceptable to the listeners. Even if an RU had been set up and a convincing Japanese speaker found few would have been taken in by its pretending dissident movement.[11]*

In August 1941 Killery formed a propaganda section (OM/P) to plan, produce, and distribute covert propaganda aimed at Japanese morale at home and abroad. It tried to stimulate anti-Japanese sentiment, and attacked the Axis. It founded Zenith, a company to make propaganda films, among them a series of shorts entitled *Oriental Magazine*. Through a secret arrangement with the *Sydney Morning Herald* it placed material in newspapers throughout the world, including sixty in the United States. An Australian firm of

---

* The idea of a black radio station was revived in May 1944; but it was again accepted that no one would believe in a revolutionary Japanese station and the idea was again shelved.

newspaper distributors opened a branch in Singapore to produce propaganda material. The services of the Malaya Broadcasting Company were also used. During the four months of its existence OM/P was directed by Sir George Sansom.

Given time and the co-operation of British agencies Killery might have built a far Eastern propaganda organization on the same scale as PWE, but he was denied both. The British Minister in Siam, in particular, objected to his propaganda efforts. When an anti-Japanese pamphlet appeared in Bangkok Crosby jumped to the conclusion that 'this foolish and pernicious propaganda' had been put out by Killery's agents, and sent a vituperative complaint to London – without accusing Killery directly. MOI detected similarities in the Siamese text with a paper Killery had sent to New York, which convinced the Minister (Mr Brendan Bracken) that Killery was in fact responsible. This led to an angry correspondence between Bracken and Dalton, who finally wrote:

I should have thought that in the circumstances you would at least have admitted that you were wrong in the accusation which you made against him [Killery] and my organization generally at last week's Ministerial meeting . . . It would give me much more satisfaction if we could make an end of this silly bickering to join with you in knocking the real enemy on the head.

To which Bracken replied that OM's propaganda activities should be closed down. When Killery later proposed a leaflet campaign for Siam Crosby recorded: 'so long as I occupy my present post in Bangkok, I can scarcely imagine myself agreeing to any such proposal'. SOE would be well advised to have as little as possible to do with Siam.

Both Killery and FEB felt that they did not have enough guidance from London about propaganda themes. The former pointed out to his Minister that while it was easy to produce material 'varied with insults and spiced with innuendo', effective propaganda depended on a full understanding of political and economic problems in the Far East. He needed a specially qualified group to study themes, for example Japan's co-prosperity campaign; Japan as a competitor in the Far East; Japan's policy in occupied China; and a dozen others. The memorandum reached the Minister two days after the Japanese invasion put paid to all OM's efforts.

A fresh start was made in 1942 when Whitehall, mindful of Killery's

plea for guidance, set up PWJC. It might be expected that in the light
of OM's failure the India Mission would have been instructed to
hasten slowly; but the propaganda objectives set in April 1942 were
on an impossible scale. They included measures to reduce production
and weaken the monetary system in Japan and the occupied
countries. Dissension between central and local government in Japan
would be fomented. Her relations with neutral countries, especially
in South America, would be weakened. Fanatical opposition to the
Japanese regime by secret societies and individuals would be
encouraged. There would be created general despondency, doubts
about the principles which guided and sustained Japan, fears for her
future, conflict over the opposing racial theories and ideologies of
Japan and her ally Germany. The peoples of South East Asia would be
instructed in the techniques of resistance, sabotage, and revolt. All
this and more was envisaged at a time when Japanese armies pouring
across South East Asia made nonsense of *any* British propaganda.[12]

The all-embracing plan was a restatement of the grandiose
psychological-warfare charter of OM, and it may be explained away
as a necessary exercise in relieving frustration. Little of the programme was attempted. Nevertheless, a few months later an even
more ambitious programme was sketched out by the India Mission's
Controller of Political Warfare, which included subversive propaganda, political corruption, currency manipulation, the suborning of
enemy troops, and even political assassination.

The feud between Dalton and Bracken confused the relationship
between the India Mission and FEB. Officials take their time from
their Ministers. Had the latter seen eye to eye they would have issued
clear directives to their outposts in the Far East. SOE would have
confined themselves to anti-Japanese subversive propaganda. FEB
would have stuck to domestic and political. As it happened, when the
Viceroy became alarmed by the flood of anti-British propaganda
broadcast from Tokyo, it was the India Mission he asked to mount a
whispering campaign to sustain morale. MOI at once pointed out
that this had nothing whatever to do with subversion and was
therefore outside SOE's charter. Mr Gladwyn Jebb (later Lord
Gladwyn) valiantly argued that there *was* an element of subversion.
The India Mission had provided an organization ready to spread
alarm and despondency among the Japanese if they succeeded in
occupying the country. This argument did not impress MOI, but

possession is nine points of the law. The India Mission had no intention of abandoning their campaign.

It was difficult in the Far East to use the sophisticated ploys employed in Europe. There a rumour could be started through 'jetsam' – notes left in telephone kiosks, letters dropped in waste-paper baskets in hotels; fake news items stamped in stop-press columns; talking on telephones known to be tapped. The India Mission had to rely on word of mouth. Rumours manufactured in Meerut were dispatched in 'discreetly written letters' which, by arrangement with the Post Office, were not censored. In North West India seven regional contacts each had between six and fifteen sub-agents who passed on the rumours and promoted discussion of them. Their task was made easier 'by the custom in India by which when an educated man goes into a restaurant or cafe, those who are illiterate or less well educated gather round him and ask him for the latest news, and urge him to express his views'. The rumour-mongers plied their trade wherever there were people to listen in parks, eating houses, religious processions, tram queues, at the docks. In Bengal rumours were sent to trusted police inspectors who farmed them out to sub-agents. There were comparable organizations in Madras, the United Provinces, and Bombay.

The whispers put out by the India Mission, tailored for the communities at which they were aimed, may seem naïve. For example, 'As soon as the Japanese troops reached the frontier of India they were struck down by cholera as if by the Gods.' One theme common to East and West was the enemy's attitude to women: 'The Japanese are enrolling Burmese women in Battalions of Comfort and Cultural Relaxation.' It was impossible to measure the success of the campaign. Agents' reports naturally made the most of their own efforts. One reported from Amritsar that 'one of the stories of our propaganda literature which has been put into propagation' had been passed on as the truth at a big Muhammadan wedding. This was a fabrication that Japanese soldiers who had been reprimanded by a Malayan imam for entering his mosque wearing boots had tortured him to death. Another success was the repetition in the North West Frontier Province of a rumour started in the Punjab that German reverses had led Hitler to put out peace feelers. Occasionally a rumour would misfire. An elaborate tale that a report of a Japanese plane shot down in flames really referred to a shooting star portending the immediate defeat of Japan was misinterpreted. People got the idea that the non-existent shooting star portended great evil for India.

Peterson was given a free hand by Linlithgow but when Wavell replaced him the position changed. The new Viceroy had formed a poor opinion of SOE in North Africa and it was only out of deference to Linlithgow's wishes that the rumour campaign continued. In February 1944 the rumours, which Wavell insisted on approving, included a crop to popularize the appointment of Mr R. G. Casey as Governor of Bengal, which had come in for criticism. Points in his favour were that he was the first former War Cabinet member to become Governor; his appointment meant closer co-operation between India and Australia; his acceptance of the post meant great personal sacrifice; and his children cycled round the city like ordinary mortals. At its peak the India Mission whispering campaign employed 220 agents.

The Mission also spread rumours throughout the SEAC area. For example, Operation *Gracie* was designed to persuade the Japanese both in the field and in Japan that so many Japanese prisoners of war with left-wing tendencies were anxious to help the Allies win the war that special training camps were being built for them. This rumour was spread by individual agents in Burma, by the IFBUs, and by SOE officers attached to BAAG (the prisoner-of-war escape organization working in China). It was supported by fake letters sent to people living in Japan. The senders' names were fictitious but the addressees were real people whose names came from Allied censorship. It was presumed that even if the Japanese censorship officials deleted the references to the disloyal prisoners of war there was a good chance they would talk about them themselves. Another rumour, that the wooden ships being built for service along the South China Coast were not seaworthy and that many were foundering soon after leaving port, was supported by a complementary rumour that the Allies now had remarkable new weapons for sea warfare – the implication being that the wooden ships were in fact perfectly seaworthy, and that in reality they were succumbing to the new weapons.

The Globe Agency was an extension of the rumour campaign. It was mooted in April 1943 to distribute 'a steady stream of doctored information' to the Indian Press. Professional journalists skilled in the art of blending falsehood with truth would be employed under an Indian figurehead, although the agency would be run by an SOE-trained British journalist. It would present the British Empire as a union in which the left wing were perfectly free to plead their case; and claim that the British people accepted that after the war a form of government to satisfy nationalist aspirations would be set up in India, Burma, and Malaya.

The India Mission was strongly in favour of the agency, as were the other interested parties – the Viceroy, the Viceroy designate (Wavell), and Selborne. One was against – the Minister of Information. Eventually, having used every stratagem he could think of to block the project, Bracken said that if the Viceroy was satisfied that the Government of India could not place material in the vernacular press without a dummy agency, he had no objection. SOE regarded this as a licence to go ahead; and in April 1944 MOI realized that their defences had been breached. Bracken immediately protested. SOE had established the agency in defiance of their agreement with his Ministry. Not so, replied SOE. He had accepted that if the Government of India wanted the agency, it could go ahead. Bracken admitted defeat. In fact his objection had been without foundation. MOI was concerned only with the dissemination of honest news. The Globe Agency was a 'black' organization which tailored the news to suit its own purposes.

Mainly because of Bracken's opposition it took the agency a year to go into action from the time it was first mooted. It opened an office in Calcutta in April 1944 and a second in Bombay in January 1945. At first it placed about thirty columns a week in 100 publications; but before long it was averaging 100 columns a week in between 300 and 400 publications. It continued until the end of the war, although it was suggested early in 1945 that the great improvement in the war news rendered its services unnecessary.

Early in 1943 the Director of Military Intelligence, India, asked the India Mission to form an 'Indian Field Broadcasting Unit' (IFBU) to carry out 'combat propaganda' in the field. An experimental unit operated in Burma from February to April 1943 using British officers with little knowledge of Japanese, and Koreans to tell the enemy front-line troops through powerful loudspeakers that their position was hopeless. They also scattered Burmese and Japanese propaganda leaflets; and took the opportunity of broadcasting news in English and Urdu to the Allied troops, who at this time had no regular news service. The commander, Major G. L. Steer, was refreshingly frank about the unit's performance. There was no evidence of success or failure, but at least it was possible to speak to a large captive Japanese audience. There was nothing to suggest that the leaflets, produced on the spot on duplicating machines, made any impact, although the Burmese who saw them politely said they were very good.

In the first six months of 1944 there were five IFBUs in the field – companies of sixty Indian troops commanded by a British officer: No. 1 Unit with XV Corps, Nos. 201 and 203 with IV Corps, No. 204 on the Assam/Burma front, and No. 2 between Mandalay and Kalewa. Each was equipped with four 'ampradiograms', devices which transmitted the human voice or gramophone records through two powerful loudspeakers located half a mile forward and a quarter of a mile apart. This enabled the unit to cover an area nearly four miles wide and up to 900 yards deep – the maximum distance the loudspeakers could be clearly heard. The speakers were now fluent in Japanese and Burmese, and the languages of the rebel Indian National Army; and they intermingled their talks with nostalgic Indian and Japanese music, using the technique of the disc jockey of a later age.* Some prisoners of war admitted they were affected by the music more than by the propaganda, which sometimes had negative results. Others thought the scripts badly prepared, and the speakers poorly briefed: 'Japanese front line soldiers from commanders down to privates are much too preoccupied and under too high tension to listen to long theoretical explanations.' What was wanted was a short powerful statement rather than a long-winded talk.[13]

It was intended that regular radio programmes from Calcutta should be rebroadcast from mobile IFBU transmitters but this proved impracticable because of poor reception in the field, and because regular programmes did not synchronize with lulls in the fighting.

Each IFBU had a two-inch mortar to fire 'leaflet bombs' – parachute flare bombs with the flare replaced by a tin canister holding 100 rolled-up leaflets printed on semi-gloss paper so that they would separate easily. The bombs could be fired up to 500 yards. When they burst at the top of their trajectory the canister split open and the leaflets floated down on the entrenched troops 'like a flight of birds'. This technique was most effective when the front was static, especially just before an Allied attack. It was difficult for the IFBUs to

---

* Early in 1945 thirty-five Canadian Japanese were recruited, mainly for IFBU work, but the war ended before they were able to go into action.

keep up with an enemy on the retreat, but of course at that time Allied superiority was the best propaganda. The IFBUs also delivered leaflets by hand, occasionally throwing bundles into enemy dug-outs; and they directed the dropping of leaflets by reconnaissance planes and light bombers. When required to replace the pen with the sword they used their mortars to fire ordinary bombs and to lay smoke screens.

They were under the command of the military formation to which they were attached, which could be frustrating. This is illustrated by two reports:

In about 5 minutes had speakers on the perimeter defences and was broadcasting surrender call through dense haze of smoke to the Japs who were about 100 yards away. In the initial stages was shot at twice but when the broadcast got going there was a tense silence and they were obviously listening. I saw figures moving through the bushes about 30 yards away. However, at the crucial stage of the broadcast when we were giving the final 'come on over' line a squadron of tanks roared up beside the village about 30 yards from the speakers and completely drowned the broadcast.

and again:

Got the speakers within 80 yards of a Jap light machine gun post and started broadcast. Put the Jap prisoner on the microphone. He was a little mike shy at first, but eventually plucked up courage and shot them a very good line. At the end of 25 minutes talking, with a nostalgic record thrown in, told the Japs that we were not going to fire again, and we would not speak for 20 minutes. During that 20 minutes they were to think over what we had told them and then when we spoke again and invited them to come over they could do so in absolute safety ... Then the spanner was thrown in the machinery. One of the tanks poured a burst into the Japs right in the middle of the 20 minutes contemplation period ... The Jap machine gun post replied and in a trice the battle was flat out again with bullets and grenades flying about like nobody's business. It was useless to continue.

The commander of the IFBU was later told that the tanks had been ordered to fire during the silent period to prevent the Japanese from using the breathing space to strengthen their position.

The IFBUs' consolidation propaganda – the preparation of the Burmese people for the return of the British – was carried out through special patrols which penetrated to villages in no man's land and behind the Japanese lines to distribute pamphlets, spread rumours, and set up markets where scarce commodities were offered at reasonable prices. A typical selection of goods offered – in order of popularity with the customer – was:

Longyis (sarongs)
Salt
Onions
Garlic
Chillies
Sugar
Blankets
Vests.

The IFBUs occasionally provided very welcome medical services. As many as 100 villagers might turn up at a sick parade. They could also be used for other purposes. One was required in September 1944 to recruit twenty trustworthy and able-bodied Burmese, to find watermen who knew the Chindwin River, and to train saboteurs. For rumour-mongering the IFBUs recruited agents who became paid employees. These men floated the same rumour simultaneously in several villages, taking care to keep secret their connection with the British, and leave it to villagers to pass on the rumour. The assembled Burmese were as a rule addressed by the IFBU commander who would assure them that the Japanese would soon be gone.[14]

There were mixed views about the value of the IFBUs. In May 1944 Slim told 11th Army Group that they had considerable intelligence and operational value, and a proposal to expand them had Mountbatten's support. The Army Group, however, thought the men would be better employed as combat troops, and fought a delaying action for twelve months. Then in 1945, in spite of Slim's earlier view, the Fourteenth Army decided that the IFBUs were not paying a reasonable dividend. XV Corps agreed that broadcasting did have some effect on isolated Japanese troops, but said that they would be destroyed in any case. 'They don't need a wireless to be played to them.' Moreover, the marketing enterprise imposed a strain on the line of communications without producing proportionate benefit. In spite of these adverse opinions the IFBUs were retained to the end of the war.[15]

The range of propaganda themes likely to be effective in the Far East was narrower than in Europe where, since the troops were more akin racially to the Allies, it was possible to see into their minds and guess what would influence them; and where there were sophisticated resistance movements to appeal to. The Burmese hill tribes were very simple-minded. Hidden meanings in the text or illustrations of a leaflet would be lost on them, many being unable to recognize their own likeness in a photograph. Equally, maps showing the progress of the Allied armies were pointless since the Karens and Kachins knew little of the world beyond their own district. Propaganda linked to tales of their valour and loyalty to the British even in the distant past was well received; and occasionally a headman would be prepared to send a leaflet message to the people of his district urging them to help the Allies. One leaflet addressed to the tribesmen failed. It depicted a bursting bomb which they took to be the rising sun, and therefore a message from Japan.

For the Burmese people at large, who had been unmoved by Allied propaganda during the first two years of Japanese occupation, a profitable line was the advertisement of the IFBU markets and the promise of better times which they symbolized. The folly of continuing to help a beaten enemy was drummed into them and they were urged to enjoy the spectacle of 'the little men on the run'. In addition to leaflets the American OWI distributed packets of seeds – beans, radishes, and tomatoes – as a gift from the American/Chinese Task Force, with the message 'Wherever the Japanese go they bring destruction. Wherever the Allies come, the fields spring up green.' OWI also offered to buy the produce of these seed packets when the Japanese had been driven out, paying in either silver rupees or salt. This upset the Burma Civil Affairs authorities, who were committed to using paper money, and could not provide the transport to carry the huge amounts of salt that would be needed.[16]

The line taken with the Indian National Army serving with the Japanese was that those who willingly surrendered would come to no harm. The enemy's assertion that prisoners would be killed was false. The sooner they surrendered the better, since they would be driven further and further from home, and end up as Japanese slaves. 'Which do you choose? Coolie labour, or death?' This sometimes had spectacular results. On one occasion 250 members of the Nehru Brigade surrendered in a body.[17]

The main themes against the Japanese were relatively simple. The certainty of defeat:

The Imperial Grand Fleet is a vanished dream . . . Who is going to help you now?

The battleships *Yamashiro* and *Fuso*, 4 carriers, 12 cruisers, and 6 destroyers are sunk.

The Burma dream is over. 50,000 of your comrades rot in these hills.

You won't be here long, son of Nippon! Terrible weapons of destruction, machines that belch a sea of fire making men into hot dust are about to be turned against you!

Soldiers of the 31st Division! Have you enjoyed yourselves in Burma this year? Where are your aeroplanes? Where will you get your food?

### The bravery of the private soldier in contrast with the incompetence of his commanders:

Brave son of Nippon! The failure of your commanders has brought your heroic efforts to nothing!

You are brave, soldier of Nippon! You have great fighting qualities which fill the British with admiration; but the bravest soldier cannot continue to fight when his commanders let him down.

Japanese soldier, please take this message to General Mutaguchi . . . You have murdered your men, General, by bringing them to Manipur. Do you remember how in March you told them that they would advance like a ball of fire and capture Imphal at a stroke?

### The appalling conditions in which they had to fight:

Here is your enemy! The rains have come. For months the skies will weep. These mountains will be soaked with water like the weeds of a river . . . Loathsome diseases will feast upon your flesh!

### Allied successes in Europe:

Invasion! Soldier of Nippon! Read and tremble! The attack on Europe has begun. The attack on Japan will come next.

Paris is free! Liberation after four years and two months of German rule.

### Nostalgic reminders of home:

Remember the good old days? Fermented bean soup. Raw fish. Broiled fish. Assorted rice. Pickles. Japanese tea. All you get now is jungle roots, grass, and filthy water.

How would you like your favourite meal served by your wife in your own home?*[18]

* This may have struck a chord. A scrawl in a captured private's diary reads: 'When I get home . . . the faces . . . raw fish, vegetables, five bowls of red-bean soup – first day. Second day – pork cutlets, vegetable salad.' And so on to 'Ninth day – cutlets, curry and rice. Tenth day – ten plates of fried noodles a la Wan Tun.' At this point the writing which has become steadily fainter disappears altogether. (SEAC War Diary 10.11.44.)

The theme that the private soldier was required to endure hardship at the front for the benefit of the war profiteer was developed in an interesting series of leaflets depicting the life-style of the profiteer. Six photographs were commissioned:

1. Profiteer at dinner waited on by pretty girls.

2. Smoking and drinking after dinner with the girls.

3. Communal bathing scene.

4. Fornication.

5. Fornication.

6. More smoking and drinking.

The production of Nos. 1, 2, 3, and 6 presented no difficulty. 'No. 4 can be produced by fake photography from an existing photograph in the possession of MI 5; but we are rather stuck at present for No. 5, for which it is suggested that a model could most easily be found at the Home Office Libraries.' In the event there was 'a lot of difficulty in getting hold of anyone to play the more stirring scenes'. Eventually suitable models were found but 'the pornographer's path is thorny and there may yet be some unforeseen hitch'. In the end the pictures were produced although it was necessary for 'a certain amount of red tape to be unwound before we got our subjects stripped for action. The results, however, are satisfactory I think, and seeing the subjects had to be photographed separately the photographer is to be congratulated on a really clever bit of photomontage.' It was hoped the pictures struck the right note of artistic debauchery. 'The background looks a bit austere to the western eye . . . but with the Japanese the play's the thing, and the scenery is kept simple.'

The caption read: 'This is the way the profiteers are living at home. Soldiers, it is not for such as these that you should die. If you surrender to us you will be well treated and your lives will be preserved to clear Japan of such scum after the war.'

The main stumbling-block the Allies had to overcome was the Japanese soldier's attitude to death and surrender, inculcated from childhood. Death in battle was glorious. His family would rejoice to hear of it. That there was no greater disgrace than to be captured was enshrined in the Japanese battle training manual. This idea was developed in a twenty-four-page pamphlet for the guidance of soldiers. 'Not to be subjected to the shame of becoming a prisoner of war while life remains is an ancient tradition of our country . . . in the present holy war a few have allowed themselves to be taken alive, but not all were victims of unavoidable circumstances.' Those captured in combat usually fell into enemy hands while stupefied by severe wounds. This is no excuse. It is the utmost disgrace to be captured alive, but if he is, the soldier must enhance his spirit, maintain a gallant attitude, and commit suicide, or escape. SEAC's Adviser on Japanese Affairs believed the only way to deal with this attitude was to find 'an emotional antitoxin'. The army had been trained to accept death in battle as an article of faith, and something must be done to show that this faith was misplaced.[19]

This led to well-intentioned appeals to reason which had little hope of success. For example:

Since the dawn of chivalry it has been understood that when a soldier has fought bravely to the end there comes a time when he can achieve nothing more . . . He can flee the field, he can die, or he can lay down his arms. The first is shameful to any warrior and cannot be contemplated. The second offers release from all problems and responsibilities, but precludes all possibility of further service to country. The soldiers are the flower of the manhood of any nation and it is to avoid the vain destruction of this flower that the civilized code of chivalry enjoins the last-named as the only honourable alternative for the soldier.[20]

This type of argument was complemented by the distribution of safe conducts. They carried a message to Allied troops saying the bearer was to be well treated, and were embellished with SEAC's emblem of hope – the phoenix rising from the ashes. Few Japanese availed themselves of this means of escape from the front line – far fewer than the number of Germans when the Allies were advancing towards Berlin. Safe conducts for the Indian National Army, which was not imbued with the fanaticism of the Japanese, were rather more successful.[21]

Prisoners of war provided ample evidence that there was no greater disgrace than surrender. Most were so ashamed that they were terrified to think that one day they must face their fellow-countrymen in Japan. One tried to commit suicide three times, once by stabbing himself with his bayonet, and twice by biting his tongue. Another who refused to give his name begged his interrogators to kill him, or let him die. 'If you should die, what name shall we put on your grave?' 'Just write "An unknown warrior who was fool enough to die in enemy hands".'[22]

It was only in Burma that there was an opportunity to use propaganda in direct support of military operations. Mobile printing units at the front produced urgent leaflets to support tactical moves – for example, an appeal to Burmese in a certain district to withhold bullock carts from the enemy, or an up-to-the-minute Japanese order of battle to show that Allied intelligence knew their exact dispositions. Some success was claimed for this 'combat propaganda'. It was recorded that Japanese soldiers had been seen in tears after reading leaflets; and again, 'A major is said to have committed suicide after reading a copy of *Gunjin Shimbun* [*Soldiers' Newspaper*]. Although reaction to reading our news sheet is not always so violent, there is constant evidence of their popularity.' There can be little doubt, however, that in combat it was Allied military superiority, the impossible terrain, inadequate rations, and other hardships that really mattered. That propaganda made little impact is suggested by the frequent repetition in official reports of the same tiny success stories – surrenders in twos and threes represented as major triumphs; four Japanese shot as they were reading leaflets; a group of twelve who left their trench in response to an IFBU broadcast, and then changed their minds and went back again; and so on.

Some Japanese prisoners were prepared to co-operate by providing an assessment of Allied propaganda; but even their evidence may be suspect. They may have tried to say what their captors wanted to hear. One at least provided a massive critical essay. At first Allied leaflets were poorly written, with many grammatical errors. Too little attention was paid to technical detail. For example, red meant communist, and black was the sign of death, so these colours should never be used. Better paper would emphasize the strength of Allied resources – and it would be less acceptable as toilet paper. Pictures of dead Japanese had been so horrific that they were counter-productive. Leaflets quoting Japanese prisoners' letters saying how well they were being treated were assumed to be fabrications. Even the accepted truth cut no ice. A leaflet pointing out that the mechanized tide of the Allied armies could not be stemmed was seen to be the truth; but it led none to surrender, so great would the shame be.[23]

Another prisoner of war reminded his captors of the Japanese proverb 'There is no gem so precious as an unknown good deed', and suggested that information favourable to the Allies, but not put out as part of their propaganda campaign, could do more than 'many thousands of words poured out under the banner of propaganda'. The admission of Japanese troops who had been captured in the Imphal campaign but later escaped that they had been well treated while in captivity was worth a thousand leaflets making the same point. The careful medical attention given to wounded Japanese in Singapore hospitals before the city fell was also powerful evidence of the humanitarian attitude of the Allies. This witness argued that honesty was the best policy. To broadcast unvarnished news, the truth of which could later be tested, would break down Japanese distrust of Allied propaganda as a whole.[24]

A soldier who was a school principal in civilian life said leaflets had no effect at all. Troops were amused by them, knowing that they were propaganda. References to the Emperor had alienated all classes. The average private thought the messages too long and the language too complicated. It was obvious that they had been written in English and translated, which produced an awkward style far removed from free-flowing Japanese. It would be more sensible for the 'propaganda expert' to state the general theme and leave it to the translator to render it in Japanese. Leaflets were more acceptable when printed rather than written by brush or pen and then reproduced. Others agreed with this verdict. 'A brush has been used but stroking of characters was not in true Japanese fashion.' These witnesses had no doubt that the leaflets in question had been written by a Chinese, which of course reduced their value to nil.[25] All the same, there was little point in trying to achieve perfection. It was virtually impossible to induce surrender.

# 11

# Prisoner-of-war recovery

THE totally unexpected end of the war in the Far East, brought about by the atomic bombs at Hiroshima and Nagasaki in August 1945, found Force 136 with plans for activities in Malaya and elsewhere in SEAC stretching far into 1946. Relief at the cessation of hostilities was mingled with regret that the India Mission was now denied the chance of capitalizing on experience gained in the last three years. There was consolation, however, in the fact that Force-136 parties were well placed to help the surviving Allied prisoners of war and interned civilians – well over 100,000 of them in the SEAC area. Together with E Group, concerned with the rescue of prisoners while the war was still on, and OSS, the Force mounted a massive operation to ensure their safety and health and to arrange for their evacuation. The joint enterprise was known as the Repatriation of Allied Prisoners of War and Internees (RAPWI).

The prisoner-of-war camps were scattered over five countries, often in remote places, and there was the danger that Japanese unwillingness to admit defeat would lead some commandants to ignore their Government's decision to surrender. Allied parties going to help the prisoners might be attacked. Equally, prisoners might take the law into their own hands and attempt a mass break-out, or do something that would lead to a pitched battle with the Korean guards, who if past performance was anything to go by, would not hesitate to retaliate in most drastic fashion. Mountbatten therefore issued an 'unshakeable order' that no camp be approached until he was satisfied beyond doubt that the surrender was holding, and had sent a special signal to go ahead. In spite of strong pleas from his Staff he refused to lift the ban until 26 August; and even then parties on the ground were authorized to approach only those camps which were known to have been abandoned by the Japanese.

Leaflets were dropped to the camp authorities, the local population, and the prisoners, care being taken to ensure that the first had their instructions an hour or two before the prisoners received theirs – either by phasing the aircraft sorties, or by circling the camps between drops. Forty Thunderbolts covered Southern Burma, where the enemy were still present, and thirty-seven Liberators the rest of SEAC, including places as far east as Hanoi and Saigon. Between 28 and 31 August they visited virtually every camp in the region, dropping twenty tons of leaflets.

The commandants were told that the war was over and that the Emperor had signed a surrender document. Prisoners must be treated with every care and attention, and without delay handed their leaflets telling them 'to remain quiet where they are'. The prisoners were told that the Japanese had surrendered unconditionally, and were asked to remain in camp, to prepare nominal rolls, and to list their most urgent needs. They were warned about the danger of suddenly eating large quantities of solid food, fruit, or vegetables. Gifts of food from the local population must be cooked. 'We want to get you back home quickly, safe and sound, and we do not want to risk your chances from diarrhoea, dysentery and cholera at this last stage.'

The leaflet operation, christened *Birdcage*, was accompanied by Operation *Mastiff* which carried men and supplies to the camps. The acceleration of Force 136's programme in support of the planned invasion of Malaya had already imposed a severe strain on the resources of the India Mission, but now a vast additional airlift was needed – far greater than the Special Duties Squadrons could cope with on their own. They were reinforced with aircraft from Nos. 159, 203, 231, and 355 Squadrons, which had not been trained for special duties, and were used in *Mastiff* only to drop stores, not men. The squadrons mustered six Lysanders, ten Dakotas, used to land men and supplies where there were suitable airstrips near camps, and a hundred Liberators. Between them they flew more than 550 sorties, their capacity being increased by removing guns, gun turrets, and ammunition, and by using the minimum crews.

Fifty four-man teams were briefed to go to the camps. They were warned to use great tact, for example by issuing instructions only through the Senior Allied Officer, whose word would carry weight with the prisoners. The latter must be persuaded to remain in or near their camp, however distasteful it might be, to facilitate evacuation and sending news of their release to relatives. They must be told to be patient, and reminded of the magnitude of the recovery operation. They would continue to be fed by the Japanese, who would administer the camps, taking orders from the RAPWI groups.[1]

Apart from sharing in the provision of these teams Force 136 packed all the huge quantities of stores required, and provided all the W/T communication. Between 16 August and 17 October 1945 over 1,000 tons of stores were packed, including 800 tons of food and over one hundred tons of clothing and personal equipment. There were thirty-eight tons of medical supplies, seventy-five tons of Red Cross parcels, and eleven tons of 'amenities'. In Calcutta at the peak of the operation – between 27 August and 12 September – twenty-four NCOs, fifty-four other ranks, and over 200 coolies worked twenty-four hours a day in eight-hour shifts. Malaya and Sumatra were supplied through the Cocos Islands, which meant ferrying stores there in Liberators from Minneriya and in Sunderland flying boats from Galle at the southern tip of Ceylon. Much of the packing in Ceylon was done in the shadow of Sigirya Rock, the fortress capital of the ancient kings. But for the ready-made Force-136 organization it would have taken much longer to get badly needed supplies to the camps.

W/T communication for RAPWI was provided through the Force-136 teams already on the ground. By the end of September they were using fifteen stations in Malaya, ten in Sumatra, and five in Java (where the India Mission had not previously operated) working to Colombo; and thirty-one in Siam and one in Indo-China working to Calcutta. Force 136 also supplied 1,500 Miniature Communications Receivers (MCR) manufactured by SOE London, which were invaluable for the reception of instructions in the camps and enabled the ex-prisoners to listen to broadcasts from India and Britain. Fifty MCRs were issued to RAPWI in Ceylon for use in transit camps for the ex-prisoners.[2]

The 35,000 prisoners in Siam were lucky in that Force 136, E Group, and OSS were present in strength and in close touch with the resistance movement, which included virtually the whole of the Siamese army and police force. They were also helped by the nearness of Rangoon from which many sorties were flown to Bangkok. By the end of September when the city was occupied by men from the 7th Indian Division most of the British prisoners had been evacuated.

Many camps heard about the Japanese surrender before the *Birdcage* leaflets reached them, through a secret radio operated at grave risk – in *The Night of the New Moon* van der Post tells how prisoners caught in Java with a radio were beheaded – through contacts made by working parties sent to a nearby town, or perhaps through newspapers smuggled into the camp. In Kanchanaburi camp in Southern Siam the news was broken at a weekly meeting between the camp authorities, a group of prisoners, and the Siamese supplier from whom they were allowed to buy tobacco and other goods out of their meagre wages. Arnold Thorne, a young lawyer serving with the Singapore Royal Artillery Volunteers and taken prisoner when Singapore fell, recollects how this man, who over a long period at great personal risk had smuggled badly needed drugs in the prisoners' purchases, held up a notebook behind the Japanese officers' backs with the words 'Japan surrenders today'.* It was some hours before the commandant admitted the war was over, and some days before an Allied officer – from OSS – who had parachuted to the neighbourhood arrived on a commandeered donkey. His face was badly gashed, which was taken to be the result of his parachute jump until he confessed that he had landed unscathed and that his wounds came from being thrown by his mount.

Colonel David Smiley, the Force-136 officer in command of the *Candle* area in Northern Siam, returned to his guerrillas on 15 August 1945 after a spell in hospital in India recovering from severe burns caused by the accidental setting-off of an explosive briefcase. In his absence his W/T operator had been told about the atomic bomb and the Japanese surrender, and warned that all Japanese commanders might not follow the Government's lead. Smiley, who had earlier been in touch with the prisoners in the nearby camp at Ubon through a Sino-Siamese girl who supplied ice to the camp authorities, was already established with his W/T operator on the top floor of the Siamese army officers' mess in the town of Ubon – evidence how much Japanese control in Siam had waned. By 23 August he had contrived to arrange for three senior prisoners to come to the mess escorted by Japanese guards who were relieved by Siamese officers before the prisoners were brought to Smiley. They gave information about immediate requirements of medical and other supplies which were passed to headquarters.

* Thorne had been lucky to survive until the end of the war. Some months earlier he was playing cards in a hut when American bombers attacked a bridge which he and his fellow prisoners had built (and which they later believed to be the inspiration for the fictitious River Kwai bridge). Three of the four who left the table to watch the planes as they sought to demolish their handiwork took cover when they saw bombs falling dangerously close. The fourth, waiting at the table for their return, was killed – along with twenty-eight others.

To Smiley's astonishment – and indeed embarrassment, for he was forbidden to visit the camp until he received the code-word* from headquarters – on 27 August Lieutenant-Colonel (later Sir Philip) Toosey and several other prisoners armed with pistols arrived without escort at his secret hide-out. To his relief the code-word came next day, and he at once drove to the camp, accompanied by the Chief of Police, to find all except the sick drawn up to raise the British and Dutch flags and sing the national anthems – a moving occasion. Smiley and Toosey were received arrogantly by the commandant until they threatened him with their pistols. He then produced whisky and food removed from Red Cross parcels. They found a room filled with the prisoners' mail for the last three years, which had never been issued to them – on the pretext that there were no interpreters to censor it.

When Smiley was briefed in India about dealing with the prisoners he asked if he might show them copies of the *Tatler* which he received regularly from London. This, he was assured, would be bad for morale. Toosey found the instruction so amusing that he insisted on displaying it on the camp notice-board so that all might share in the joke.

Nevertheless, not all prisoners were able to be so light-hearted. Many suffered permanent psychological damage. The experience of one member of Force 136's Anglo-Dutch Country Section, Lieutenant-Commander B. W. Lefrandt who parachuted into Northern Achin in Sumatra at the beginning of July 1945, suggests that headquarters may have had a point in urging special care. That the war was over may have been all that mattered for most, but many were shattered to learn for the first time of the death of close relatives. Lefrandt believed that specially trained parties should have been sent in to cater for these unfortunates, but of course the sudden end of the war made it virtually impossible. He himself had a traumatic experience. His young daughter, who had been interned with his wife and son, could not believe that he was her father; and it was four years before they could settle down to a normal family life again.

There was still some fight left in the Japanese forces in Sumatra, which justified Mountbatten's reluctance to give RAPWI parties their heads in approaching prisoner-of-war camps. Moreover, prisoners there were less fortunate at the time of liberation than many of their

* *Goldfish* for Siam; *Swansong* for Malaya.

brothers in South East Asia, since the country was at the end of the queue for an Allied invasion. At the time of the surrender there were on the ground only three SOE parties, which had arrived as recently as 28 June, 1 July, and 4 July, and had had little time to establish themselves. They were also hindered by the hostile attitude of the natives, and when they arrived they had no idea that the war would end almost immediately and that their task would not be to pave the way for an invasion, but to help to evacuate prisoners of war. One party bound for Kotaradja was blocked by the Japanese and went to Medan instead. Another was hampered by some members of the Kempei Tai. Eventually five more groups were sent in; and three were dropped into Java – SOE's first activities in that part of the Dutch East Indies since the days of the Oriental Mission.

The sense of disappointment at the time taken to evacuate prisoners from Sumatra is reflected in one account of events in the Sungei Geron camp ten miles from Palembang. Frank Brewer, a member of 101 STS and later of Colonel Dalley's 'Dalforce', joined a small group after the dispersal of Dalforce on 14 February 1942, intending to link up with a left-behind party understood to be in preparation in Sumatra; but he was captured near Banka Island. He has recorded:

Release from our POW camp was a gradual and haphazard business. Allied forces did not arrive to take the Japanese surrender and to take charge of us and arrange our evacuation in any formal way. Very late in the day an officer was sent to take charge of affairs . . . It was not until 1 September that we received newspapers by an air-drop which gave us some idea of the problems faced by SEAC in coping with POW release.*

It was perfectly understandable that prisoners who for years had been dreaming about the day when they would be freed should see themselves as forgotten men, and find it difficult to appreciate the difficulties in which the totally unexpected cataclysm had landed the whole of SEAC, including the India Mission. Only when Captain A. W. Fordyce of Force 136 arrived in Sumatra on 15 September – a month after the Japanese surrender – was the evacuation of prisoners taken seriously in hand. Eventually he had under him seven British and two Dutch officers, four W/T operators, and two medical orderlies. In addition to organizing the assembly and evacuation of

_____
* Information to author.

over 3,000 prisoners of war, he controlled 22,000 Japanese troops, 7,500 of them on guard duties, and provided for 4,000 destitute Javanese coolies who had been working for the occupying forces.

Since the greater part of Burma had been reoccupied by the Allies before the Japanese surrender, the recovery of the relatively small number of prisoners there presented few problems. By 19 September the final evacuation – from a camp at Tavoy – had been completed. An incident in Burma, however, provided further evidence of the wisdom of waiting until it was certain that the Japanese had accepted the idea of surrender. Through a failure of W/T communication Major Turrall, operating with Force 136 in Karenni, did not receive the order forbidding contact with the enemy; and on 16 August he crossed the Kyaukkyi Chaung accompanied by a single Karen guerrilla to take the surrender of the local Japanese forces. They received his claim that the war was over with scepticism, which increased when the area was heavily machine-gunned by British fighters, concluded that he was an agent on a propaganda mission, and made him prisoner.

The guards amused themselves by 'partially throttling' from time to time the boatman who had ferried them across the Kyaukkyi Chaung, but he and the Karen soon escaped. Turrall was kept tied up, subjected to face-slapping, blows from a rifle butt, and threats of torture to make him confess he was a spy. On 21 August he managed to free himself and make a dash for the jungle, but he was recaptured and again beaten up. Only when a British plane dropped leaflets announcing the Emperor's agreement to surrender did his captors begin to suspect he might be telling the truth and agree to regard him as an emissary of the British forces. The Japanese commander asked him to provide a letter saying he had been well treated but Turrall recorded what had actually happened, adding as a concession, 'For reversal of treatment I wish to express my appreciation.' Finally, he was escorted some distance through the Japanese lines and left on his own, still deep in enemy territory, and certain to be attacked by any Japanese patrol he encountered. Happily he got back to the Kyaukkyi Chaung unscathed; and after a lengthy swim downstream made his way back to his guerrillas.

In French Indo-China more than two-thirds of the 11,000 prisoners and internees were French, most of whom remained in the country to rejoin the army or return to their civilian jobs. The others, mainly British and Dutch, were flown to Rangoon by Special Duties

Dakotas based at Mingaladon. At the time of the surrender there were six clandestine groups available to help prisoners, comprising 310 Europeans (an increase of about forty since immediately after the Japanese coup) and about 300 natives (a significant decrease of more than 600 since the coup). The French Military Mission to SEAC took a particular interest in the *Mastiff* operation largely because of their concern to re-establish French authority in the country at the earliest possible moment. They drew up a parallel plan on 15 August 1945 to send eighty men of the French Secret Intelligence Service – *Directeur Général Études Recherches* (DGER) – to carry out preliminary reconnaissance in the neighbourhood of Hanoi, Saigon, Phnom Penh, and Hue as soon as the surrender was made official. Later these teams were to be supplemented by naval paratroops and the 5th Colonial Regiment. The latter did not reach Saigon until November, however, by which time all the prisoners had been liberated; and law and order was in the hands of the 80th Brigade of 20th Indian Division which arrived in Saigon at the beginning of October.

In Malaya most of the 42,000 prisoners were in the Singapore area, many of them in Changi Gaol. The first RAPWI party (Operation *Snooper*) reached Singapore on 30 August to find that the Japanese had accepted the surrender and were co-operating; and two days later they established W/T communication with Colombo. The Force-136 parties up-country – where there were more than 5,000 prisoners, dispersed in several camps – were, as were their brothers in Burma and Siam, under strict orders to keep their guerrillas in the jungle to avoid clashes with the Japanese which might prolong the conflict and incidentally put prisoners' lives at risk. This was a difficult task since the Malayan People's Anti-Japanese Army (MPAJA) had been eagerly awaiting the Allied invasion, and the chance of revenge after years of occupation. The slaughter of 20,000 Chinese, thrown into Singapore Harbour and machine-gunned, had not been forgotten. At the time of the surrender the Force-136 Group with the 4th (Selangor) Regiment of the MPAJA (commanded by Lieutenant-Colonel Broadhurst) was in the jungle a few miles north of Kuala Lumpur, where they were joined by John Davis who had come down from Perak to be nearer the centre of things when the invasion began.

Davis and Broadhurst told headquarters it would be virtually impossible to keep the guerrillas in the jungle now that the war was over, but that if they left it they would be tempted to slip away to deal with any Japanese they could find. It was therefore conceded that they should occupy territory no longer controlled by the Japanese, which in practice meant the countryside as opposed to the towns. This provided an effective safety-valve and the 4th Regiment set up headquarters in a derelict hospital near the village of Serendah twenty miles north of Kuala Lumpur. Three days later the Japanese broke the truce by attacking the police station where the guerrillas had established themselves, killing a guard and seizing two British Liaison Officers. The MPAJA dispersed to nearby buildings and there was every sign that a major battle was developing, which might set off a widespread chain reaction – and also throw doubt on the wisdom of allowing the guerrillas to leave the jungle.

In Davis's words:

Immediate and if possible non-aggressive action was needed to regain control and prevent the incident from spreading. Fortunately I had a Union Jack which had been dropped in to us some time before, so with Broadhurst and Lau the Chinese commander of the MPAJA and with our Gurkha support group flying the flag but with arms at the shoulder, we set off down the road just as dawn was breaking. We brushed aside two Japanese sentries who tried to bar our way as we approached the police station, and by the time we arrived had worked ourselves into such a state of simulated anger and indignation (we were in fact very nervous) that we must have been quite impressive. Anyhow, the 'bluff' worked. The Jap company commander quickly handed over the two British officers and agreed to call his men off. This, however, was easier said than done as they were busily engaged with the MPAJA who were still holding out in the buildings behind. It took a good half hour of flag waving, shouting, and blustering before we got the two sides lined up facing each other along the main road, still glowering, but at last under control.

Of the Force-136 parties elsewhere in Malaya which immediately went to the help of the prisoners in the neighbourhood some came across camps hitherto unknown to the Allies. One was found near Kachau in Selangor with 1,300 internees; and another near Ipoh with 300 Indians. In South Johore Operation *Carpenter* looked after 1,000 Indians, and smaller camps were administered by Operation *Fighter* at Gong Gajah and Operation *Multiple* at Raub. These final activities may have been but a shadow of what Force 136 and the guerrillas had for many months been training to carry out; but at least their ability to act quickly brought relief to thousands of prisoners of war and internees who might otherwise have had to wait much longer for repatriation, especially in Malaya, Burma, and Siam; and the members of the Force on the ground in these countries had the satisfaction of knowing that their immediate presence saved many lives.

# Conclusion

HAD the Oriental Mission been allowed to establish left-behind parties in Malaya well before the Japanese invasion – as it desperately tried to do – it would then have been in a position to carry out special operations in the accepted sense. Well-trained and well-equipped groups in the mountainous jungle regions could have been supplied by air, and with effective direction from military headquarters might have posed a serious threat to the invaders' lines of communication; but with the defeat of the army (which a powerful resistance movement could have delayed and perhaps even prevented) the possibility of special operations on the European pattern disappeared. SOE London failed to recognize this fundamental fact, and by saddling the India Mission (which found itself compelled to direct activities in countries many hundred miles distant) with a European charter they put it in a difficult position from the very beginning.

At first the Mission had three functions: subversive political activity; sabotage; and the dissemination of subversive propaganda. Later the task of raising and arming guerrillas was added. It soon transpired that the second of these activities was beyond the Mission's capability. Nevertheless London constantly urged Colin Mackenzie to carry out sabotage, which they deemed to be 'the heart and hub of special operations'. They pressed for the infiltration of civilians in civilian clothes ('as far as natives wear clothes'), which the military could not ask of soldiers.* They deprecated the Mission's failure to do a single thing

to fulfil the proper role of SOE in India . . . In sabotage – our most important sphere of action – we have made no headway whatsoever . . . the nearest we have got to it is through cables sent *from* here *to* India, suggesting fair fields

---

* On 30 May 1943 the War Office told C-in-C, India that the COS had decided that 'No member of the armed forces . . . should be sent on military operations, however hazardous, in civilian clothes, except in the case of subversive activities for which civilian clothes are essential.' The men must be volunteers and warned that if caught they were likely to be shot without trial. (India Office Records L/WS/1/1296.) Of course SOE were equally powerless to order men to act as agents.

for sabotage . . . To contend that a sabotage and Fifth Column organization is not practicable is to accept the gospel of despair and defeatism . . . .

The War Office went out of its way to remind C-in-C, India that one of SOE's main functions was 'sabotage of selected installations, dumps, bridges, important transportation, and other agencies vital to the enemy effort'.

The India Mission, for its part, did not suggest to London that sabotage of the nature prescribed was out of the question, but mistakenly devoted much time and effort to planning the impossible. For example, at the end of 1943 it examined the whole of its territory with a view to sabotage. Possible targets included oil storage tanks and refineries in the Dutch East Indies, docks and shipyards in Hong Kong and Singapore, the important coal-mines in North China, and – which savours of barrel-scraping – wooden shipbuilding in various places. London was assured that sabotage operations would definitely be carried out against oil targets in Sumatra, and that a party would attack industrial objectives in the neighbourhood of Hong Kong. Not one of these proposed operations took place; and indeed the only sabotage missions worthy of the name were the attack on Axis ships in Goa, the destruction of 50,000 tons of shipping in Singapore harbour, and Ivan Lyon's disastrous second attempt against Singapore. When it is borne in mind that Japanese shipping losses in the Far Eastern war totalled 8,617,234 tons, the India Mission's contribution becomes insignificant; and it is arguable that the use of submarines on such operations was counter-productive, inasmuch as the submarines had to forgo attacks which might have cost the Japanese higher losses. Perhaps the only justification for an operation like *Jaywick* was the beneficial effect on Allied morale and the adverse effect on the morale of the enemy.

As late as June 1945 when Mackenzie visited London there was pointed criticism in headquarters of the Mission's failure to carry out a sabotage programme. Mackenzie might have taken the opportunity to explain the difficulties. Instead he agreed that there was scope for sabotage in Manchuria and North China; but before it could be established that this was still a pipe-dream the war ended.

It is not easy to take stock of the performance of an organization and to decide whether it is adequately fulfilling its assigned role; but it is surprising that the India Mission in its self-examination never faced up to the fact that in the Far East the function to which SOE headquarters and COS gave the highest priority simply did not exist. Its failure to do so created a functional vacuum; and, since an organization abhors a vacuum no less than does nature, the Mission had to find other functions to employ its capacity, or go out of business. The vacuum was filled with a great increase in guerrilla work, which was of course included in the Mission's charter, and in the undertaking of intelligence work, which was not. That this led to a subliminal somersault is clearly revealed by Lieutenant-Colonel Cumming's analysis of SOE's performance in the Burma campaign, made with a view to defining its objectives in the forthcoming invasion of Malaya. The three objectives were to provide intelligence, to identify bombing targets for the RAF, and to take offensive action as auxiliaries to the regular effort. None of these activities was a special operation in the accepted sense. Cumming saw no place for sabotage or subversion. Yet no one in the Mission seems to have questioned whether the self-approved change in terms of reference was a change for the better.

Although the India Mission's revised charter of August 1942 did authorize guerrilla activities, which in the event became the Mission's most important contribution, doubts about the wisdom of undertaking this work persisted all through the war, at least in London. When the War Office raised the question of guerrillas with Wavell in 1942 he replied almost apologetically that the India Mission had hitherto taken a leading part in organizing them, but 'arrangements are now being made for them to relinquish this leading part . . .'. Guerrilla work should be left to the regular forces. About the same time George Taylor wrote to Mackenzie: 'I do not think that SOE should attempt to organize guerrilla bands with the object of carrying out paramilitary activities to assist the regular forces. This is always much better done by a special branch of the army itself.' In June 1945 a member of the SOE Council (Air Vice-Marshal A. P. Ritchie) said that Force 136 was wrong to devote so much effort to guerrilla activities. 'It is for consideration how far this extraneous work is militating against our carrying out our appointed task . . . I refrained from saying all this at the meeting [at which Mackenzie had been present] as it would not have come well after Mr Mackenzie's report.' Gubbins agreed that the India Mission was paying too much attention to paramilitary affairs.

The India Mission could have met this headquarters criticism by pointing out that by common consent its guerrillas had played a significant part in the Allied victory in Burma; but it was much more difficult to justify its incursion into the intelligence field. Of course, to support its own operations it needed specialized intelligence which was of value to the common pool, but that was hardly justification for converting it into a full-blown intelligence organization. The nature of the intelligence required for planning special operations was quite different from that required for ordinary military purposes; and even if this self-evident truth was not accepted, the intelligence function had been specifically ruled out by Selborne in November 1943 when he wrote: 'The collection of secret intelligence is not a function of SOE, although it inevitably obtains in the course of its other activities secret intelligence which is passed on to SIS' – which was right and proper. All the clandestine organizations provided intelligence as a by-product, but that did not mean that they should allow intelligence-gathering to take precedence over their particular activity.

It must therefore be asked whether Mountbatten was right to allow SOE to become an intelligence-gathering agency in competition with ISLD, the founder member of the intelligence club in the Far East. ISLD had been almost entirely wiped out when the Japanese overran Malaya and Burma, but by the end of 1943 was very much back in business – more in business than SOE realized, thanks to the extreme secrecy of its operations. It was inevitable that there should be rivalry between the two organizations since they were operating independently in the same territories with the same objective. There was, for example, competition for sea and air transport, which in Mountbatten's words 'went to the most alert and astute bidder' – and not necessarily to the most desirable enterprise.

There is a wealth of evidence that the rivalry was counter-productive. In January 1944 SOE's Operation *Gustavus VI* and ISLD's *Mud* shared the same submarine (*Tally Ho!*) to land two parties in Malaya. Although the SOE party had no difficulty in making contact with their rendezvous junk, they 'considered it too dangerous to land either personnel or stores'. However, the *Gustavus* dispatching officer vetoed the landing of the *Mud* party 'in accordance with an agreement which exists between the two organizations', despite the fact that the submarine commander (Lieutenant-Commander L. W. A. Bennington) was satisfied they could have made their way ashore without prejudice to *Gustavus*. He also recorded: 'The cooperation between the authorities responsible for Operations *Gustavus* and *Mud* is not very apparent' – a shrewd and tactful Royal Naval understatement. This was by no means an isolated incident.

Relations between the two bodies became so strained that a two-man team (one member from the headquarters of each organization) visited the Far East to pour oil on troubled waters. In fact, about the time the team arrived in SEAC relations were improving, especially at the operational level, but the visiting firemen contrived to add fuel to the flames. In particular, the SIS representative became obsessed with the idea that P Division, which was responsible for approving operations and allocating the necessary resources, was discriminating against ISLD. Nevertheless, by the time preparations for the invasion of Malaya were complete, a satisfactory *modus vivendi* had been achieved. SOE was made senior partner and authorized to carry out all dealings with AJUF. ISLD maintained liaison officers with the Force-136 Groups working with the guerrillas; and all intelligence, except target and tactical reports for the immediate use of the army and air force, was to be channelled through the ISLD network. No doubt this complicated arrangement would have worked, had it been put to the test; but surely a single intelligence organization would have worked better.

Mountbatten himself may have had misgivings about his handling of the irregular forces in his command. In his final report on the campaign in South East Asia he refers to the difficulty of co-ordinating the activities of the twelve clandestine, semi-clandestine, and quasi-military organizations which he found on arrival in India in November 1943; these he contrasts unfavourably with OSS which comprised 'intelligence both gathering and process-ing, secret operations, counter-espionage, and black propaganda; in fact all those items provided by a dozen organizations on the British side were virtually merged under one head by the Americans'. Had the Supreme Commander taken a leaf out of the American book and rationalized his secret organizations, he would have made life much easier for himself and his Command. He would have had the strong support of Slim, who saw the need for something to be done.[1] That the Fourteenth Army Commander did not get his way can hardly be attributed to lack of persistence. He tried for six months but he had a campaign to win and his energies were required in other directions. In any case he had no direct control over SOE or ISLD. The nearest SEAC came to rationalization was the agreement in principle, which was never implemented, to amalgamate Force 136 and Z Force – which would have reduced Mountbatten's irregular bodies from twelve to eleven.

It is easy to see from this distance what might have been done. Had ISLD been provided with the resources allocated to SOE – thereby forestalling the entry of Force 136 into the intelligence market – and taken over the functions of V Force and Z Force, the provision of intelligence would have been much improved. The India Mission should never have been allowed to build up a paranaval force, a costly and totally unsuccessful enterprise; but the task of maritime sabotage should have been left to the highly professional COPP. When SEAC headquarters undertook political warfare the India Mission should have ceased to have any connection with this activity. Had all this been done Force 136 would have been free to concentrate on the job to which it had gravitated naturally – raising guerrillas and conducting paramilitary activities in support of the regular forces. It might then have become a formation directly under the Fourteenth Army, instead of being attached to SEAC headquarters at one remove from the army. This would have eliminated the need for a separate supply system in the field, for an elaborate system of liaison officers to keep Force 136 in touch with the needs of the army, and for a super-secret communications network which hampered the Force's efficiency as a paramilitary organization.

The position actually reached at the end of the war was very different. ISLD, traditionally charged with the task of providing military intelligence, found itself playing second fiddle to SOE, whose charter ruled out intelligence-gathering, and whose Minister and headquarters were convinced that it was not a special-operations function. A senior member of ISLD wrote after the war:

It was my own candid opinion then and remains so that SOE and ISLD should have amalgamated, pooling all resources and using the best officer and agent material available. The aims as far as intelligence went were the same, the methods of obtaining were the same, the methods of transport were the same.

It is perhaps surprising that this officer did not question why SOE was operating in the intelligence field at all.

The fact that the India Mission found itself undertaking tasks for which it was not originally designed was something of a handicap for the management of the organization; but even when allowance is made for this, it may seem that sometimes operations were not as well conducted as they should have been. The severe criticism from agents in respect of training, briefing, stores dispatch, and signals cannot easily be discounted. No doubt the man in the field is always critical of the treatment he receives at the hands of his brother at comfortable headquarters, be he diplomat, business man, soldier, or agent. Some adverse reports may have been generated by personal animosity. Ritchie Gardiner, in commenting on those provided at the end of hostilities by his Burma field groups, wrote: 'perusal of one Area Commander's report might give the impression that the Country Section and Calcutta HQ in general were thoroughly incompetent'. This is certainly true if the report in question is believed; but of course it may be exaggerated or misleading. Again, Gardiner wrote: 'Some reports I consider good, others not so good, and with a number of the views expressed I do not agree. They serve a useful purpose, however, in giving another side of the picture.' Quite: but it is difficult to decide which side of the picture reflects the truth. Since the purpose of the Group Leaders' reports was to help future operations, they naturally dwelt on what went wrong rather than on what went right. If some activities were incompetent by any standard (for example the first submarine mission to Siam)* and if others were less successful than they might have been, it must be remembered that special operations were new and unsuited to the conditions in the Far East. Moreover, no one could expect every mission to go without a hitch.

There can be nothing but praise, on the other hand, for the performance of the operatives of the Oriental and India Missions, starting with the Malaya left-behind parties' – European and Chinese – attempts to slow the Japanese advance, a forlorn hope rewarded with death in the field, years in a prison camp, or beheading by a Japanese sword; the even more hopeless task of their brothers in Siam condemned to inevitable failure by the British Minister; the fighting retreat of the Burma hillmen in 1942, led by Noel Stevenson, not formally a member of SOE but whose name cannot be omitted; and the epic walks out of Burma by Steven Cumming, Ritchie Gardiner, Eric Battersby, and others. The catalogue is lengthy. The noble action of Warren in remaining with the troops in Sumatra to face with them

* See pp. 105–6.

imprisonment by the Japanese, when it was open to him to go to India with the other SOE men who were to live to fight another day. The years spent by Spencer Chapman, Davis, and Broome and their fellows in the Malayan jungle in the most primitive conditions, and the steadfastness of the Chinese and Malay resistance under constant threat of Japanese attack. The resolution of the unwarlike Siamese, who willingly left their studies in England to parachute into the unknown dangers of their occupied homeland. The part played by SOE's Dutchmen, no less resolute, but who had fewer opportunities to further the Allied cause. The missions of François de Langlade, de Gaulle's emissary, into Japanese-controlled French Indo-China, and the stubborn retreat of the Free French into China from that country, where their brave resistance had been sadly hindered by the doctrinaire anti-colonial policies of the Americans, who even denied them ammunition to save themselves from the common enemy. The outstanding success of Ivan Lyon's tiny fleet in bearding the Japanese in Singapore harbour and sinking 50,000 tons of their shipping, and the more glorious failure of his second enterprise in Singapore when he perished along with the whole of his gallant company. Scores of actions carried out in Burma by the guerrillas and their British leaders behind Japanese lines in support of the advance of the regular troops. The brilliant deception with which Tan Sri Ibrahim bin Ismail foiled his Japanese captors in Malaya. The currency black market organized in China by Walter Fletcher, which saved the Allies millions of pounds. The invaluable contribution of the Special Duties Squadrons of the RAF, supplemented by the submarines of the Royal Navy and the Royal Netherlands Navy, without which few agents could have reached the occupied countries. Nor must the hundreds of FANYs be forgotten. Although denied the opportunities for unbelievable heroism afforded to their sisters in the West, they played an essential part in running the machine in India, Ceylon, China, and later Burma.

Mackenzie, who commanded the India Mission for the whole of its life, earned the respect both of SOE London and the men who served under him. Taylor wrote in 1944:

No-one can visit India without being impressed by Colin Mackenzie; by his exceptional grip on the working and personnel of his group; by his capacity to simplify and without delay to go to the root of any problem; and by his remarkable sense of timing and diplomacy. The high regard in which he is held in SEAC, in GHQ India, and in the Viceroy's Department is obvious. Not less impressive is the respect with which all members of his group, scattered as it is all over India and China, have for his judgement; the faith they have in his capacity to produce the right solution for all problems; and the personal affection in which he is held.

In his account of the Burma campaign Slim pays a well-deserved tribute to the efforts of Force 136:

Our own levies led by their British officers were a most valuable asset and had a real influence on operations. They were tactically controlled by wireless from Army Headquarters, told when to rise, the objectives they should attack, and given specific tasks. They could not and were not expected to stand up to the Japanese in pitched battles but they could and did in places harry them unmercifully. Their greatest achievement was the delaying of the 15th Japanese Division in the Loikaw-Mawchi area, thus enabling IV Corps to reach Toungoo first, but they have rendered almost equally valuable services. They had an excellent jitter effect on the Japanese, who were compelled to lock up troops to guard against attacks on the lines of communication.[2]

Thanks to the dropping of the atom bombs two questions remain unanswerable. First, what would Force 136 have accomplished in the other countries of SEAC had the war in the Far East run its expected course? There is little doubt that in Malaya it would have made at least as great a contribution as it had done in Burma, still of course in the paramilitary field. The Chinese guerrillas there were well trained and well armed and the treatment their fellows had suffered at the hands of the invaders, especially in the early days, provided them with an incentive to give the strongest possible support to an Allied expeditionary force throwing out the Japanese. In Siam Force 136 was already working in close co-operation with a widespread and potentially powerful resistance including large numbers of the police and the army. It seems inevitable that an Allied invasion would have made short work of the Japanese whose morale by this time must have been steadily declining. There would have remained Sumatra and French Indo-China, where there was no sign of whole-hearted resistance, and indeed where Force-136 parties would have found themselves fighting alone, or, more likely, against the guerrilla forces whom they would have expected to be their allies. The difficulties which Force 136 would have faced in these two countries are well illustrated by the events of the immediate post-war years.

The second question which must remain unanswered is, would Mountbatten and SOE headquarters have faced up to the fact that Force 136's activities could only become more and more purely military, and accepted that there was no scope in the Far East for special operations in the accepted sense? Would they have decided to make the Force's personnel an irregular extension of the military forces, rather than a body subject to terms of reference which it was incapable of carrying out, thanks to the peculiar circumstances of the Far East? Had the projected Allied invasions of the territories remaining in Japanese hands followed quickly one upon the other, it seems likely that there would have been no change, on the ground that the known devil was to be preferred. On the other hand, if there had been a significant interval between two campaigns, it is conceivable that someone would have faced up to the fact that it would make sense to use Force 136 for what it was – a straight paramilitary force – to remove from it the inhibiting shackles of super-secrecy which impaired its efficiency in the field, and to put it directly under the army commander – an instrument which he could use as he saw fit where and when it would be most effective. But this is mere speculation. It is on its performance in Burma that Force 136 must be judged, and that it succeeded there in spite of the innumerable difficulties is a tribute both to the management of the India Mission and to its operatives in the field.

# Primary sources

*(other than SOE papers)*

*Public Record Office*

| | |
|---|---|
| ADM 199 | War History Cases |
| AIR 27 | Squadron Operations Record Books |
| AIR 28 | Station Operations Record Books |
| CAB 66 | War Cabinet Memoranda |
| CAB 79 | War Cabinet, Chiefs of Staff Committee, Minutes |
| CAB 80 | War Cabinet, Chiefs of Staff Committee, Memoranda |
| CAB 91 | War Cabinet, Committees on India |
| CAB 96 | War Cabinet, Committees on Far East |
| CAB 106 | Historical Section, Archivist and Librarian Series |
| CAB 121 | Special Secret Information Centre Files |
| CAB 122 | British Joint Services Mission, Washington Office Files |
| CAB 127 | Dalton Papers |
| FO 371 | General Correspondence, Political |
| FO 898 | Political Warfare Executive |
| FO 954 | Avon Papers |
| PREM 3 | Prime Minister's Office Papers |
| WO 106 | Directorate of Military Operations and Intelligence Papers |
| WO 172 | War Diaries, South East Asia Command |
| WO 193 | Directorate of Military Operations, Collation Files |
| WO 203 | Military Headquarters Papers, Far East |

# Select bibliography

Ian Adamson, *The Forgotten Men* (Roy, 1965).

Louis Allan, *Sittang – The Last Battle* (Macdonald, 1973).

——, *Singapore 1941–1942* (Davis Poynter, 1977).

Ralph Barker, *One Man's Jungle – a Biography of Spencer Chapman* (Chatto and Windus, 1975).

John Beamish, *Burma Drop* (Elek Books, 1958).

John Bowen, *Undercover in the Jungle* (Kimber, 1978).

Duncan Brelis and William Peers, *Behind the Burma Road* (Robert Hale, 1964).

D. S. Clemens, *Yalta* (OUP, 1972).

Brian Connell, *The Return of the Tiger* (Evans Brothers, 1960).

John Cross, *Red Jungle* (Robert Hale, 1957).

Charles Cruickshank, *The Fourth Arm: Psychological Warfare 1938–1945* (OUP, 1981).

Nancy Davidson, *Winning Hazard* (Low, 1947).

F. S. V. Donnison, *British Military Administration in the Far East 1943–46* (HMSO, 1956).

Geoffrey Evans, *The Johnnies* (Cassell, 1964).

Ian Fellowes-Gordon, *Amiable Assassins: the Story of Kachin Guerrillas in North Burma* (Robert Hale, 1957).

M. R. D. Foot, *SOE in France* (HMSO, 1966).

Sir Andrew Gilchrist, *Bangkok Top Secret* (Hutchinson, 1960).

Duncan Guthrie, *Jungle Diary* (Macmillan, 1946).

John Haseman, *Thai Resistance Movements during the Second World War* (N. Illinois U.P., 1978).

Denis Holman, *The Green Torture* (Robert Hale, 1962).

Peter Kemp, *Alms for Oblivion* (Cassell, 1961).

Oliver Lindsay, *At the Going Down of the Sun* (Hamish Hamilton, 1981).

Ronald McKie, *The Heroes* (Angus and Robertson, 1960).

Roy MacLaren, *Canadians Behind Enemy Lines, 1939–1945* (University of British Columbia Press, 1981).

Alistair Mars, *HMS Thule Intercepts* (Elek Books, 1956).

Ian Morrison, *Malayan Postscript* (Faber and Faber, 1942).

——, *Grandfather Longlegs* (Faber and Faber, 1947).

W. Stanley Moss, *A War of Shadows* (Boardman, 1958).

G. Peacock, *The Life of a Jungle Walla* (Arthur Stockwell, 1958).

Edwin Ride, *BAAG* (OUP, 1982).

G. Sabattier, *Le Destin de l'Indochine* (Paris, 1953).

Mamoru Shinozaki, *My Wartime Experiences in Singapore* (Institute of South East Asia Studies, 1973).

Ian Skidmore, *Escape from the Rising Sun* (Leo Cooper, 1973).

Sir William Slim, *Defeat into Victory* (Cassell, 1956).

F. Spencer Chapman, *The Jungle is Neutral* (Chatto and Windus, 1949).

Bickham Sweet-Escott, *Baker Street Irregular* (Methuen, 1965).

D. Thatcher and R. Cross, *Pai Naa: the Story of Nona Baker* (Constable, 1959).

Ian Trenowden, *Operations Most Secret. SOE: the Malayan Theatre* (Kimber, 1978).

Sir Laurens van der Post, *The Night of the New Moon* (Hogarth, 1960).

Dame Irene Ward, *FANY Invicta* (Hutchinson, 1955).

# Notes

## Origin

1. CAB 127 206 (2.7.40; 16.8.40).
2. FO 954 24, ff. 107–8; 123–4; 125–9.
3. PREM 3 409/6 (7, 13, 14, 21, 23, 24, 27, 29.9.43; 11.10.43).
4. WO 193 605, nos. 1A, 9A, 11A.

## PART I

### Chapter 3

1. WO 203 3306 (18.12.43).
2. WO 203 610 (17.6.42).
3. WO 203 3306 (29.4, 4.6, 29.6, 28.9.44); WO 203 4332 (17.11.44), no. 2A.

### Chapter 4

1. WO 172 1703 (17.1.44).

### Chapter 5

1. AIR 27 1065–8; 1174–5; 1460–2; 1760–4; 1765–9; 2151; AIR 28 405.
2. AIR 27 1761 (24/5.1.45); AIR 27 1066 (31.7/1.8.45).
3. AIR 28 405 (May 1945).
4. Ibid.
5. AIR 27 1776 (20/1.2.45).
6. SEAC War Diary (28.6.45).
7. Ibid.

### Chapter 6

1. ADM 199 1885, f. 25.

### Chapter 7

1. WO 172 1724 (7.8.44).
2. AIR 27 1760.

## PART II

### Chapter 1

1. Ian Morrison, *Malayan Postscript* (Faber and Faber, 1942), pp. 158–9.
2. F. Spencer Chapman, *The Jungle is Neutral* (Chatto and Windus, 1949), pp. 91–2.
3. Stevenson's unpublished account, pp. 256, 261.
4. WO 203 5712 (this file contains several accounts of these operations, including one by Stevenson).
5. WO 193 605 (12.4.41).
6. CAB 120 615 (16.4.41).
7. WO 193 607, no. 1A; WO 193 911, no. 65.
8. WO 193 606 (26.5.41); WO 193 911, no. 86.
9. WO 193 911, nos. 68, 77; WO 193 605, nos. 85A, 86A.
10. CAB 96 1, ff. 58b, 65b, 239, 344–348b; CAB 96 4 (FE (41) 177).
11. WO 106 5035; WO 193 609 (13, 24.2.42).
12. CAB 120 517 (14.10.41).
13. CAB 120 615.
14. CAB 106 40; CAB 120 518 (25.6.42).
15. CAB 106 45, p. 24.

### Chapter 2

1. ADM 199 1879, ff. 355–6.
2. ADM 199 1882, f. 67.
3. Ibid., ff. 159–60.
4. Ibid., f. 83.
5. Ibid., ff. 128–31; ADM 199 1885, ff. 132–82.
6. ADM 199 1884, ff. 111–13.

## Chapter 3

1. FO 371 35977, f. 43.
2. Ibid., f. 74.
3. Ibid., ff. 73, 84.
4. ADM 199 1882, f. 45; ADM 199 1865, f. 289.
5. *Thai Politics 1932–1957*, vol. i, p. 421.
6. Ibid., p. 425.
7. FO 371 35977, ff. 147–51; FO 371 35978, ff. 119–20; FO 371 41844, ff. 89, 113–14.
8. CAB 66 43, f. 20; FO 371 41844, f. 176.
9. FO 371 41845, f. 77.
10. Ibid., ff. 37, 43, 102–3.
11. Ibid., ff. 73–4; FO 371 46560, f. 35.
12. FO 371 41845, ff. 43, 102–3.
13. Ibid., f. 43.
14. Ibid., ff. 101, 108–10.
15. Ibid., ff. 183, 185.
16. FO 371 46560, ff. 24, 79.
17. Ibid., ff. 72–3.
18. Ibid., ff. 101–2; FO 371 46561, ff. 3–10.
19. FO 371 46560, f. 152.
20. Ibid., ff. 13–14.
21. Ibid., f. 247.
22. WO 203 4407 (11.7.45).
23. FO 371 46562, f. 4.
24. Ibid., ff. 41, 100; WO 203 4340, no. 69A (2.7.45); WO 203 4413, no. 16 (1.7.45); no. 19 (3.7.45); no. 21 (7.7.45); no. 24 (13.7.45).

## Chapter 4

1. CAB 96 1, f. 58b.
2. FO 371 41723, ff. 4, 7, 12–13.
3. CAB 122 1168, no. 1 (30.9.43).
4. FO 371 35935 (21.11.43).
5. FO 371 41723, ff. 6, 20.
6. CAB 122 1168, nos. 11–17.
7. FO 371 41723, ff. 156, 163.
8. CAB 79 81, f. 348.

9. CAB 122 1169, no. 33; CAB 122 1177 (2.3.45); CAB 80 92, ff. 248 ff.
10. CAB 80 92, ff. 248 ff.; CAB 122 1168, nos. 22–7, 35–7, 40A, 51A; CAB 122 1177 (2.3.45); FO 371 46304, f. 59; CAB 80 89, f. 126 (13.11.44); CAB 80 91, ff. 90 ff.
11. FO 371 46304, f. 90; CAB 80 92, f. 248; CAB 122 1177 (2.3.45).
12. FO 371 46304, ff. 115–16.
13. G Sabattier, *Le Destin de l'Indochine* (Paris, 1953), pp. 71, 80.
14. FO 371 46305, ff. 50 ff.
15. Ibid., ff. 135, 136, 166, 188, 195.
16. AIR 27 1761 (26.4.45).
17. FO 371 46306, f. 84.

## Chapter 5

1. FO 371 31751.
2. WO 193 911 (24.2.42); WO 193 609 1A.
3. FO 371 31751.
4. ADM 199 1879, ff. 348, 362.
5. Ibid., ff. 377–82.
6. CAB 121 304 (11.43).
7. PREM 3 147/3, ff. 128–37, 141, 144–56; PREM 3 147/5, ff. 218–53; PREM 3 147/3, ff. 318, 360.
8. ADM 199 1882, ff. 246–50.
9. Ibid., f. 109b; ADM 199 1863, ff. 109–15.
10. ADM 199 1882, f. 248.
11. Ibid.
12. Ibid., ff. 246–8; CAB 120 307 (6.44).
13. ADM 199 1882, ff. 254–5.
14. Ibid., ff. 235–6.
15. ADM 199 1884, f. 142.
16. Ibid., ff. 235–41.

## Chapter 6

1. FO 371 46196; WO 172 1757.
2. FO 371 46304, ff. 54, 57, 92, 110, 131, 157.

## Chapter 7

1. WO 172 1724 (6.8.44).
2. WO 203 476, no. 13.
3. WO 203 56, no. 1; WO 203 367, no. 1.
4. WO 203 4332, no. 16A; WO 203 5748 (15.7.44).
5. WO 203 4332 (17.11.44); WO 203 5748 (2.10.44).
6. WO 203 5748 (28.12.44).
7. WO 203 53, no. 4 (2.1.45).
8. Ibid. (16.2.45); WO 203 367 (4.1.45).
9. WO 203 53 (9, 13, 29.1.45; 9.2.45).
10. WO 203 54 (4.4, 25.5.45); WO 203 367 (6.6.45).
11. WO 203 53 (2.1.45).
12. Ibid. (29.1.45).
13. WO 203 4403 (31.1.45).
14. FO 371 46334B (F 1036/G: 2, 20.2.45).
15. F. S. V. Donnison, *British Military Administration in the Far East 1943–46* (HMSO, 1956), pp. 348–9.
16. WO 203 58 (13.2.45); WO 203 4332, no. 33A (27.2.45).
17. WO 172 1751 (26.2.45); WO 203 4332, no. 30A (27.2.45); WO 203 4404, no. 7.
18. WO 203 56 (27.3.45).
19. CAB 91 3 (29.3.45); FO 371 46334B (F 2007–9/G: 2.4.45).
20. WO 203 4464, no. 31 (20.4.45).
21. Ibid., nos. 31A, 33A (9.5.45).
22. Ibid., no. 9A (31.3.45); no. 41A (14.5.45).
23. WO 203 4404 (15.5.45).
24. WO 203 2124A (2.6.45).
25. Donnison, p. 395.
26. WO 203 59 (16.5.45).
27. WO 203 54 (11, 13, 21.5.45).
28. WO 203 4398, no. 25B (21.7.45).
29. WO 203 4332, no. 70A (5.7.45).

## Chapter 8

1. ADM 199 1885, f. 43.
2. Ibid., f. 61.
3. Ibid., f. 62.
4. Ibid., f. 69.
5. Ibid., f. 80.
6. ADM 199 1882, ff. 46–8.
7. Ibid., ff. 172–4; ADM 199 1885, ff. 81–99.
8. ADM 199 1882, ff. 74–6.
9. Ibid., ff. 84–7.
10. Ibid., ff. 209–13.
11. Ibid., f. 223.
12. ADM 199 1883, ff. 352–9.
13. Ibid., f. 357.
14. ADM 199 1884, ff. 135–6.
15. Ibid., ff. 216–17.
16. ADM 199 1883, f. 4.
17. D. Thatcher and R. Cross, *Pai Naa: the Story of Nona Baker* (Constable, 1959), p. 179.
18. WO 203 4332 (18, 27.2.45).
19. WO 203 4403, no. 79A (19.4.45); WO 203 3884 (20.2.45).

## Chapter 9

1. FO 371 41552 (26, 29.9, 5.10.44).
2. Ibid. (5.9, 29.9, 2.11.44).
3. Ibid. (13.10.44).

## Chapter 10

1. WO 203 5653.
2. FO 898 273.
3. WO 172 1709 (25.3.44).
4. WO 172 1703 (12.1.44); WO 172 1713; WO 203 5179, no. 52 (29.4.44); WO 172 1723 (4.8.44).
5. WO 172 1705 (4.2.44); WO 172 1708 (9.3.44); WO 172 1709 (23.3.44); WO 172 1713 (7.5.44); WO 172 1715 (29.4.44).
6. WO 203 3981 198A (24.12.44); 205A (3.1.45).
7. WO 172 1722 (26.7.44); WO 203 5183 (17.7.44).
8. WO 203 5180 (17.6.44).
9. WO 203 4332, no. 17A (18.5.45); WO 203 5189 (28.7.45).

10. FO 898 266 (8.10.40; 27.2.41; 13.3.41); WO 203 5653.
11. FO 898 266 (27.2.42).
12. FO 898 273 (23.4.42).
13. WO 203 5792.
14. WO 172 1711 (6.4.44); WO 172 1722 (21.7.44); WO 172 1723 (30.4.44).
15. WO 203 53, no. 48B; WO 203 3312; WO 203 3331.
16. WO 203 3881 21B; WO 203 3997, no. 14A; WO 203 5806; WO 172 1722 (21.7.44); WO 172 1725A (21.8.44); WO 172 1700 (13, 15, 21.12.43).
17. WO 203 5394.
18. WO 172 1725A (21.8.44); WO 203 5394.
19. WO 172 1719 (26.6.44); FO 371 41819 (F 5570).
20. WO 203 5394.
21. WO 172 1713 (4, 8.5.44); WO 172 1720A (6.7.44).
22. WO 203 5806.
23. WO 203 5807.
24. WO 203 5792.
25. WO 172 1724A (21.8.44); WO 203 5792; FO 371 41810, f. 292.

## Chapter 11

1. WO 203 4332.
2. Ibid.

## Conclusion

1. CAB 106 77.
2. CAB 106 48, p. 29.

# APPENDIX 1

# Force 136 – principal establishments

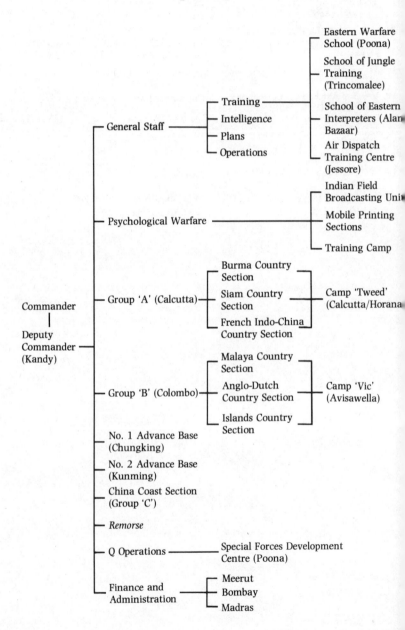

At the end of the war in the Far East Force 136 comprised:

| | Kandy | Calcutta | Colombo | Training Schools | China and elsewhere | Total |
|---|---|---|---|---|---|---|
| Officers | 87 | 63 | 29 | 110 | 46 | 335 |
| Other ranks | 69 | 57 | 17 | 326 | 133 | 602 |
| Indian army | | 66 | 26 | 534 | 44 | 670 |
| FANY | 89 | 153 | 266 | 45 | | 553 |
| Civilians | 79 | 117 | 58 | 13 | 5 | 272 |
| Total | 324 | 456 | 396 | 1028· | 228 | 2432 |

There were 600 operational officers and other ranks in the field in Burma and Siam, and 400 in Malaya.

# APPENDIX 2

# Operation *Galvanic*: SOE personnel with AJUF Group I, Selangor

## GROUP LIAISON TEAM

### (Signal plan – GUITAR)

Lt.-Col. D. K. Broadhurst (SPROUT) GLO
Capt. A. R. G. Morrison (APPLE) A/GLO
Sgt. J. C. Reynolds (MARROW) W/T
Yiu Ming Tek (LEEK) Int.

Sgt. B. C. Lee (PEAR) Coder
Sgt. F. A. Bailey (PLUM) W/T
Capt. Holman (SPADE) MO
Sgt. Goodyear (FORK) MOrd

## PATROL LIAISON TEAM

*GALVANIC ORANGE* (Serendah)

(Signal plan GUITAR ORANGE)

Maj. P. T. Thompson-Walker
(PARSNIP) PLO
F/O J. Robertson (CARROT) 2 i/c
Seah Tin Toon (TOMATO) W/T
Sgt. O. Wong (GUAVA) Int.
Sgt. G. Elvidge (TURNIP) W/T

## PATROL LIAISON TEAM

*GALVANIC GREEN* (Kerling)

(Signal plan GUITAR GREEN)

Maj. C. E. Maxwell (SWEDE) PLO
Lt. J. R. Prosser (WURZLE) 2 i/c
Sgt. T. Collins (SQUASH) W/T
Sgt. B. L. Chinn (HARICOT) Int.

## PATROL LIAISON TEAM

*GALVANIC BLUE* (Sempak)

(Signal plan GUITAR BLUE)

Maj. A. J. Hunter (SPUD) PLO
Capt. R. S. Davies (CABBAGE) 2 i/c
Tong Shu Shan (BEAN) W/T
Huang Yih Hsia (CAULI) Int.
Cpl. K. Faulkner (ONION) W/T

## PATROL LIAISON TEAM

*GALVANIC BROWN* (Kajang)

(Signal plan GUITAR BROWN)

Capt. I. A. Macdonald (BRINJAL) PLO
Capt. M. Levy (PUMPKIN) 2 i/c
Sgt. T. Henney (CHIVE) W/T
Sgt. H. W. Fung (KALE) Int.

## PATROL LIAISON TEAM

*GALVANIC SLATE* (Kachau)

(Signal plan GUITAR SLATE)

Capt. K. R. Heine (SHALLOT) PLO
Capt. H. Fraser (CHILLIE) 2 i/c
Sgt. D. Tack (ENDIVE) W/T

Tsun Man Yang (LETTUCE) W/T
Sgt. R. W. Lew (MAIZE) Int.

*Abbreviations:* GLO Group Liaison Officer; PLO Patrol Liaison Officer; W/T W/T Operator; MO Medical Officer; MOrd Medical Orderly; Int. Interpreter.

# APPENDIX 3

# Note on the Office of Strategic Services (OSS)

THE United States Office of Strategic Services (OSS) combined the functions of the British SOE and ISLD (the latter being the Far Eastern manifestation of SIS) and operated in all the countries where SOE operated, except French Indo-China. The first OSS team, which arrived in the Far East in 1942, was under the command of General Stilwell in northern Burma. When SEAC was formed towards the end of 1943 it included an OSS unit responsible to Mountbatten through the Commanding General, China-Burma-India (CBI) theatre. In April 1944 SEAC's OSS unit moved to Kandy with the rest of SEAC headquarters, its operations being co-ordinated with those of the other clandestine bodies through SEAC's P Division. OSS were principally active in Siam where in collaboration with Force 136 they laid the foundation of active resistance to the Japanese.

OSS operated radio stations at five points in India, two in Ceylon, and four in Burma. Their stations at Chittagong and Rangoon were used to broadcast 'black' radio programmes to enemy-occupied territories. They had forty-seven W/T stations throughout the SEAC area in communication with headquarters at Kandy.

Like Force 136 they had their own schools for the training of agents destined for clandestine operations, including Siamese, Burmese, Karens, Malays, and Indonesians. The basic course lasted five weeks and included intensive instruction in weapons, demolitions, codes, aircraft recognition, intelligence-reporting, and order of battle, as well as maritime, physical, field, and survival training. Before leaving on an operation agents were given two or three weeks specialized training in a jungle area. W/T operators were required to train with their equipment under the field conditions they were likely to meet.

OSS records show that the guerrillas under their control accounted for 5,428 Japanese killed, with a further 10,000 probably killed or seriously wounded. Fifteen Americans lost their lives, and 184 guerrillas. Eighty-seven Americans were parachuted into occupied territories, and 147 natives; and at the beginning of 1945 OSS was in control of over 9,000 guerrillas, when they employed 131 officers and 418 enlisted men.

OSS ran a weather-reporting service which provided the USAAF 19th Weather Region, Calcutta, and the British Joint Meteorological Centre, Colombo, with weather information from twenty-five points in enemy-occupied territory covering an area from Singapore to north-eastern Siam.

OSS also provided information about codes, and the location and frequencies of Japanese weather stations which enabled the Allies to make use of Japanese weather information over the whole of SEAC.

In all, OSS mounted 122 operations, using submarines, Liberators, Catalinas, and C 47s. Sixteen sorties went to Burma, seventeen to Malaya, eight to Sumatra, ten to the Andaman Islands, and seventy-one to Siam. There was one operation to Indo-China at the beginning of September 1945 for the rescue of prisoners of war.

# Index